Krzysztof Piotrowski

Distributed Shared Memory and Data Consistency

Krzysztof Piotrowski

Distributed Shared Memory and Data Consistency

for Wireless Sensor Networks - Assessment of the feasibility

Südwestdeutscher Verlag für Hochschulschriften

Impressum/Imprint (nur für Deutschland/only for Germany)
Bibliografische Information der Deutschen Nationalbibliothek: Die Deutsche Nationalbibliothek verzeichnet diese Publikation in der Deutschen Nationalbibliografie; detaillierte bibliografische Daten sind im Internet über http://dnb.d-nb.de abrufbar.
Alle in diesem Buch genannten Marken und Produktnamen unterliegen warenzeichen-, marken- oder patentrechtlichem Schutz bzw. sind Warenzeichen oder eingetragene Warenzeichen der jeweiligen Inhaber. Die Wiedergabe von Marken, Produktnamen, Gebrauchsnamen, Handelsnamen, Warenbezeichnungen u.s.w. in diesem Werk berechtigt auch ohne besondere Kennzeichnung nicht zu der Annahme, dass solche Namen im Sinne der Warenzeichen- und Markenschutzgesetzgebung als frei zu betrachten wären und daher von jedermann benutzt werden dürften.

Coverbild: www.ingimage.com

Verlag: Südwestdeutscher Verlag für Hochschulschriften GmbH & Co. KG
Heinrich-Böcking-Str. 6-8, 66121 Saarbrücken, Deutschland
Telefon +49 681 37 20 271-1, Telefax +49 681 37 20 271-0
Email: info@svh-verlag.de

Approved by: Cottbus, BTU, Diss., 2011

Herstellung in Deutschland:
Schaltungsdienst Lange o.H.G., Berlin
Books on Demand GmbH, Norderstedt
Reha GmbH, Saarbrücken
Amazon Distribution GmbH, Leipzig
ISBN: 978-3-8381-3159-7

Imprint (only for USA, GB)
Bibliographic information published by the Deutsche Nationalbibliothek: The Deutsche Nationalbibliothek lists this publication in the Deutsche Nationalbibliografie; detailed bibliographic data are available in the Internet at http://dnb.d-nb.de.
Any brand names and product names mentioned in this book are subject to trademark, brand or patent protection and are trademarks or registered trademarks of their respective holders. The use of brand names, product names, common names, trade names, product descriptions etc. even without a particular marking in this works is in no way to be construed to mean that such names may be regarded as unrestricted in respect of trademark and brand protection legislation and could thus be used by anyone.

Cover image: www.ingimage.com

Publisher: Südwestdeutscher Verlag für Hochschulschriften GmbH & Co. KG
Heinrich-Böcking-Str. 6-8, 66121 Saarbrücken, Germany
Phone +49 681 37 20 271-1, Fax +49 681 37 20 271-0
Email: info@svh-verlag.de

Printed in the U.S.A.
Printed in the U.K. by (see last page)
ISBN: 978-3-8381-3159-7

Copyright © 2012 by the author and Südwestdeutscher Verlag für Hochschulschriften GmbH & Co. KG and licensors
All rights reserved. Saarbrücken 2012

To all those that made it possible..

Contents

Contents	3
1 Introduction	**7**
1.1 Research area	7
1.2 Research objectives	8
1.3 Contributions	9
1.4 Structure	10
2 Related work	**11**
2.1 Wireless Sensor Networks	11
2.1.1 Hardware	12
2.1.2 Software	24
2.1.3 Applications	31
2.1.4 Evaluation means	33
2.2 Distributed Shared Memory	34
2.2.1 DSM classification	36
2.2.2 Consistency models	47
2.2.3 Fault tolerance	58
2.2.4 Communication Issues	60
2.3 Data sharing and consistency related examples in WSN	62
3 The WSN related aspects of a DSM realization	**87**
3.1 Request forwarding	88
3.2 Replication strategy	90
3.3 Dependent request forwarding	95
3.4 Master copy discovery	97
3.5 Master copy migration	98
3.6 Instance filtering	100
3.7 The access transparency	103
3.8 The operating system adaptation layer	107

| | | 3.9 The operation span . . . . | 108 |

4 The tinyDSM Middleware   115
- 4.1 The goals 115
- 4.2 The architecture and services 117
- 4.3 The distributed shared memory abstraction 121
- 4.4 The policy parameters 126
  - 4.4.1 Identification policy parameters 127
  - 4.4.2 Replication policy parameters 128
  - 4.4.3 Reliability policy parameters 129
  - 4.4.4 Optimization policy parameters 130
  - 4.4.5 Access rights policy parameters 131
- 4.5 The implementation details 131
  - 4.5.1 The functional interface 132
  - 4.5.2 The data structures 137
  - 4.5.3 The communication interfaces 169
  - 4.5.4 The Replication Logic module 173
  - 4.5.5 The Event Logic module 175
  - 4.5.6 The operations 176

5 Consistency Model Evaluation   187
- 5.1 The evaluation setup 187
- 5.2 Consistency models without synchronization 200
  - 5.2.1 Atomic or Strict Consistency 200
  - 5.2.2 Linearizability 201
  - 5.2.3 Sequential Consistency 208
  - 5.2.4 Causal Consistency 215
  - 5.2.5 PRAM or FIFO Consistency 215
  - 5.2.6 Cache Consistency 218
  - 5.2.7 Processor Consistency 220
  - 5.2.8 Slow Memory 220

6 Conclusions   223
- 6.1 Future work 226

Bibliography   227

A Policy Parameters–Identification   245

B Policy Parameters–Replication   249

C	Policy Parameters–Reliability	253
D	Policy Parameters–Optimization	255
E	Policy Parameters–Access rights	261
F	Policy Parameters–Future improvements	263

Used Abbreviations	267
List of Figures	270
List of Tables	273
List of Listings	276

Chapter 1

Introduction

This chapter introduces the objectives of this work. First, it sketches the area involved in the presented research, names its advantages and open issues that define the state of the art and the required improvements. Further, the research objectives are specified and the contributions are explained. Finally, the structure of this thesis is presented.

1.1 Research area

Wireless sensor networks (WSN), also known as cyber-physical systems are data oriented distributed systems consisting of a potentially large number of small and cheap devices (sensor nodes or simply, nodes) able to sense, process and transmit data. The nodes use these capabilities to interact with the environment, they are installed in, i.e. they monitor or control it. The range of WSN applications is very broad and limited only by the imagination of the application engineers. Their applications include, but are not limited to, monitoring and control systems to interact with individuals, buildings, vehicles, home and industry appliances as well as a broad range of military and homeland security applications. Sensor nodes differ in the applied hardware, but usually the resources of the nodes are constrained; they have limited energy and computation power, but are expected to work properly for time periods up to ten years. Thus, the application engineering is a challenging task that has to be done carefully, taking into account the scarce resources of the nodes. There exist two extreme ways of application programming for sensor nodes. They can be categorized as low level and high level programming. The low level programming tries to optimize the code as much as possible, most of the software modules are written from scratch, exactly according to the requirements of a specific application. This approach results in very efficient, but usually also very inflexible code. Additionally, the development time and costs are high and the low level optimizations are often based on try and fail approaches and thus, error prone. On the other hand, the high level programming tries to abstract everything, making the programming easy and fast, but neglects taking the available resources into consideration. An approach for programming wireless sensor networks that provides low level control with high level application development time is not available.

In order to perform their tasks, the nodes have to collaborate and the data exchange is the basic means to allow cooperation. The exchanged data can have various meaning and importance levels, starting with simple measurements, through intermediate data computed based on the measurements, ending with state or process coordination data. I.e. the core task of WSNs is data or information handling. The currently running application defines the level of required quality, regarding the storage and transmission. There exists no standard for describing the data quality in wireless sensor networks nor a means that allows for easy adapting data quality in WSNs to the application needs. In the domain of large, high performance distributed systems, the quality of the data provided by shared data storage can be described using one of the defined memory models. The nodes in the network are only a kind of data collection and carrier system and the state of single nodes in the network should not affect the overall goal of the distributed application. Thus, different mechanisms can be applied, in order to improve the data availability in case of failures, e.g., the data can be replicated on multiple nodes. This implies the issue of the consistency of the stored replicas. Means to provide a defined quality of data in shared data storage with replicated data for wireless sensor networks did not attract much research in recent years. But, applying the standardized description of the data quality as it is used in wired networks to WSN as well as appropriate means to enforce those data could enable faster application development based data sharing service modules with clearly defined quality of the data storage, they provide.

1.2 Research objectives

The aim of this work is to investigate the means to exchange data between nodes while providing the specified quality of the data. Since data sharing is an already elaborated subject in the domain of large distributed systems, the means to be investigated in this thesis are also inspired by these solutions and follow the ideas known from the large computers.

But since the features of these two distributed systems differ radically, these original concepts have to be reconsidered in the context of wireless sensor network. The results shall support the application development for wireless sensor networks, by offering a set of data quality descriptors or models and mechanisms to achieve these.

In order to achieve this goal several technical and scientific objectives have to be investigated. First, the specific character of the wireless sensor networks has to be analyzed. This includes all the aspects, the hardware, with its constrained resources, as well as the software, with the current programming approaches and methodologies. Further, the distributed shared memory (DSM) abstraction has to be investigated, as a prominent example of the data sharing mechanism for large distributed system. Here it is necessary to understand the required mechanisms as well as the classification of the particular approaches with respect to the data quality and the features, they provide, i.e., the consistency models and the ways they can be implemented. Then, it is necessary to investigate the intersection of the two worlds, by considering the DSM related mechanisms within the WSN domain and proposing lightweight mechanisms to provide similar results with reduced resource consumption. In order to verify the proposed mechanisms and combinations of these, they have to be evaluated within the wireless sensor network context. And to provide the support for application development with the use of the proposed mechanisms, a specification for defining the data quality has to be created and the way a definition is transformed into an implementation has to be specified.

1.3 Contributions

This thesis investigates the feasibility of the provision of the distributed shared memory abstraction in the wireless sensor networks domain. The thesis analyses the individual memory consistency models defined for the DSM systems for large distributed systems as data storage quality measures and evaluates the feasibility of their realization in the WSN context. These consistency models are disassembled into a set of mechanisms that can be parameterized and used separately or in combinations to implement application specific consistency models. Based on that approach, a standardized and flexible framework for implementing data consistency in wireless sensor networks is proposed. This framework consists of a WSN middleware that provides the DSM abstraction with a standardized interface which can used to define the chosen data consistency. This standardized interface of the middleware allows implementing applications that are independent from the data consistency model and evaluating these with multiple models.

The data handling parameters allow fine tuning of the data consistency. This approach simplifies the application development by providing a tailor-made data exchange module automatically. A tool translates the description of the parameterized data handling mechanisms into an application specific instance of the WSN middleware that fulfills the needs of the application.

Thus, the burden of programming the consistency model into the application is taken from the developer by providing a tool that translates the description of the parameterized mechanisms into an application specific instance of the middleware that fulfills the needs of the application.

The proposed framework allows also practical data consistency related research in the wireless sensor network domain. This framework was used to evaluate the feasibility and costs of the chosen data consistency models in a practical approach. The implementations of these models generated by the tool were successfully executed on real wireless sensor nodes working as a network and exchanging data. This framework was also practically tested within the FeuerWhere [18] project, funded by the German Ministry of Education and Research.

1.4 Structure

This work is organized in six chapters, where the first one introduces the thesis and its objectives.

Chapter 2 provides the information about the state of the art in the individual areas involved in the research for this work. It starts with the introduction to the underlying distributed system, i.e., the wireless sensor network, providing an evaluation of the WSN systems together with their limitations. Then, the distributed shared memory abstraction is introduced and the different aspects of the DSM abstraction are initially evaluated in the WSN context. The chapter closes with some example approaches that combine these two areas and are related to the research presented in this work.

Chapter 3 discusses the mechanisms and principles that allow the application engineers to adjust a DSM system for WSN to their needs. The aspects of a DSM implementation, mentioned in Chapter 2, are deeper evaluated in the WSN context.

Chapter 4 introduces the tinyDSM middleware that was designed within this work, to provide the practical framework for the proof of concept. It starts with discussion on the main features the middleware should provide, i.e., the way of providing the distributed shared memory abstraction and supporting the application developer, taking into consideration the specific environment it should work within–the wireless sensor network. After discussing the set of functions the middleware provides and its interfaces, the details on the realization of the middleware are provided together with the methodology how to use it.

Chapter 5 evaluates the memory consistency models, introduced in Chapter 2 and provides the implementations of the chosen models within the tinyDSM framework. The implementations are also evaluated regarding their operation costs.

Chapter 6 concludes the thesis and gives the outlook for future work.

Chapter 2

Related work

This chapter provides the information about the state of the art in the individual areas involved in the research for this work. It starts with the introduction to the underlying distributed system, i.e., the wireless sensor network, providing an evaluation of the WSN systems together with their limitations. Then, the distributed shared memory abstraction is introduced. Due to the importance of the DSM concept in the area of distributed processing many systems with different features were proposed and implemented. However, only one of these systems (A Linda [8] derivate–TeenyLime [56]) takes into account the WSN as the underlying distributed system. Thus, this introduction of the DSM concept is extended by the evaluation of the different aspects of the DSM abstraction in the WSN context. The chapter closes with some example approaches that combine these two areas and are related to the research presented in this work.

2.1 Wireless Sensor Networks

A Wireless Sensor Network (WSN) is a specific type of a distributed system. It consists of a (potentially large) number of small computers with limited resources connected by means of (potentially unreliable) wireless communication. These computers, also referred to as (sensor) nodes or motes, may be equipped with sensing or acting capabilities, or both and the target application of such a system is to interact with the environment in any possible way, e.g., by sensing it, influencing it and even using it to obtain energy needed for operation. Thus, the term *wireless sensor network* has a rather principal meaning and covers all the new classes of cases in this research area known as Wireless Sensor and Actor Network (WSAN) or as Cyber-Physical System (CPS). Additionally, different classes of wireless sensor networks regarding their application, like Body Area Network (BAN) or more specifically a Medical Body Area

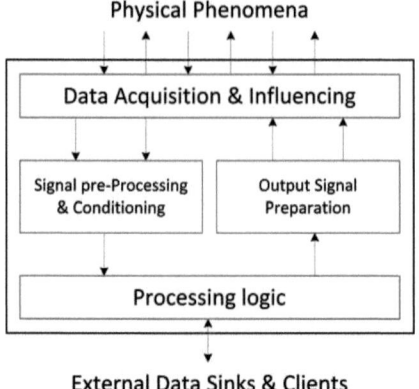

Figure 2.1: High level idea of a WSN application

Network (MBAN) or Wireless Body Area Network (WBAN) are covered by the general term as well.

The high level idea of the WSN application is presented in Figure 2.1. The rectangle represents the network of nodes, a distributed system that interacts with some physical phenomena, processes the data collected and probably, provides the data to some external systems or users.

This section first introduces the hardware used in WSNs to specify the magnitude of its limitations and then presents the software solutions used in these systems.

2.1.1 Hardware

The main components of the nodes, the WSN consists of, are the processing unit, the radio unit, the energy source and a set of sensors and actuators. These components are enough for a node to provide the basic functionality, i.e., to interact with the environment, process the data and communicate with other nodes.

The simplified architecture of a sensor node presented in Figure 2.2 is usually extended to provide additional functionality and to optimize the existing functionality. An extended architecture of a sensor node is depicted in Figure 2.3. It already goes into details of the hidden building blocks that a WSN node contains, i.e., the processing unit provides input and output functionality and requires different kinds of memory to fulfil its tasks. RAM memory is necessary for storing the local data, the program (or code) memory and the flash (or general, non-volatile) memory for local permanent data, like configuration. The external storage is used for larger data blocks, like logs or copies of the program.

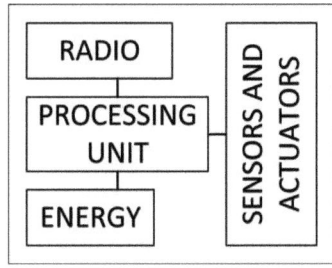

Figure 2.2: A simplified architecture of a wireless sensor node

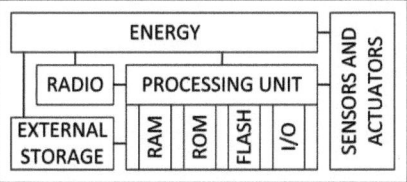

Figure 2.3: An extended architecture of a wireless sensor node

The basic concept of WSN was that the hardware shall be very inexpensive, allowing deployment without further maintenance or collecting of nodes. Many projects were involved in the elaboration of the WSN node hardware [173, 60, 59, 78], the term *mote* was invented at the University of California, Berkeley that was one of the centers were the research on the area started. The advances in technology allowed the node hardware to be miniaturized and self-contained. Thus, application specific nodes can be very small and highly integrated.

For research and to enable easy development and debugging several WSN node hardware platforms build from off-the-shelf components were proposed. A good comparison of the publicly available sensor node platforms can be found in [123]. It compares the most widely used platforms like the TmoteSky from Sentilla [48] (now available as TelosB [104] from MEMSIC [46]), MICA2 [102], MICAz [103], IRIS [101] from Crossbow (now MEMSIC), the SHIMMER from Shimmer Research [185] and the Sun SPOT (Small Programmable Object Technology) [105] from SUN (now Oracle [47]).

Other interesting wireless sensor hardware platforms are the EZ430-Chronos [115] from Texas Instruments [120] and the high-performance Imote2 [100] from Crossbow (now MEMSIC). The implementation presented in this work was done for the IHPNode hardware platform (see Figure 2.4) developed at the IHP [84] and mentioned in [171]. The main parameters of the above mentioned platforms are collected in Table 2.1. Since the SHIMMER and TmoteSky platforms are just derivates of the TelosB, they are not mentioned in the review.

Figure 2.4: The IHPNode hardware platform

Table 2.1: Sensor node hardware platforms build from off-the-shelf components

Platform	μC	f_{max} [MHz]	RAM [KB]	Code [KB]	Storage [MB]	Radio
MICAz	ATmega128L [54]	8	4	128	0.5	CC2420 [108]
MICA2	ATmega128L	8	4	128	0.5	CC1000 [110]
IRIS	ATmega1281 [52]	8	8	128	0.5	CC2420
TelosB	MSP430F1611 [119]	8	10	48	1	CC2420
IHPNode	MSP430F5438A [116]	25	16	256	4	CC1101 [112] CC2500 [111] CC2520 [109]
Chronos	CC430F6137 [114]	20	4	32	-	CC430F6137 (CC1101)
Sun SPOT	AT915SAM9G20 [51]	400	1024	8192	-	CC2420
Imote2	PXA271 [150]	416	256 + 32768	32768	-	CC2420

The different sensor node platforms can be divided into three main groups, depending on the architecture of the processing unit. They use either an 8-bit microcontrollers, e.g., one from the AVR family [43] from Atmel [44], or a 16-bit microcontroller, like one from the MSP430 family [107, 117, 113] from Texas Instruments or a 32-bit microcontroller based on an ARM core [145]. This parameter determines the available computational power of the platform, but on the other hand, it also specifies the energy costs related to the processing unit. This knowledge allows choosing the processing unit according to the expected complexity requirements of the application and influences the choice of energy sources.

Table 2.2 provides the energy consumption data for the Atmel ATmega128L micro-

Table 2.2: The energy consumption profile of the Atmel AT128L microcontroller

Mode	Frequency	Vcore	Power	Energy/MIPS
Active	8 MHz	5 V	85 mW	10.625 mWs
Idle	8 MHz	5 V	40 mW	-
Active	4 MHz	3 V	15 mW	3.75 mWs
Idle	4 MHz	3 V	6 mW	-
PowerDown	-	3 V	15 μW	-

Table 2.3: The energy consumption profile of the Atmel AT1281 microcontroller

Mode	Frequency	Vcore	Power	Energy/MIPS
Active	8 MHz	5 V	50.0 mW	6.3 mWs
Idle	8 MHz	5 V	13.5 mW	-
Active	4 MHz	3 V	9.6 mW	2.4 mWs
Idle	4 MHz	3 V	2.1 mW	-
Active	1 MHz	2 V	1.0 mW	1.0 mWs
Idle	1 MHz	2 V	0.3 mW	-
PowerDown	-	3 V	3 μW	-

Table 2.4: The energy consumption profile of the Atmel ATx128A4 microcontroller

Mode	Frequency	Vcore	Power	Energy/MIPS
Active	1 MHz	1.8 V	0.47 mW	0.47 mWs
Active	1 MHz	3 V	1.71 mW	1.71 mWs
Active	2 MHz	1.8 V	0.92 mW	0.46 mWs
Active	2 MHz	3 V	3.30 mW	1.65 mWs
Active	32 MHz	3 V	34.20 mW	1.07 mWs
Idle	1 MHz	1.8 V	0.14 mW	-
Idle	1 MHz	3 V	0.45 mW	-
Idle	2 MHz	1.8 V	0.29 mW	-
Idle	2 MHz	3 V	0.90 mW	-
Idle	32 MHz	3 V	14.40 mW	-
Active ULP	32 kHz	1.8 V	54 μW	1687.50 mWs
Active ULP	32 kHz	3 V	225 μW	7031.25 mWs
PowerDown (LPM4)	-	3 V	0.3 μW	-

controller used in the MICA2 and MICAz nodes. This is the least efficient processing unit from all used in all the platforms, but it is also the oldest one. It works only with supply voltage higher than 2.7 V, what reduces its application spectrum. Its successor, the ATmega1281 (see Table 2.3) used in the IRIS platforms provides already better figures in this area. It has also the double of its RAM memory and works with lower

Table 2.5: The energy consumption profile of the Texas Instruments MSP430F1611 microcontroller

Mode	Frequency	Vcore	Power	Energy/MIPS
Active	1 MHz	2.2 V	0.726 mW	0.73 mWs
Active	1 MHz	3 V	1.5 mW	1.50 mWs
Ultra Low Power	4 kHz	2.2 V	5.3 μW	1375 mWs
Ultra Low Power	4 kHz	3 V	27 μW	6750 mWs
Idle (LPM0)	-	3 V	225 μW	-
PowerDown (LPM4)	-	3 V	0.6 μW	-

Table 2.6: The energy consumption profile of the Texas Instruments MSP430F5438A microcontroller

Mode	Frequency	Vcore	Power	Energy/MIPS
Active Flash	25 MHz	3 V	27.0 mW	1.08 mWs
Active RAM	25 MHz	3 V	13.5 mW	0.94 mWs
Active Flash	12 MHz	3 V	9.3 mW	0.79 mWs
Active RAM	12 MHz	3 V	4.5 mW	0.375 mWs
Active Flash	8 MHz	3 V	5.5 mW	0.6875 mWs
Active RAM	8 MHz	3 V	2.7 mW	0.3375 mWs
Idle (LPM0)	-	3 V	210 μW	-
DeepSleep (LPM4,5)	-	3 V	0.3 μW	-

supply voltages starting from 1.8 V. But, these two microcontrollers are already outperformed by the new Atmel microcontrollers, e.g., the ATxmega128A4 [53], whose energy consumption data can be found in Table 2.4. It is a combined 8-bit and 16-bit computing unit, not used in any of the presented platforms, but a very interesting candidate for new solutions. The two older AVR microcontrollers work with clock frequencies up to 16 MHz, the new one allows setting it at 32 MHz. The AVR family members perform most of their operations in a singe clock cycle, and thus, their clock frequency affects the MIPS performance directly.

The next group of microcontrollers is the 16-bit MSP430 family from Texas Instruments. Table 2.5 presents the energy consumption data for the MSP430F1611 [119]. Due to its very good energy efficiency, low supply voltage (as low as 1.8V) and rich set of integrated peripherals it was very popular and used in many sensor node platforms. The most famous is the TelosB platform that was an inspiration for many other, like the SHIMMER or EPIC [75]. The MSP430 microcontroller provides better performance than the ATmega1281 or ATmega128L, even though it requires more than one clock cycle for most of its operations. An example of such a performance comparison for these two microcontroller families are cryptographic operations [169, 163].

Table 2.7: The energy consumption profile of the Marvell PXA271 microprocessor

Mode	Frequency	Vcore	Power	Energy/MIPS
Active	416 MHz	1.35 V	570 mW	1.37 mWs
Idle	416 MHz	1.35 V	186 mW	-
Active	104 MHz	0.90 V	116 mW	1.12 mWs
Idle	104 MHz	0.90 V	64 mW	-
Active	13 MHz	0.85 V	44 mW	3.38 mWs
Idle	13 MHz	0.85 V	10 mW	-
Standby	-		1.7 mW	-
DeepSleep	-		0.1 mW	-

Table 2.8: The energy consumption profile of the Atmel AT915SAM9G20 microprocessor

Mode	Frequency	Vcore	Power	Energy/MIPS
Active	400 MHz	1.0 V	50 mW	0.125 mWs
Idle	-	1.0 V	20 mW	-
Active	500 Hz	1.0 V	8 mW	16000 mWs
Backup	-	1.0 V	9 μW	-

The MSP430F1611 works at the maximum frequency of 8 MHz, what reduces its performance and has only 48 KB of code flash memory, what reduces the complexity of the applications that may run on platforms based on that microcontroller. The small memory size was due to the 16-bit addressing space and its von Neumann architecture. But, this problem was solved by the extension of the addressing space to 20-bit in the newer members of the MSP430 family. One of these new microcontrollers is the MSP430F5438A [116] used in the IHPNode platform. This microcontroller works with clock frequency reaching 25 MHz. Table 2.6 presents its power consumption data. An interesting feature of the MSP430 family members is that the energy consumption can be further reduced by more than 50% if the programs are executed from RAM.

The 32-bit processors from the last group are far more complex than the simple microcontrollers presented so far. They require more complex power supplies, due to separate voltages for the core and input-output circuitry, but they also provide much more functionality. The lower core voltage helps reducing the overall power consumption. They also work with clock frequencies above 400 MHz delivering enormous performance. However, this performance is compensated by higher energy consumption. The energy consumption data for the PXA271 [150] from Intel [45] (now Marvell [99]) are given in Table 2.7. Actually, this microprocessor is well known from mobile Personal Digital Assistant (PDA) class devices. It delivers enormous performance but

Table 2.9: Energy consumption profiles of the processing units used in WSN hardware platforms

μC	Energy/MIPS	@Frequency	Off Power
ATmega128L	3.750 mWs	4 MHz	15.0 μW
ATmega1281	2.400 mWs	4 MHz	3.0 μW
ATxmega128A4	1.070 mWs	32 MHz	0.3 μW
MSP430F1611	1.500 mWs	1 MHz	0.6 μW
MSP430F5438A	0.680 mWs	8 MHz	0.3 μW
PXA271	1.120 mWs	104 MHz	100.0 μW
AT91SAM9G20	0.125 mWs	400 MHz	9.0 μW

it contradicts with the idea of small and energy efficient wireless sensing devices. The AT915SAM9G20 [51] from Atmel is an ARM core based microprocessor with support for Java [106] programming language, what is used by the Java based Sun SPOT platform. Its energy consumption data provided in Table 2.8 shows that it is much more energy efficient than the PXA271. However, what can be seen for these two processing units is that the energy cost of one MHz is acceptable only for higher frequencies. Thus, advanced power management mechanisms are required in order to save energy.

Table 2.9 provides a summary of the energy requirements for all the mentioned processors. The power figures for the 8-bit and 16-bit microcontrollers are all provided for supply voltage equal to 3 V and for code running from flash memory. Reducing the supply voltage could further reduce the power consumed. And running the program from RAM memory on the MSP430 microcontrollers requires additional memory management overhead, but reduces the power consumption by more than 50 %. The clock frequencies are given according to the specifications from respective data sheets. However, for the ATmega128L, ATmega1281 and MSP430F1611 the energy consumption per MHz should also apply for higher clock frequencies, e.g., 8 MHz. The very attractive per MHz power consumption of the AT91SAM9G20 is caused by its high clock frequency and by very low core voltage, i.e., only 1.0 V. The AT91SAM9G20 can be used as the second processor that can be used on demand, but in general, the 32-bit processors are not considered further as potential main processing units for sensor network hardware.

The WSN node hardware platforms can be further differentiated based on the radio module they use. All the mentioned platforms use radio transceiver modules from Chipcon (now Texas Instruments). The CC1000 [110] used in the MICA2 platform was one of the first integrated low power transceivers working in the sub-GHz frequency bands (315 MHz, 433 MHz, 868 MHz and 915 MHz). Table 2.10 provides the energy consumption data for this transceiver. Its disadvantage is relatively low data rate, however its overall power consumption figures (especially in the 433 MHz band) are

Table 2.10: The energy consumption profile of the Texas Instruments CC1000 transceiver

Mode	Power	Energy/kbit	Comment
RX @433 MHz	27.9 mW	363 µWs/kb	optimum
RX @433 MHz	22.2 mW	289 µWs/kb	low current
RX @868 MHz	35.4 mW	461 µWs/kb	optimum
RX @868 MHz	28.8 mW	375 µWs/kb	low current
Power Down	0.6 µW	-	
Idle	2.6 mW	-	
TX @433 MHz	26.7 mW	348 µWs/kb	-5dBm
TX @433 MHz	31.2 mW	406 µWs/kb	0dBm
TX @433 MHz	44.4 mW	578 µWs/kb	5dBm
TX @433 MHz	80.1 mW	1042 µWs/kb	10dBm
TX @868 MHz	41.4 mW	539 µWs/kb	-5dBm
TX @868 MHz	49.5 mW	645 µWs/kb	0dBm
TX @868 MHz	76.2 mW	992 µWs/kb	5dBm
VCC 2.1 V–3.6 V			
Max. datarate 76.8 kbps			

very good.

As the complexity of the network protocols and the requirements of communication grew, the data rate provided by the CC1000 and its support for protocols became insufficient. Its successors are the CC1101 [112] and CC2500 [111], pin and logic compatible transceiver chips working in the sub-GHz bands and the 2.4 GHz band, respectively. These two transceivers differ in the applied radio front end, and thus, differ in the efficiency and possible output power settings. But they both work with wider voltage supplies, i.e., starting from 1.8 V. In contrast to the CC1000, in the receive mode (RX) the CC1101 transceiver is more energy efficient in the 868 MHz band than in the 433 MHz (see Table 2.11). The CC2500 performs similar to the CC1101, but provides lower output power and the transmission costs are higher if using the same data rate (see Table 2.12). These two radio modules, the CC1101 and CC2500 are used on the IHPNode hardware platform developed at the IHP [84]. This allows low power and high data rate communication in both, 868 MHz and 2.4 GHz frequency band using similar settings and the same parameters.

The above mentioned transceiver chips provide only basic support for the protocols, e.g., simple addressing and the clear channel assessment (CCA). Thus, the remaining part has to be realized in software. In order to standardize the applications, reduce the complexity of the software and improve the performance new transceiver chips with more protocol hardware support were developed. One of the first IEEE 802.15.4 [159] and ZigBee [11] compliant transceivers is the CC2420 from Chipcon (now Texas

Table 2.11: The energy consumption profile of the Texas Instruments CC1101 transceiver

Mode	Power	Energy/kbit	Comment
RX@433MHz	46.2 mW	1203 μWs/kb	38.4 kbps
RX@433MHz	49.2 mW	197 μWs/kb	250 kbps
RX@868MHz	45.3 mW	1180 μWs/kb	38.4 kbps
RX@868MHz	48.9 mW	196 μWs/kb	250 kbps
Power Down	0.6 μW	-	
Idle	5.1 mW	-	
TX@433MHz	39.3 mW	78 μWs/kb	-6dBm, 500 kbps
TX@433MHz	48.0 mW	96 μWs/kb	0dBm, 500 kbps
TX@433MHz	87.6 mW	175 μWs/kb	10dBm, 500 kbps
TX@868MHz	49.2 mW	88 μWs/kb	-6dBm, 500 kbps
TX@868MHz	50.4 mW	101 μWs/kb	0dBm, 500 kbps
TX@868MHz	90.0 mW	180 μWs/kb	10dBm, 500 kbps
TX@868MHz	102.6 mW	205 μWs/kb	12dBm, 500 kbps
VCC 1.8 V–3.6 V			
Max. datarate 500 kbps			

Table 2.12: The energy consumption profile of the Texas Instruments CC2500 transceiver

Mode	Power	Energy/kbit	Comment
RX@250kBaud	51.9 mW	208 μWs/kb	normal
RX@250kBaud	45.0 mW	180 μWs/kb	low power
RX@500kBaud	54.9 mW	110 μWs/kb	normal
Power Down	1.2 μW	-	
Idle	4.5 mW	-	
TX	45.0 mW	90 μWs/kb	-6dBm, 500 kbps
TX	63.6 mW	127 μWs/kb	0dBm, 500 kbps
TX	64.5 mW	129 μWs/kb	1dBm, 500 kbps
VCC 1.8 V–3.6 V			
Max. datarate 500 kbps			

Instruments). It provides hardware support for packet handling, encryption using advanced encryption standard (AES) [6] and authentication, and thus reduces the burden of the software. However, the price for this increased functionality is the slightly increased energy consumption compared to the simple transceivers (see Table 2.13). Due to its features, the CC2420 is very popular and extensively used in the sensor node platforms. It is used by the most of the above mentioned WSN node hardware platforms, i.e., it is applied in MICAz, IRIS, TelosB, Sun SPOT and Imote2. This provides, at least from the physical layer (PHY) perspective, the possibility for all

Table 2.13: The energy consumption profile of the Texas Instruments CC2420 transceiver

Mode	Power	Energy/kbit	Comment
RX	56.4 mW	226 μWs/kb	
PowerDown	60 nW	-	
Idle	1.3 mW	-	
TX	29.7 mW	119 μWs/kb	-15dBm
TX	33.0 mW	132 μWs/kb	-10dBm
TX	42.0 mW	168 μWs/kb	-5dBm
TX	52.2 mW	209 μWs/kb	0dBm
VCC 2.1 V–3.6 V			
Datarate 250 kbps			

Table 2.14: The energy consumption profile of the Texas Instruments CC2520 transceiver

Mode	Power	Energy/kbit	Comment
RX	66.9 mW	-	wait for sync
RX	56.4 mW	-	wait for sync low power
RX	55.5 mW	222 μWs/kb	receiving
Power Down	525 μW	-	LPM1
Power Down	90 nW	-	LPM2
Idle	4.8 mW	-	
TX	77.4 mW	310 μWs/kb	0dBm
TX	100.8 mW	403 μWs/kb	5dBm
VCC 1.8 V–3.8 V			
Datarate 250 kbps			

these nodes to communicate with each other.

Like the CC2420, its successor, the CC2520 uses direct symbol spread spectrum (DSSS) to increase the link budget. The data rate is thus reduced, but higher ranges can be achieved with lower transmitting power and the robustness is increased. Table 2.14 shows that the CC2520 provides slightly worse energy efficiency, compared to cc2420, but is more flexible in use. The general purpose pins are freely programmable and can provide the microcontroller with direct information, so it does not need to read the registers of the transceiver. The CC2520 provides also higher transmitting power and lower supply voltage (starting from 1.8 V instead of 2.1 V) compared to its precursor. The CC2520 is used as the third radio module at the IHPNode platform to provide it the possibility to communicate with platforms equipped with CC2420 transceivers.

Other interesting radio transceivers that are very attractive for the wireless sensor node development are the AT86RF212 [50] and the AT86RF231 [49] from Atmel. These

Table 2.15: The energy consumption profile of the Atmel AT86RF212 transceiver

Mode	Power	Energy/kbit	Comment
RX	27.6 mW	27.6 µWs/kb	1 Mbps
RX	26.1 mW	26.1 µWs/kb	low power, 1 Mbps
Power Down	0.6 µW	-	
Idle	1.2 mW	-	
TX	39 mW	39 µWs/kb	0dBm, 1 Mbps
TX	51 mW	51 µWs/kb	5dBm, 1 Mbps
TX	75 mW	75 µWs/kb	10dBm, 1 Mbps
VCC 1.8 V–3.6 V			
Max. datarate 1 Mbps			

Table 2.16: The energy consumption profile of the Atmel AT86RF231 transceiver

Mode	Power	Energy/kbit	Comment
RX	30.9 mW	15.5 µWs/kb	normal mode, 2 Mbps
RX	36.9 mW	18.5 µWs/kb	high sensitivity, 2 Mbps
PowerDown	60 nW	-	
Idle	1.2 mW	-	
TX	34.8 mW	17.4 µWs/kb	0 dBm, 2 Mbps
TX	42.0 mW	21.0 µWs/kb	3 dBm, 2 Mbps
VCC 1.8 V–3.6 V			
Max. datarate 2 Mbps			

are also IEEE 802.15.4 and ZigBee compliant and work either in the 2.4 GHz band (AT86RF231) or in the sub-GHz band (AT86RF212). The energy consumption data for these two transceivers is provided in Table 2.16 and Table 2.15. According to the specification these two transceivers allow data rates reaching one Mbps (AT86RF212) and two Mbps (AT86RF231). Combined with the power consumption these two chips provide very good energy consumption per Kbps. The AT86RF212 is used in the latest version of the Mulle hardware platform from Eistec [1].

Table 2.17 provides the summary of the energy consumption data for all the mentioned radio transceivers. The values are given for the supply voltage equal to 3.0 V and the transmission costs per one kbit are calculated according to the datasheet for a normalized data rate equal to 250 kbps if available. It can be seen, that the transceivers from Atmel have very attractive energy consumption parameters, even if used at lower data rate than the maximum.

For customers and researchers that need a combination of hardware components that is not available on the market in any platform a custom design is needed. Here, two main options are available, either constructing a completely new hardware platform

Table 2.17: Energy consumption profiles of the radio transceivers used in WSN hardware platforms

Transceiver	RX	TX	Comment
CC1000	289 μWs/kb	406 μWs/kb	76.8 kbps, 433 MHz
CC1101	197 μWs/kb	192 μWs/kb	250 kbps, 433 MHz
CC2500	208 μWs/kb	254 μWs/kb	250 kbps
CC2420	226 μWs/kb	209 μWs/kb	250 kbps
CC2520	222 μWs/kb	310 μWs/kb	250 kbps
AT86RF212	110 μWs/kb	156 μWs/kb	250 kbps
AT86RF231	124 μWs/kb	139 μWs/kb	250 kbps

Figure 2.5: The Tandem Stack hardware platform

from scratch or constructing it from available building blocks. The former option is time and cost consuming, but gives the largest flexibility of the design. There are again two options, either commercially available integrated circuits (IC) can be used or application specific integrated circuits (ASIC) can be developed. Developing ASICs is even more time and cost consuming. The IHPNode is an example of completely new platform build from scratch using commercially available ICs.

The building of a sensor node hardware platform from prefabricated modules allows fast prototype development and is less error prone, since the building blocks are usually logically separated modules that are already tested functionally and electrically. The building block approaches like EPIC [75] propose using prefabricated modules that can be soldered on a larger main board and approaches like the Tandem Stack (see Figure 2.5) developed at the IHP and the one proposed in [176] propose using LEGO like approach with standardized connectors to construct a stack of modules constituting the sensor nodes. The approach presented in [176] allows also using field programmable gate array (FPGA) to be used as the processing units for even more flexibility.

The above discussion on energy consumption of radio modules and processing units is due to the fact that these components are the most utilized components of a wireless sensor node, and thus, are in the largest part responsible for the energy consumption. The wireless sensor nodes are usually powered by batteries or other low capacity energy sources, like solar cells. Thus, the efficiency of the chosen hardware influences the prospected lifetime of the application with some given energy source. Usually, the voltage provided by batteries differs in dependence of the remaining capacity. And this is the reason why the wide range for accepted supply voltage is an advantage.

The capacity of a standard AA alkaline battery is about 2.5 Ah [169]. Different battery manufacturer can define this capacity differently, but usually it is specified for a cut-off voltages equal to 0.8 V. What means that the battery voltage drops from the initial 1.6 V down to 0.8 V. Assuming a linear voltage drop, the average voltage is equal to 1.2 V, resulting in 3 Wh of energy that can be delivered by a single battery. Thus, two AA alkaline batteries in a series deliver about 6 Wh of energy with a voltage range between 3.2 V and 1.6 V. Moving the cut-off voltage above 1.8 V limits this value to about 5 Wh, but allows specifying the amount of energy that can be used by the most of the mentioned radio and processing units. For example, the MSP430F5438A running at 8 MHz can work for about 26471 billion clock cycles with this amount of energy (40 days). Similar, the CC1101 can transmit or receive about 91.4 Gbit of data at the data rate of 250 kbps, what equals to more than 100 hours of constant transmission.

The above hardware evaluation shows that the applications in the wireless sensor network are highly energy efficiency driven. Additionally, the unreliable and contention prone communication means require sophisticated protocols in order to provide both, reliability and energy efficiency. The following section presents the WSN software layer that actually cannot be evaluated without considering the underlying hardware.

2.1.2 Software

The software that has to be executed on WSN hardware has to take into account its limitations. Thus, care has to be taken on the optimal implementation. However, just like in the case of the hardware platform design, there is a trade-off between the most optimal realization and the time and costs needed for its development. Again, modular approach may result in slightly less optimal implementation, but can reduce the development time radically.

Operating Systems

An operating system for wireless sensor networks is a set of hardware drivers and simple services combined with some programming concept. They provide a programming framework to speed up the development and provide code reusability. A survey on current operating systems for wireless sensor networks can be found in [183].

The operating systems for Wireless Sensor Networks are restricted by the specific nature of wireless sensor nodes. These devices have constrained memory, processing power and energy resources, what makes the standard operating systems unusable for them. The operating system for wireless sensor networks needs to fulfil the following requirements:

- Limitation of code and data memory usage

- Energy management, Memory management, Device management (peripherals)

- Concurrency mechanisms, scheduling, multitasking, multi-threading

- Real-time operation, Robustness

- Low level hardware abstraction, API to application developers

- Modularity, application-specific configuration, parameterizing

TinyOS TinyOS [137] is an event driven programming framework for embedded systems. It is a set of independent components that allow building an application-specific operating system for each application. The components are implemented in nesC, a dialect of C programming language, which has a very low memory foot print. The execution model of TinyOS is based on commands, asynchronous events and tasks. A command is a request to a component to perform some function, for example reading a sensor. The completion of the operation is signaled by the correspondent event, following the hardware split-phase way of working. Events can be signaled to the handlers written by an application developer or can be signaled completely asynchronously, e.g., by hardware interrupts. Commands and events can post tasks, i.e., non-preemptive, running to completion deferred procedures executed by the TinyOS FIFO scheduler.

Components encapsulate set of commands they provide and events they signal, specified by interfaces. The component has two classes of interfaces: interfaces it provides and interfaces it uses. The interfaces are the definition of the interaction of the component with other components. Interfaces contain both commands and events. Command is implemented by the provider of the interface and event is implemented by the user of the interface.

An application connects the components using wiring, which is independent from the component implementations. Only used components are included in the application binary.

There are two types of components; modules and configurations. A module provides a code written in nesC with extension for calling and implementing commands and events. Configurations wire other components together by connecting interfaces used by components to interfaces provided by other components. Interfaces can be wired multiple times and this fan-out is transparent to the caller as long as the return type has a function that combines the results of all the calls.

The nesC dialect has limitations when compared to the C language. The compiler knows the complete function call graph of the program, what removes the cross-module calls overhead. Function pointers are not allowed. The dynamic memory allocation is not supported by nesC, what prevents memory fragmentation and allocation failures.

The concurrency model in TinyOS consists of non-preemptive tasks and also of interrupt handlers, which are signaled asynchronously. Tasks are atomic to each other, but not to interrupt handlers, commands and events invoked by those tasks. To avoid data races it is possible to use atomic sections of code, which are running atomically.

The communication in TinyOS is based on Active Messages, where packets are associated with one byte handler ID. The received Active Message is dispatched using an event to all the handlers being entitled to receive this type of messages. Active Message provides an interface to the serial port and to the radio and in the latter case may abstract the used protocol modules, allowing more general applications.

TinyOS provides also support for energy saving. To reduce the power usage, the processor and all the subsystems can be put into a low-power mode every time, when there are no tasks in the queue. The components save their states in the memory for later resumption.

Due to the cross-component optimizations and whole-program compilation, TinyOS produces smaller and faster code than the original hand-written C code.

Contiki Contiki [74] is an operating system developed for power constrained devices, such as wireless sensor nodes. It is implemented in the C programming language. Contiki offers a possibility to upload the applications or services at run-time, without the need of uploading the entire system as a single binary image. Thus, this allows saving energy and time needed for the transmission of code updates, since the application binaries are smaller than the complete system binary.

Contiki is a hybrid combining the event-driven kernel as the base of the system with a preemptive multi-threading library that can be optionally included for applications that require it. Kernel, program loader, drivers for communication hardware and supporting libraries constitute the core of the system. The core is compiled and installed on the device before the deployment and is not modified.

The Contiki system consists of the core and processes. A process is a service or application, where a service implements functionality that is used by other processes, i.e., it is a kind of a shared library. The program loader is used for loading the applications into the system on the device. The communication between processes is done by posting the events. The events can by synchronous or asynchronous. There is also a polling mechanism, where polling can be seen as a high priority event scheduled in-between each asynchronous event.

The kernel consists of a scheduler dispatching events to processes and calling processes' polling handlers. The event handlers are not preempted by the scheduler, thus they run to completion. Only the interrupts can preempt the events.

The kernel uses single stack for execution of all processes. Stack space is reduced due to rewinding the stack between each invocation of event handlers. The kernel does not support power saving, but the applications can implement such a mechanism.

A service layer manages the services by keeping the track of running services and providing the way for finding the installed services. A service consists of the interface and of the process implementing the interface.

The sizes of the generated binaries to be installed on the nodes is usually larger than that of TinyOS.

Reflex The Reflex [206] operating system implements the basic abstraction for the event flow model. The implementation is divided into three layers. The lowest layer–the kernel–consists of the interrupt handlers, energy managing units and the scheduler. The middle layer–the runtime library–offers the event flow mechanisms, which are used by the third layer–the application. The third layer contains also the drivers, which are able to be directly influenced by the interrupts. The Reflex is implemented in the C++ programming language.

The application is built using activities, i.e., C++ objects that are managed by the scheduler. The activity can be run, triggered, locked and unlocked. The triggering of an activity can be configured regarding the frequency. An activity has an execution state, i.e., it may be idle, running, scheduled or interrupted. But the interrupted state is only possible in case when preemption is allowed. If the activity is locked, then it cannot be planned.

The handling of the interrupts in Reflex is realized in two steps. After the interrupt occurs, the wrapper-routine detects what kind of interrupt occurred and executes the common interrupt handler, which saves all the volatile registers. After the synchronization with the scheduler, the specific handler for the interrupt is called.

The application is built from components, i.e., C++ classes containing activities, interrupt handlers, variables and functions. The components are connected using the interfaces in a configuration that additionally contains the parameters and the instantiation of the components.

The Reflex operating system provides the scheduling framework, where the chosen scheduling method does not influence on development of the activities.

Reflex implements the following scheduling schemes:

- First come first serve scheduling–the activities are put on the list and are processed one by one

- Fixed priority scheduling–the activities are put in the queue according to the priorities they have. There are three variants of the scheme: non-preemptive scheduling, preemptive scheduling and preemptive scheduling with minimal interrupt lock

- Earliest deadline first scheduling–the activities are placed in the queue according to time which is left until their reach their deadline

- Time triggered scheduling–the activities are connected with the system clock. The scheduler determines the execution order in time.

IHPOS The IHPOS operating system [171] was developed within this work. It provides a software development framework for the IHPNode hardware platform. It simplifies the application development and allows verifying the application behaviour and parameters with very low additional overhead. Due to the lack of support for the MSP430F5438A microcontroller in the mspgcc [69] the IHPOS was originally developed in the Code Composer Studio [118] integrated development environment (IDE). However, since the microcontroller is supported by mspgcc4 [23], the IHPOS can be also used in a Linux based software development environment.

IHPOS consists of drivers and services. The drivers have the direct access to the hardware and the services abstract the functionality provided by the drivers. The services provided by the IHPOS are:

- identity–provides the node identity based on some specific hardware data, e.g., unique identity stored in an identity chip or flash memories,

- interrupt–controls the interrupt handling, allows registering the handler functions for interrupts and notifies these on interrupt,

- radio–allows using the radio transceivers available on the hardware platform,

- scheduler–allows registering and scheduling parameterless tasks for later execution,

- timer–provides the functionality provided by the real time clock (RTC) and timers available on the hardware, i.e., allows measuring time, reading out the current time and periodic or time delayed execution of parameterless functions.

- sensors–provides a standardized interface to sensors, i.e., allows reading passive sensors, enabling and disabling active sensors and handling of the measurements they provide.

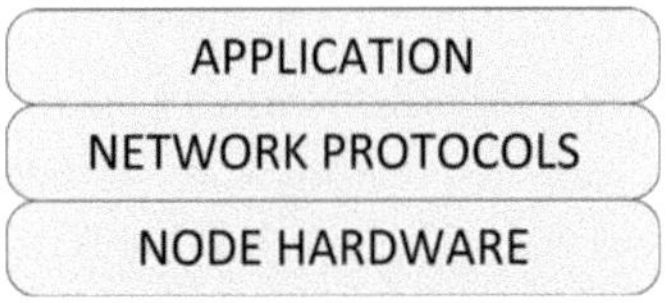

```
┌─────────────────────┐
│     APPLICATION     │
├─────────────────────┤
│  NETWORK PROTOCOLS  │
├─────────────────────┤
│    NODE HARDWARE    │
└─────────────────────┘
```

Figure 2.6: The simplified WSN protocol stack

Since the system was designed for a specific hardware platform it naturally covers the features the platform provides. However, the services provide a standardized interfaces, what allows supporting also different hardware, after some adaptations and exchanging the set of hardware specific drivers. Thus, an application using this interface could be run on different hardware without modifications.

The scheduler is based on a list of registered task that are permanently monitored and run to completion if scheduled. An active task can reschedule itself and runs to completion, i.e., it can be only preempted by a hardware interrupt. The tasks are not prioritized and the order is determined by the task registration order.

Protocols

Figure 2.6 presents a simplified protocol stack used on sensor nodes. The *application* uses the *protocols*, which use the specific *hardware drivers* of the communication modules.

This simplified stack is a result of the function melting of the standard ISO-OSI protocol stack. The hardware may represent the physical layer (PHY). It is hardware platform dependent, but is usually hidden by a hardware abstraction layer to provide a standardized and hardware independent interface to the upper layers. The protocols layer include the medium access control (MAC), routing and transport. In WSN, these three layers are often hard to separate. The session, presentations and application layers are melted into the application layer in Figure 2.6.

In order to provide energy efficient and robust communication between the nodes in the WSN it is very important that the protocol stack supports this. The medium access defines the power efficiency and allowed duty cycling, i.e., periodic switching of the radio hardware off to save energy. And since the energy consumed by the radio constitutes the larger part of the overall power consumption the MAC protocol becomes the central part of the networking.

The main aim of the MAC layer is to coordinate the access to the common medium for all the nodes in the network to avoid collisions and, as a result, to increase the throughput and reliability while decreasing the latency. If several nodes are able to send their data then the sending approaches need to be coordinated or the data may be lost due to packet collisions. And even if the coordination mechanisms are applied it can happen that the sent data will be demolished by a node that is not aware of the coordination or behaves incorrectly. Also external sources of radio signals operating in the same frequency can cause data destruction. In order to cope with such data losses additional mechanisms can be applied that verify the successful delivery of a packet and retransmit it if necessary. More sophisticated approaches can try to avoid a channel that is too busy or jammed.

The used communication technology defines the MAC layer addressing and the possible transmission schemes, e.g., it can support unicast only, broadcast only, both or even multicast.

If an assumption can be made that all the nodes in the WSN create a single-hop network and thus, are in communication range of each other, then the choice of the MAC protocol features is simplified because several medium access issues, like hidden terminal problem do not exist. Anyway, the link reliability cannot be assumed static, due to the dynamic character of the network, i.e., new nodes may be installed and they can move independent from each other causing changes in the links between the nodes and maybe even temporal link breaks.

Other important factors that influence the MAC layer are the desired topology and the way the data is accessed. The topology can represent the flow of the data, i.e., every two nodes exchanging data are connected by a link. Thus, the topology in a network can range from a star-topology with a central node to a fully connected mesh, where all the nodes exchange some data between each other. The data access can be based on data pulling or pushing. Pulling is from the definition asynchronous and pushing can be either synchronous or asynchronous. This description induces the simplest medium access mechanism with a star topology and a master node that pulls all the other nodes for their data or pushes data to them. In such an implementation of WSN the master node is usually a kind of base station that also provides the interfaces to the external data clients. From the MAC protocol perspective the master node plays the role of the coordinator.

The wireless medium can be multiplexed in code (CDMA), space (SDMA), time (TDMA) and frequency (FDMA). An important question is if the nodes belonging to different WSNs can exchange data or if the networks are logically separated and the communication in foreign network is actually to be treated as noise. In the latter case the physical separation can be achieved and the interference can be minimized by using the medium multiplexing. Best suited is frequency multiplexing. The space multiplexing is de facto used automatically as long as the WSNs are not in close proximity of each other. Code multiplexing can be too expensive for low power wireless devices. Time multiplexing is best suited to be used for coordination of the communication between nodes in a WSN not for separation of different WSNs. Thus, the main MAC protocols for WSNs use TDMA and the access is random [3], contention-based [213, 77, 204, 174] or scheduled [79, 92, 162, 214, 181, 216, 30]. The schedule of the access can also be created as a result of a contention phase.

The main advantages of schedule-based protocols is that they provide more predictable communication latency important for QoS and allow duty-cycling, i.e., saving energy by switching the radio off while there is no communication planned for a particular node. However, they need time synchronization or means to compensate the clock drift [31] and can be not flexible enough for networks with high dynamics, either in the topology or data flow changes. On the other hand, pure contention-based MAC protocols require more energy or need sophisticated hardware supporting wake-up radio to support duty cycling, but they are far more flexible and usually provide smaller, but sometimes not predictable, communication latency. Most of the schedule-based protocols provide a contention phase, where the nodes can compete for the time slots in the scheduled phase, but this increases the flexibility together with the increase of the coordination overhead and latency. Schedule-based MAC protocols are best suited for regular transport of regular data pieces. To cope with irregularities they need to be in range with the provided flexibility. Indeed, most contention-based protocols provide active/sleep cycles as well, and thus, provide kind of scheduling. This results in approaches trying to combine the best from contention-based and schedule-based mechanisms as a trade-off of their features. These advantages and disadvantages need to be analysed on application basis.

The routing and transport protocol layers for wireless sensor networks are rather application specific and these layers are often combined in one for optimization reasons. Like for the MAC protocols there is no standard solution and dozens of approaches with different features are proposed [9, 10, 215, 70].

The networking is the part of the WSN that is mostly exposed to noninvasive security threats. Thus, it is also the part that receives the most concern regarding being secured. The security approaches focus on many different aspects of networking, e.g., MAC [184, 36, 127], routing [128, 4, 193], code update [67] or collaborative authentication [68], just to mention a few. There are also approaches that combine the security mechanisms depending on the application needs [132, 164].

2.1.3 Applications

The wireless sensor networks have a very broad spectrum of applications. This section gives the idea of the typical applications that influence the research on WSN. Survey-like collections of examples of these are presented in [12] and in [155]. In general, these applications can be divided into several classes depending on the role of the sensor nodes.

sense and store This class involves individual non-cooperative nodes that only sense and store the data. The collected data is harvested from the network using a wireless mobile device and the evaluation of the data happens in a central point.

sense and forward Extends the first in that it uses the neighboring nodes to forward the sensed data to a stationary or mobile sink. The data is provided in raw or is only initially preprocessed, e.g., filtering out implausible data or data aggregation.

sense, detect and forward In this third class of applications, the nodes either individually or cooperatively process the data they have measured and are able, e.g., to detect some events. The result of the processing is forwarded to the sink.

sense, detect and react The last class enables the nodes to react to the detected events, i.e., the nodes can use some actuators to adapt to or maybe even to influence the changes in the measured phenomena.

The WSN applications can be further divided regarding their specific application area. The research on WSN was mainly initiated by military applications. In [139] a framework for distributed computation to track multiple targets in the sensor field is presented. This kind of application can be used in the general surveillance application area, but the military variant assumes also operating behind the enemy lines. The general research on intrusion detection using wireless sensor networks touching several aspects, like target tracking and classification is presented in [13]. The WSAN4CIP European project [178] proposes the use of wireless sensor networks to protect the critical infrastructure, what is an important aspect of homeland security. It relies on the security framework for WSN developed within the UBISEC&SENS project [177]. An example homeland security application developed based on this framework is presented in [90].

Another application area that significantly influenced the WSN research is environmental monitoring. Many different applications fall into this class, starting with agricultural monitoring systems. They help achieving ideal grow conditions, e.g., for wine grapes [122] and also allow profiling the results of wine production by monitoring (and externally influencing) the temperature, ground and air humidity and amount of sunlight.

Environmental monitoring applications include monitoring on and inside of a glacier in Norway [149], monitoring of an active volcano in Ecuador [209, 208] and application of WSN in oceanography [200]. In short, these applications allow monitoring changes in the environment or monitoring of the potentially dangerous elements of the environment. The system presented in [189] also belongs to the second group. It is a sensor network based system to predict land slides caused by monsoon rains in the western India. The aim of the system is to predict not only to detect them.

Another aspect of monitoring the nature is habitat monitoring. The famous example from this application class is the ZebraNet with all its consideration, i.e., hardware, software aspects as well as the deployment experience and results [124, 217, 144].

The application area that gathers more and more interest is patient monitoring, or more general medical monitoring. Architectures of systems for patient monitoring using wireless sensor networks are proposed in [160, 15]. The reliability and ease of use are the most important requirements for such systems.

Monitoring of first responders, like fire fighters is an application that combines the features of medical monitoring and homeland security. The system developed within the FeuerWhere project [18] monitors the vital and environmental parameters of each fire fighter and allows improving the safety of these forces by early detection of dangerous situations [172, 171].

The above examples are not the complete and exhaustive collection of the WSN applications. But, as shown by these examples, the spectrum of WSN applications is limited only by the imagination of researchers. To summarize, the wireless sensor networks are best suited for applications with huge amount of data to be collected in parallel and in distributed manner.

2.1.4 Evaluation means

The development of WSN protocols and applications requires reliable evaluation mechanisms to verify their correctness. Due to the complexity of the WSN as a distributed system and the huge amount of parameters that can influence the way of working, usually the verification can be realized only for some chosen set of conditions.

The testing in a real deployment requires the nodes to provide output data to allow monitoring the application flow. Such a requirement may cause changing the run-time conditions, since it may induce delay and additional traffic. Thus, the events in such a real life deployment may be also hard to observe. This is the reason why WSN simulators and emulators are applied in the evaluation process.

Since the environment is that complicated, the simulators and emulators allow verifying correctness of the ideas in different aspects. TOSSIM [135, 136] is included in the TinyOS and allows verifying the algorithms implemented with nesC language in a hardware independent way, by simplifying the networking and specific hardware features.

Avrora [203, 63] focuses on the emulation of the AVR microcontroller family and allows precise evaluation of the compiled code for MICA platforms. It also allows executing the code for the specific radio transceivers. However, the radio channel

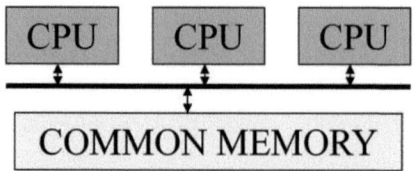

Figure 2.7: A shared memory system

simulation is simplified.

Castalia [29] can be used in order to evaluate algorithms with more precise channel simulation. It is a module for OMNET++ that tries to model the wireless channel as exact as possible. However, the implementation of the evaluated algorithms is not WSN hardware related, i.e, does not take into account resource constraints.

There are many different simulators for WSN applications with different features and focus [190, 41, 195, 175, 205, 83]. Surveys on these can be found in [98] and in [76].

The comparison of the real life evaluation and simulation is like a separate research area [165, 17]. The real life measurements can be used to enhance the simulation results [95].

2.2 Distributed Shared Memory

The Distributed Shared Memory (DSM) provides an abstraction of a common memory in a physically distributed system. It tries to combine the advantages of two classes of systems with multiple processing units: tightly coupled multiprocessors and loosely coupled multiprocessors, i.e., the shared memory systems and multi-computers. This subject is a fundamental part of distributed systems and already a mature research area, it has been studied thoroughly [140, 179, 125, 191, 42, 180, 197, 198, 158].

The shared memory multiprocessors have a common memory available to all the processors equally (see Figure 2.7). This approach allows easy programming of the mechanisms to exchange data between the processing units, also denoted as nodes. The content of the shared memory is always consistent as long as the accessing rules are clearly defined, e.g., using arbitrage, and the interface does not allow parallel modifications leading to undefined state of the data. However, the single interface to the memory may become a bottleneck if the number of accessing nodes grows or the frequency of accesses increases. Due to that the scalability of the approach is limited.

On the other hand, in a system consisting of loosely coupled multiprocessors, also denoted as a multicomputer system, each processing unit is equipped with its own memory (see Figure 2.8). Thus, exchanging data between processing units requires

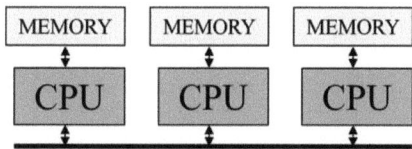

Figure 2.8: A loosely coupled multiprocessor system

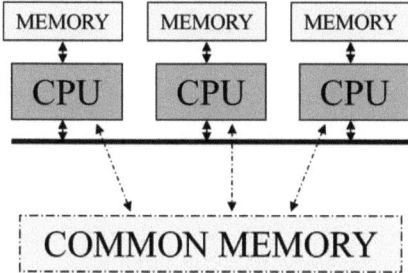

Figure 2.9: A distributed shared memory system

message passing via the interconnecting network. However, this approach lacks at the transparency of the access and complicates the programming of the data exchange. Additionally, it induces problems with the consistency of the data stored in the memories of each unit. But, it provides high scalability due to the lack of a common memory bus and possible ways to optimize the access to remote data.

Thus, the DSM abstraction tries to overcome the scalability problems of the tightly coupled multiprocessors while keeping their ease of programmability and data reliability by distributing the shared memory over multiple loosely coupled multiprocessors and providing mechanisms that hide the management layer from the processes running in the system. The DSM logically implements the shared memory model on a physically distributed memory system. The main idea is to provide a globally shared virtual memory system available for every unit in the system (see Figure 2.9). This improves the scalability of the algorithms designed for shared memory systems since it allows implementing them on a loosely coupled multiprocessor with very small changes, if any. However, the processing units in a DSM system usually suffer from contention and latencies in accessing the shared memory, which actually induces a trade-off between the performance and scalability.

The research on the optimizations in the DSM area was strongly inspired by the previous research in the areas of non uniform memory access (NUMA) architectures and multiprocessor cache systems. In these systems a processor issues the access requests to its memory management unit. If the access refers to a locally unavailable memory location an event called a *miss* or a *fault* is captured and triggeres appropriate actions.

2.2.1 DSM classification

During the implementation of a DSM system several decisions have to be taken. These design choices are discussed in the following sections.

Memory management algorithm

One of the main goals of a DSM is the static and dynamic distribution of shared data across the system in order to minimize access latencies. It is possible to distinguish three options for the access to a shared data in the DSM systems.

The first one is a *fixed* location of a single copy of the shared data item, which resides in the memory of a fixed node, which handles the access requests from other nodes. Only the accesses from the node that stores the single copy of the data are handled locally, all other requests require inter-node communication.

The second one is the *migration* of the data item. It also implies a single copy of the shared data item, but this copy *migrates* to the accessing node for exclusive use. In this case, the access is optimized if a single node performs several operations on the data item in a row.

The last, third strategy is the *replication* of the data item, which allows multiple copies of the data item to reside simultaneously in the local memories of different nodes. This reduces the delay and increases the parallelism while accessing the shared data item. However, the write operations are much more complicated due to the coherency issues of the multiple copies.

Combining these access methods for read and write operations it is possible to distinguish between four memory management algorithms as presented below.

Central Server–Single Reader/Single Writer (SRSW) This algorithm is the simplest to implement, but it also provides the lowest parallelism. The only copy of the shared data item is located at one node (the central server), who is performing both the read and write operations on request of other nodes (see Figure 2.10). This algorithm is easy to implement and avoids all problems related to data consistency, since the central server takes care of the serialization of accesses and synchronisation. However the central server is the single point of failure and may also become the bottleneck of the system.

Migration–Single Reader/Single Writer (SRSW) Similar to the central server algorithm, in the migration algorithm there is only one copy of the data item maintained in the system. However, the control over this copy is to some extent distributed in the system, i.e., any node can obtain the copy from the node that currently holds it and perform

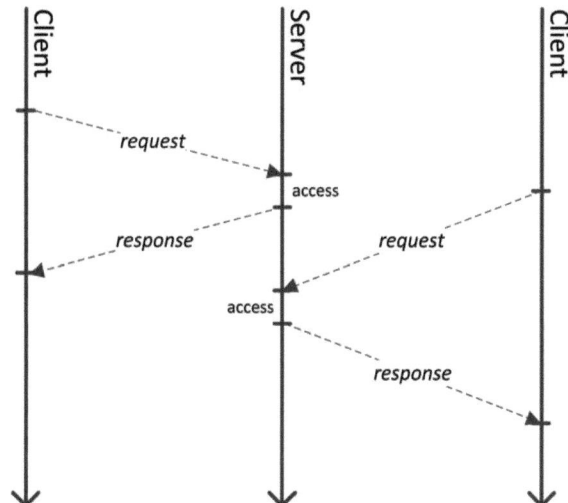

Figure 2.10: The flow of a *central server* algorithm

a read or write operation on it, but only one node at a time can hold a copy of the data item (see Figure 2.11). If the requesting node has the copy of the data item locally it does not need to send anything to any remote node and can perform the read or write operations locally. This optimizes the access in case one node performs several operations in a row. This algorithm also has no consistency problems and the accesses are synchronized. But, if frequent accesses are generated from two or more nodes thrashing may occur.

Read Replication–Multiple Reader/Single Writer (MRSW)   In the read replication algorithm multiple read only copies of the data item exist and only one of them is a read/write copy. Thus, the average cost of the read operation is reduced, since the algorithm allows read operations to be simultaneously executed locally at multiple nodes. However, a write operation becomes more expensive, because it is necessary to obtain the writable copy (or upgrade the read only copy to allow writing) and to invalidate all the other read only copies before the write operation on the exclusive copy can be performed (see Figure 2.12).

For the consistency reasons it is crucial to invalidate all the read only copies. This can be achieved by maintaining a list of nodes that hold the copies, i.e., the *copy set*. It is important to specify who is responsible for keeping this information. For this purpose the term *owner* of the data item can be introduced. Depending on the definition for the current DSM implementation the ownership can be fixed node or it can be dynamic and, e.g., change every time the data item migrates.

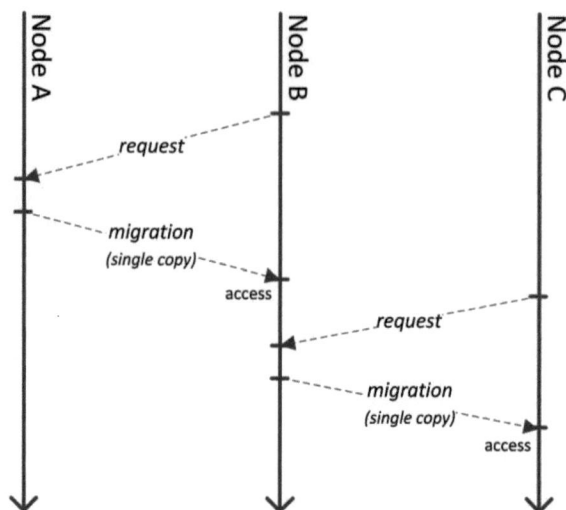

Figure 2.11: The flow of a *single copy migration* algorithm

The read replication algorithm is appropriate for systems, in which the read operation is dominant.

Full Replication–Multiple Reader/Multiple Writer (MRMW) The last algorithm is the full replication algorithm. In this algorithm multiple read/write copies exist in the system. The read operation is performed locally and the write operation causes an update of other copies. It usually reduces the costs for the write operation, but introduces problems with keeping the copies coherent in presence of multiple write operations. In order to keep the copies coherent it is necessary for the write operations to be properly sequenced. This can be done by the *sequencer*, a node that orders the write operations allowing the updates of each to be recognized and ordered as well (see Figure 2.13).

In the WSN context the replication has the advantage of improving the data availability. The initial idea behind WSN is that the applications are rather data centric, thus, the nodes are regarded as data carriers and their temporary or permanent disappearing shall not affect the data. In such a case, the replication of data is a must. But there is still the option of the replica character, i.e., if the copies are read only or writable as well. Depending on the foreseen realization the complexity of these both options may be similar. The read replication requires invalidation of all the copies and the full replication requires the delivery of an update to all the replica holders. Additionally, for the full replication in WSN either requires the use of a sequencer or an algorithm to solve the write-write conflict problem. The easiest example of the latter is the use of timestamps to identify each value, where the value with the highest

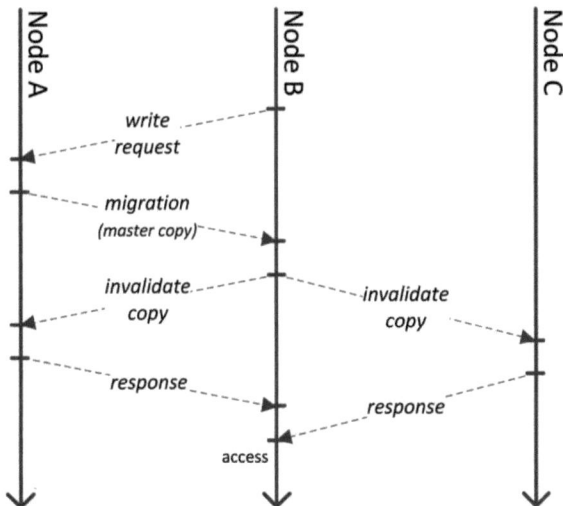

Figure 2.12: The flow of a *read replication* algorithm

timestamp overrides the others. However, this requires a global time synchronization.

Coherence control protocol

For the programmer to use the DSM system correctly, it is necessary to know the memory coherency semantics it provides. The most intuitive coherency semantics is the atomic access known from the shared memory systems, i.e., once a memory location was written, any successive access operates on the written value. However, in a distributed system this semantics may be unfeasible since it requires serialization of data accesses. This is especially important in presence of replicas of the shared data. The data is replicated on different nodes allowing parallel read operations at almost no cost. But, the write operation may become expensive to achieve the defined level of data coherency, i.e., to provide the expected behaviour in case of the read operation. Thus, it is necessary to involve a coherence protocol that takes care about the serialization of accesses. There are two classes of coherence control protocols derived from the classical cache coherence models:

- *write-invalidate*–all the replicas can be freely read, but if one of them is about to be written, all others have to be invalidated before the write access is allowed.

- *write-update*–all the replicas can be read and written, but after a write access no accesses are allowed until all the replicas are updated to the written value.

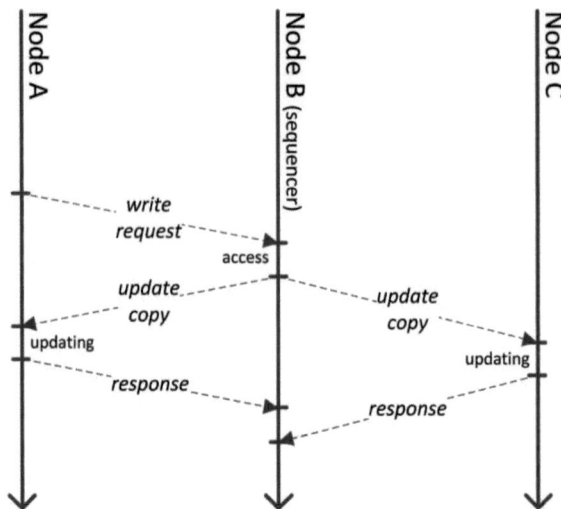

Figure 2.13: The flow of a *full replication* algorithm

In order to avoid ambiguity in the differentiation between terms *coherency* and *consistency*, they are further on distinguished following the definition from [158]. Thus, *coherency* is a general term for the semantics of memory operations and *consistency* refers to a specific kind of memory coherence. The consistency models are further described in Section 2.2.2. The actual realization of a coherency control protocol depends on the chosen memory management algorithm and the consistency model that shall be supported.

as already mentioned, in the WSN context the replication is the preferred data storage model. And the decision between the write-invalidate and write-update coherency control protocol models is mainly driven by the consistency model to be supported and the allowed costs to be spend. The invalidation actually involves a two step approach, i.e., the replicas are first invalidated, and then fetched from the source as needed. The update, in contrast, combines the invalidation of the current replica with an update of its value. Thus, update is more preferable since it also propagates the new value of the shared data increasing its availability. Both these approaches can cause consistency issues, i.e., in the time between the operation initialization and its completeness different nodes can read either the old value or the new one (or none in case of invalidation protocol).

Table 2.18: Hardware DSM implementations [179]

Implementation	Type of algorithm	Consistency model	Granularity unit	Coherence policy
Memnet	MRSW	Sequential	32 bytes	Invalidate
Dash	MRSW	Release	16 bytes	Invalidate
SCI	MRSW	Sequential	16 bytes	Invalidate
Merlin	MRMW	Processor	4 bytes	Update

Implementation level

The choice, if the DSM shall be realized in hardware, software or as a hybrid approach, is one of the most important and fundamental design choices. It influences many other parameters of the realization of a DSM system.

DASH [133], Memnet [64], SCI [121] and Merlin [148] are examples of a DSM systems realized entirely in hardware (see Table 2.18). A hardware realization is assumed to be transparent for any software running on top of it, i.e., there is no need for any software support. But, on the other hand, the hardware realization may be also less flexible.

A software realization also assumes that there is no special support from the hardware and uses software protocols to achieve its goals. These protocols can be realized as the operating system support or as a separate library. It can also be realized as an extension to a programming language that supports compile time inserting of synchronization and control primitives to manage the accesses to shared data. Examples of software DSM include Munin [16, 35], Clouds [182], Ivy [141], Mermaid [218], TreadMarks [58], Blizzard [187], Mirage [80], Linda [8], Orca [14], Midway [21, 22], Agora [26], Amber [40] and Brazos [192] (see Table 2.19).

A hybrid realization combines the advantages of both, hardware and software approaches. It allows performing critical operations in its hardware part to improve the performance, while enabling the flexibility of the software part. Examples of hybrid DSM approaches are Shrimp [97], FLASH [130], Alewife [38] and Plus [27] (see Table 2.20).

None of the WSN hardware platforms introduced in Section 2.1.1 provides hardware support for DSM. The low power microcontrollers do not even have a memory management unit (MMU), so the memory accesses are direct and no local caches are used, so a trapping of an access is not possible. Thus, the only way to implement the DSM for the most common WSN platforms is the software realization. And the most attractive and efficient solution to provide the DSM abstraction for this target environment is a middleware (or service) layer that is compiled together with the application code. A stand alone and multi purpose solutions can be too inefficient and generate large

Table 2.19: Software DSM implementations [179]

Implementation	Type of algorithm	Consistency model	Granularity unit	Coherence policy
IVY	MRSW	Sequential	1Kbyte	Invalidate
Mermaid	MRSW	Sequential	1 Kbyte, 8 Kbytes	Invalidate
Munin	Type-specific (SRSW, MRSW, MRMW)	Release	Variable size objects	Type-specific (delayed update, invalidate)
Midway	MRMW	Entry, release, processor	4 Kbytes	Update
TreadMarks	MRMW	Lazy release	4 Kbytes	Update, invalidate
Blizzard	MRSW	Sequential	32-128 bytes	Invalidate
Mirage	MRSW	Sequential	512 bytes	Invalidate
Clouds	MRSW	Inconsistent, Sequential	8 Kbytes	Discard segment when unlocked
Linda	MRSW	Sequential	Variable (tuple size)	Implementation dependent
Orca	MRSW	Synchronization dependent	Shared data object size	Update

code, so it may be too expensive for the resource limited WSN hardware platforms. A tailor-made middleware that provides exactly the features required by the application helps to save these. Even if the application and its requirements to the DSM change, then the nodes in the network usually have to be reprogrammed with the new version of the application, so the adapted DSM middleware can be redistributed as well. Thus, this solution does not limit the flexibility of the DSM middleware.

Structure and granularity

These are two closely related features of a DSM realization. The first specifies if the shared memory area is an unstructured linear memory space containing the data words, or if the shared data is structured and represented by programming language types, objects or other structures, e.g. associative memory cache lines. The structure is to some extent influenced by the implementation level. For instance, if the DSM is realized in hardware, then the shared memory is usually unstructured, since it is easier for the hardware to handle the shared memory as a virtual block of memory words,

Table 2.20: Hybrid DSM implementations [179]

Implementation	Type of algorithm	Consistency model	Granularity unit	Coherence policy
Plus	MRMW	Processor	4 Kbytes	Update
Alewife	MRSW	Sequential	16 bytes	Invalidate
Flash	MRSW	Release	128 bytes	Invalidate
Typhoon	MRSW	Custom	32 bytes	Invalidate custom
Shrimp	MRMW	AURC, scope	4 Kbytes	Update, invalidate

without requiring the knowledge on its internal structures.

The granularity specifies the size of the coherency unit, i.e., the size of an indivisible data unit that is managed by the DSM. It can be equal to the size of the defined data structure in the structured realizations or be a multiple of it. For unstructured realizations the granularity may be defined on the single word, on the defined block of words or on the page level.

The choice of granularity induces several issues. A large size of the coherency unit reduces the number of remote accesses due to the locality of reference. However, large blocks may cause false-sharing, i.e., individual and independent data items may be located in the large sharing unit causing a sharing conflict, because the accessing nodes presume they share the data, but they actually use different parts of it. Larger sharing units increase also the possibility of contention.

Small send and receive buffers in the WSN hardware radio modules limit the size of the packets that can be transmitted without additional overhead. Additionally, larger packets cause higher values of the packet error rate (PER), due to the higher possibility of packet collisions. Thus, it is reasonable to choose the maximum size of the sent packets to be relatively small, e.g., smaller that 64 bytes. This induces small sizes for the synchronization blocks, i.e., the DSM realizations for WSN are more likely to be fine granular. Within this small granularity unit any structuring is possible, i.e., it may be either structured or unstructured shared memory area.

Data location and access

If a node want to access a shared data item that is not available locally it needs to locate it first. If the data is not migrating and not replicated, then the task is trivial, since the data location is fixed. But still, it may be necessary to locate it once, if it is accessed for the first time.

In DSM systems with data migration or replication the task is more complicated.

Although these two approaches differ in accessing the data, they both share the problem of allocating the responsibility for the data item management. The specification of the responsibility requires defining nodes with special functions regarding the shared data:

- *manager*–the node responsible for managing the write access to the shared data item.

- *owner*–the node that currently owns the only writable copy of the data item. It distributes update or invalidation messages for the data item.

It is possible that these special functions are merged in one. For replicated data items it is necessary to maintain a *copy set* that contains the nodes who hold a replica of the data item.

Several ownership algorithms are proposed in [142]. In [180] these algorithms are also only analyzed regarding their application in the MRSW memory management algorithm. However, with minor modifications they can be applied for similar purposes also in other memory management algorithms. They can be divided in two main classes: fixed ownership and dynamic ownership.

Fixed ownership Each shared data item has a fixed owner. Thus, the location of the data item can be known and distributed a priori, or the location can depend on some characteristics of the data, e.g., it can be specified using hashing functions. No other node has direct write access to the data item, thus, every write access has to be performed by the owner. Thus the owner is also the manager of the data item. This solution is preferable if the most of the write operations come from a single node.

Dynamic ownership The ownership moves from node to node. In order to locate the owner the manager keeps the track of the ownership migration. And since the write access to the data is controlled by the manager it has the information available.

Centralized management A node is the manager of all the shared data items and keeps track of the current owners of each data item. In order to access the data a node has to contact the manager. The manager can also queue both read and write requests. This approach is also called the *monitor-like* centralized manager approach. In its improved version the manager only maintains the copy set and the information on the current owner for each data item.

Distributed management Since the centralized management can present a bottleneck in the system it is a natural choice to allow distribution of the management task. In this case the situation is similar as described above for the ownership, i.e., there is a need to locate the manager prior to accessing the data item. Similarly, the manager function can be assigned either in a fixed or a dynamic way. In the first case, each manager manages a predefined set of data items and the mapping of data item to its manager works similar as in the case of fixed ownership.

For the dynamic distributed manager assignment the following schemes are proposed:

- *broadcast*–the nodes manage the data items they currently own. A node that wants to access the data item broadcasts the request in order to locate the data. The current owner provides the new one with the management data, i.e., it moves with the data.

- *dynamic*–the management information is distributed in a loosely way, i.e., every node keeps the information on a potential manager of each shared data item. If a node requires the access to the data item it contacts the potential manager, who can forward the request further if it is not managing the data item anymore. The information on the manager is updated as possible, e.g., on receiving of an data invalidation message.

- *distributed copy sets*–every node that has a valid replica manages the copy set. A read request can be realized by any node with a valid replica and the answering node adds the requester to its copy set. The invalidation messages are propagated in waves, i.e., starting from the owner node, each node propagates them to the nodes from its copy set.

In a DSM realization for WSN, a fixed ownership scheme is generally disadvantageous. Regarding the ownership of the writable copy of a shared data item which is additionally replicated to increase the availability, the fixed owner can be a potential single point of failure, i.e., if the owner disappears, the shared data cannot be written anymore. Thus, to increase the robustness, it is reasonable to apply one of the dynamic ownership schemes. It is even reasonable to have backup owners, who take the responsibility of the data in case the primary owner disappears. However, such a solution requires a clear definition of the ownership transfer to avoid consistency issues if two or more nodes act as owners.

Heterogeneity

If the DSM system shall allow sharing data between heterogeneous nodes it is necessary to take different data representations into account. This includes, e.g., different sizes of standard types on different hardware architectures, as well as different representation of these in memory (little-endian/big-endian) and different boundaries for alignment. This issue requires a throughout analysis of the desired features to be provided and the potential hardware architectures that shall be supported, since data converting may be expensive.

In a WSN application it is also required that the different kinds of nodes use hardware radio modules that are compatible at the physical layer. It is also necessary to take the architectural differences of the processing units into account. Additionally, if the heterogeneity shall also involve the software layer it is necessary that the packets are constructed in a way that they are acceptable by each kind of operating system (or software stack, in general).

Scalability

Scalability is one of the reasons to use DSM approaches and the driving force for its development. Thus, if scalability is a primary goal of the implemented DSM system, then it is necessary to avoid any bottlenecks that can limit it.

The WSN is a specific network, its characteristics and the shared medium is one of the main factors that influence scalability. Assuming the use of a single carrier frequency, the broadcast medium causes the nodes in the radio range to receive all the transmitted packets. Even if mechanisms that avoid reception are applied, one communication usually prohibits another one, reducing the bandwidth available for other nodes. Thus, adjusting the transmission power helps improving the scalability, i.e., lower transmission power limits the direct communication range, but, it also limits the interference range. Setting the sending power too high may cause that only few of the nodes may be able to transmit their data. But, setting the sending power too low, may cause that the transmitted data cannot reach the closest nodes. Thus, the sending power controls the amount of nodes that can be reached and interfered, as well. A higher sending power with constant spatial density increases the virtual density of the network and may increase the packet error rate (PER).

Another factor that jeopardizes the scalability is the use of globally acting mechanisms. Any mechanism that involves global knowledge and communication reduces the scalability of the approach. Of course, it is of advantage to provide mechanisms that adapt to the current deployment and scale well.

In the WSN application area it is reasonable to be able to specify the acting range for the applied operations. Anyway, having a globally shared data may require at least a minimum set of global knowledge, but depending on the required features, the use of global scope operations can be minimized. A globally shared and migrating data item may require a global action during the write (possibly in combination with data migration) or during the read operation. In the first case, the information on the data migration may be globally propagated, so each node that needs to read the item in the future, knows the current owner. However, this solution also requires storing part of the information on the shared data item and may also cause metadata coherency issues, even if the data itself is not replicated. Additionally, if the write operations are more frequent than the read operations, then it is reasonable to combine the read operation with a discovery mechanism, which globally searches for the current owner of the shared data item. This solution has an additional advantage that it does not require any storage for the metadata on the shared data, since this global knowledge does not necessarily require to be continuous.

Another feature that improves scalability is the spatially limited replication. In WSN it may happen that nodes disappear temporarily when the links between them change, e.g., due to environment changes. Some nodes may even disappear permanently if their energy sources are exhausted. The data replication assures that the data is available even if the source node disappears. And, since the data in WSN is usually locality bound (especially the taken measurements), the replication can be limited to a specific range, to reduce its costs and actually to make the DSM approach network size independent.

Replacement strategies

In case of data sharing involving migration or replication the local memory of a node may become full. In such a case it is necessary to specify which data items shall be replaced by the new ones. The most often used replacement strategies are similar to those from caching:

- least recently used,
- random replacement.

But, since the aim of the data replication in WSN applications is also the increase of the robustness, no data shall be simply removed by the nodes. Thus, the node, who is the owner of the shared data item should not remove it from its local storage. The replica holders, should not remove their replicas, since they increase the data availability. If it is necessary and desired, then to avoid holding a data item forever, the individual pieces can have defined validity periods. It requires additional overhead, but allows more optimal handling of the shared data.

2.2.2 Consistency models

The shared data can be replicated in order to increase the system performance and data availability. The system performance increase is caused by the ability to access the data concurrently. The availability increase is caused by the redundancy of the data in the system, what additionally increases the reliability of the system making it less failure sensitive. Ability to perform parallel operations and reliability are two very important features of a distributed system. But the replication induces also additional

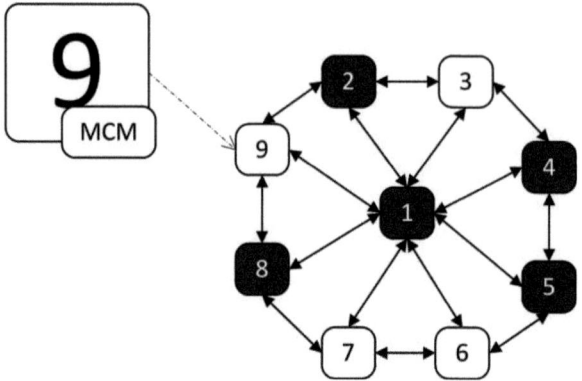

Figure 2.14: An example of a system with replicated data

problems, i.e., there is a need to assure concurrency and replication transparency. What means, that the fact that the data is replicated, has to be hidden from the client. Atomic update is a desired property of the system that helps achieving replication transparency.

An example system for managing replicated data is shown in Figure 2.14. A data item is replicated on the nodes represented by black shapes. The nodes represented by white shapes are those without a replica of the data item. All the nodes are equipped with a memory coherency manager (MCM) module as depicted for the node number nine. These modules on the nodes are responsible for inter-node communication to achieve the chosen data coherency and also to access remote data. The responsibility for the management of the replicas is shared between the MCMs. As a node (*client*) accesses the shared data, it may be necessary to involve its MCM to access the nodes (*data servers*) that hold the replicas of the data item. The client node can be also a data server, if it holds a replica of the accessed data item.

The client may read or write the data stored in the system. Assuming that the replication transparency is provided, the read request of the client needs only to be delivered to any of the data servers. But depending on the underlying realization of the protocol it may happen that the MCM forwards the request to more than one data server in order to be able to reply to the request with the most recent data. The three options for the realization of a read operation by the front end are as follows:

- *master*–in order to ensure the most recent data the master copy has to be read.
- *any*–any of the replicas can be read.
- *quorum*–the MCM must read from a quorum in order to get the most recent data.

On the other hand, in an ideal case, a write request should be delivered to all the replicas atomically, to provide the replication transparency and consistency. But, due to different consistency requirements of the applications there are also less strict possibilities. The options for the realization of a write operation are as follows:

- *master*–the write requests are delivered to the master copy and the MCM of the data server that manages the master copy propagates the request to the other replicas.

- *all*–the write requests are propagated atomically to all the replicas and they are serialized.

- *available*–the write requests are propagated atomically to all non-faulty replicas. The faulty replicas have to update their data after recovery.

- *quorum*–the write request is propagated atomically only to a quorum.

- *gossip*–the write request is delivered to any replica and the MCM of the data server that manages this replica propagates it to other replicas using a gossip protocol.

The combinations of these operations provide different possibilities for consistency realizations as well as different performance figures.

The master-read/master-write combination involves the data server that holds the master copy for both, reading and writing of the data. In this case the concurrency is completely neglected, but there is no problem with consistency and the replicas are stored on the other data servers only for the purpose of the failure of the master copy holder, i.e., if the master data server fails it can recover the most recent state of the data based on the other replicas. However, the master-read and master-write operations cannot be performed if the data server that holds the master copy fails.

The support for concurrency would be increased if reading from data servers other than the one that holds the master copy is allowed. In the ideal case reading any of the replicas, i.e., providing any-read operation, should by sufficient. However, the distribution of write requests to the other replicas from the master copy requires time that already causes consistency issues. Thus, it would require atomic propagation of the updates in order to support the any-read operation.

If an atomic update protocol is available, then it is also possible for the write operations to be initialized at any replica of the data and they are atomically propagated to all the replicas, resulting in the any-read/all-write combination. But, in the presence of failures the all-write operation cannot be guaranteed to be successful, what makes the any-read operation a probabilistic approach as well, i.e., it cannot be guaranteed to return the most recent value of the data item. A solution would be the any-read/available-write combination, but with additional limitations of the any-read in case the replica to be read just recovered from a failure. In such a case it is necessary for the replica to recover completely and to update its state before it can be regarded as available.

A solution to the problem of potential inconsistencies in the set of replicas of a shared data is to use the quorum-read operation. In this case the read operation is regarded as successful if a quorum of replica holders is accessed and returns the data. In order to provide the right number of replicas of a data item x to constitute the read quorum on that data item–RQ(x), it is necessary to use an appropriate write operation, i.e., the quorum-write. The quorum-write operation is regarded successful if a write operation reaches the write quorum on the data item x–WQ(x).

In order to avoid conflicts between two quorum-write operations performed on the data item x it is necessary that the write quorum is larger than the half of the total number of replicas of the data item x–REP(x). If the number is smaller or equal to the half of the REP(x), then none of the potentially parallel write operations gets the majority of the replicas. In such a case, two partitions of contradictory replicas exist and no unambiguous judgement on the latest value of the data can be made. On the other hand, in order to assure that the quorum-read operation returns the most recent value of the data item, it is necessary that the read quorum includes at least one replica that belongs to the write quorum. Thus, the sum of the two has to be larger than the total number of replicas, i.e., it is required that the read and write quorums on the data item x overlap, for the system to be able to provide the most recent value of the data item x. These two rules can be expressed as follows:

$$2 * WQ(x) > REP(x) \tag{2.1}$$

$$RQ(x) + WQ(x) > REP(x) \tag{2.2}$$

Since the number of data servers to be accessed during the operation influences its costs, the defined sizes of the quorums can be chosen according to the ratio between the amounts of read and write operations. The case where RQ(x) is equal to one requires the WQ(x) to be equal to REP(x) and is actually the any-read/all-write combination. If failures shall be tolerated the write quorum cannot be equal to REP(x) and can be reduced to the non-failed replicas, resulting in available-write operation. However, in this case the read quorum has to be greater than one, thus, any-read is not sufficient to ensure the most recent data to be returned by the read operation. This way, the quorum-read/quorum-write combination provides the tolerance to replica failures FT(x) that specifies the maximum number of replicas that can fail without causing the read operation to return the value other than the most recent. The FT(x) is specified by the read quorum as follows:

$$FT(x) = RD(x) - 1 \qquad (2.3)$$

A possible realization of the quorum operations is to associate the values of the shared data items with version numbers. On the write operation the highest version number from the write quorum is incremented and used to identify the new value that is further written to the write quorum. On the read operation the read quorum is queried and the value with the highest version number is returned as the most recent one.

For large data items it is possible to provide the quorum operations without the need to store the replica on every node. Some of the nodes, called *ghosts*, take a passive part in the replication, but active in the voting, i.e., they store only the information on the latest version of the data item.

Many applications do not require such a high data consistency as provided by the combinations described above. If the number of read operations exceeds the number of write operations and the ordering of operations can be relaxed, then it is possible to use the gossip-write operation. In this case, the write operation is provided to any replica and is further propagated like a gossip, i.e., the data servers compare their knowledge and these with newer data provide it to the others. The read operation in this case is the any-read.

The above mentioned access operations in presence of replicas show that it is possible to realize DSM systems that provide diverse performance and data consistency figures and also that these two parameters are contradictory. Thus, there is a trade-off between the performance measured as the cost of the operations and the consistency that represents the quality of the data.

In order to specify the constraints of the DSM realization and to allow applications to adapt to a more of less standardized memory coherency semantics, several consistency models have been defined. These model definitions are inspired by the cache coherency models for multiprocessor cache systems that were further relaxed for NUMA architectures. The chosen consistency model is a contract between the DSM system and the application, in which the DSM system promises the chosen level of memory coherency if the access is realized in a specified way.

The consistency models are also a well studied subject and information on these can be found in many publications. Survey like presentations of consistency models can be found in [5, 153, 179, 42, 125, 191, 180, 197, 158]. There has also research been done on the performance evaluation and optimization [85, 34, 86, 38], for both software and hardware.

The following paragraphs present the chosen consistency models used in DSM implementations. These are introduced here and their implementation feasibility and operation features in the WSN environment are further discussed in Chapter 5.

Models without synchronization

In consistency models without explicit synchronization each operation triggers the synchronization process. Thus it is hidden from the application designer, who does not need to care about specifying explicit synchronization points.

Atomic or Strict Consistency This is the strictest of all the consistency models and is defined in [196] as follows:

Any read to a memory location x returns the value stored by the most recent write operation to x.

It means that all writes to memory must be visible by all nodes at the same time. Implementation of strict consistency requires the existence of absolute global time so the memory read/write operation can be correctly ordered. It requires all read and write operations to be executed atomically and sequentially, i.e., it requires real-time ordering of operations and disallows overlapping of these. It provides that a read operation returns the most recent value and that all write operations are completed before a data item can be read. The complexity to implement the strict consistency is very high and usually it is used as a benchmark for more relaxed consistency models.

Linearizability As defined in [93] a system is linearizable if its operations are timestamped and the following condition is fulfilled:

The result of any execution is the same as if the read and write operations by all processes on the data store were executed in the same sequential order. If $ts_{op1}(x) < ts_{op2}(y)$ then OP1(x) should precede OP2(y) in this sequence.

The linearizability assumes timestamping of operations. The clocks of the nodes need to be loosely synchronized. The timestamps are used by all nodes to agree on the global order of the operations. Linearizability is weaker than strict consistency, but it is said to be stronger than sequential consistency [197].

Sequential Consistency Sequential consistency is defined as follows [131]:

The result of any execution is the same as if the operations of all the processors were executed in some sequential order; and the operations of each individual processor appear in this sequence in the order specified by its program.

All the machines see the same sequence of write operations. This model is slightly weaker than the atomic consistency. There is no need for real-time ordering of the accesses. Compared to the atomic consistency the sequential model allows the access operations to cause different delay of execution what can result in commuted appearances of these operations observed by the processors. Thus, sequential consistency does not guarantee that the read operation returns the value most recently written by another node.

It can be implemented in distributed systems since time does not play a role. There is a need for a global sequencer that stamps the write operations with a sequence number. The operations issued by a single processor have to appear in the global sequence in the order they were executed. The operations issued by different processors do not have to appear in the sequence according to the strict consistency, but the order of them has to be the same for all the processors in the system. Thus, important is the sequence of operations and all nodes have to agree on the order in which the observed effects take place. This consistency model is equivalent to the concept of *one-copy serializability* known from database systems [20].

Causal Consistency In [7] the causal consistency is defined as follows:

Writes that are potentially casually related must be seen by all processes in the same order. Concurrent writes may be seen in a different order on different machines.

Two operations are causally related if, e.g., the second one relies on the result of the first one. The causal consistency requires the ordering of operations that are causally related. All other operations are regarded as concurrent and can appear in the sequence observed by different processes in different order.

Pipelined RAM (PRAM) Consistency (FIFO Consistency) The pipelined RAM (PRAM) consistency model is defined in [143]. It can be described as follows:

Writes done by a single process are received by all other processes in the order in which they were issued, but writes from different processes may be seen in a different order by different processes.

The idea of the PRAM consistency is as follows. Assume a multiprocessor system, where every processor has a local copy of the shared data item. On read the processor simply accesses the local copy of the shared data item. On write it updates the local copy and broadcasts the update to other processors. Thus, all processors observe the order of writes done by a single processor in the same order, but writes done by different processors can be observed in different order by different processors.

In this consistency model all writes from a single process are pipelined and the writing process does not have to wait for each one to complete before starting the next one. All writes issued by different processes are concurrent. The advantage of PRAM consistency is that it is easy to implement.

Cache Consistency (Coherence) Cache consistency was introduced in [89], coherence in [87]. They are synonymous and provide a shared data item related weakening of the sequential consistency, which requires that all accesses to a single shared data item or location in the shared memory area are observed by all the processes in the same order.

Processor Consistency The processor consistency is defined as follows [89]:

A multiprocessor is said to be processor consistent if the result of any execution is the same as if the operations of each individual processor appear in the sequential order specified by its program.

Similar to the PRAM consistency, the operations issued by a single process have to appear to any other process in the order as they were executed at the issuing process. Operations from different processes are regarded as concurrent, i.e., can appear in any order. Additionally it requires that the accesses to a single memory location or shared data item are observed by all processes in the same order.

Thus, processor consistency combines the features of PRAM consistency and cache consistency. Processor consistent systems are easier to build then sequentially consistent systems since they reduce the sequential consistency to every single process and memory location individually.

Slow Memory Slow memory introduced in [96] is a location related weakening of the PRAM consistency. A system is slow memory if all the processes agree on the order of the writes to each location issued by a single process. Like in the PRAM consistency model, the writes have to be immediately visible locally.

Models with synchronization

Consistency models with explicit synchronization require that the application designer (or the compiler) explicitly puts the synchronization operations in the application code to indicate that they are required.

Weak Consistency A memory system is weakly consistent if it enforces the following restrictions [73]:

- *accesses to synchronization variables are sequentially consistent,*

- *no access to a synchronization variable is issued in a processor before all previous accesses have been performed, and*

- *no access is issued by a processor before a previous access to a synchronization variable has been performed.*

Weak consistency relaxes the requirements of the consistency even further and reduces the synchronization of the shared data from every operation to chosen synchronization points only. In order to do that it introduces a notion of synchronization variable associated to the data store. Weak consistency enforces consistency on a group of operations, not on a single operation. Performing a synchronization means that all local shared data items are brought up-to-date, i.e., the local writes are propagated to other copies and remote writes are brought to the local copy. The synchronization is done for the local data of the process, i.e., if a process wants to get the most recent value for a read it needs to perform synchronization first and synchronization after a write assures that the written value is available to all processes that synchronize before reading.

(Eager) Release Consistency A DSM system supports the release consistency if the following rules are followed [87]:

- *before an ordinary access to a shared variable is performed, all previous acquires done by the process must have completed successfully,*

- *before a release is allowed to be performed, all previous reads and writes done by the process must have completed, and*

- *the acquire and release accesses must be processor consistent (sequential consistency is not required).*

The release consistency extends the weak consistency by introducing two types of synchronization operations–the *acquire* and *release* that are used to indicate that the process enters and leaves the critical section. This helps to distinguish between two synchronization tasks–the updating of local copies before entering the critical section and propagating local writes to remote copies after leaving it. This split of synchronization operations allows easier implementation and provides the lock mechanism for the shared data. Starting the data access the process acquires the exclusive access to the data store and on release unlocks the data.

Similar to weak consistency, a process is only assured about the most recent data if it acquires the access to the data store. The acquire and release operations do not need to be applied to all the shared data, it is possible that it is only applied to a chosen set of data items. These data items are said to be protected.

(Lazy) Release Consistency In order to optimize the synchronization operations the lazy release consistency disables the immediate forwarding of local writes to other processes on release operation [129]. On the acquire operation, the process that performs the operation obtains the most recent data for the local copy of the data. This allows to reduce the effort related to updating the remote copies only to the situations where it is absolutely necessary, i.e., only if the other processes require the data. This optimization allows reducing the amount of messages exchanged between remote processes. It also allows multiple acquire-release sections to be performed in a row without synchronizing the data.

Entry Consistency The entry consistency was introduced in [21]. A DSM system supports the entry consistency if it follows the following rules:

- *an acquire of a synchronization variable is not allowed to perform with respect to that process until all updates to the guarded shared data have been performed with respect to that process.*

- *before an exclusive mode access to a synchronization variable by a process is allowed to perform with respect to that process, no other process may hold the synchronization variable, not even in non-exclusive mode.*

- *after an exclusive mode access to a synchronization variable has been performed, any other process' next nonexclusive mode access to that synchronization variable may not be performed until it has performed with respect to that variable's owner.*

The entry consistency relaxes further the release consistency by allowing multiple synchronization variables and requiring each shared data item to be associated to some synchronization variable. It also uses acquire and release, but these operations are applied for each shared data item or each set of data items separately. Thus, entering the critical section the process has to state explicitly which shared data items are to be acquired.

A synchronization variable is owned by the process that last acquired it. Another process that wants to access the variable, i.e., wants to acquire the shared data it protects, has to ask the owner. Thus, the owner may perform multiple acquire-release sections without any communication with other processes. Several processes can own the synchronization variable in a non-exclusive mode, so they can read but not write the protected data.

The entry consistency allows several processes operating on different data items to run in parallel. However, this causes more synchronization overhead and may induce concurrency problems like dead locks.

Client centric models

Client centric consistency models consider the state of the copies regarding the content and one accessing process. These models take into account that the client process may change its connection point to the network of replica holders. Thus may access different replicas at different stages of the replication process, depending on the realization of the update propagation. In this case the client may be considered as one of the nodes in the network, one that can move. These consistency models were defined in [201, 202] and initiated by the Bayou system [66].

Eventual Consistency   The eventual consistency is defined as follows:

If no updates take place for a long time, then all the replicas will gradually become consistent.

Eventual consistency uses epidemic or gossip protocols as introduced in [65] to propagate the updates in the system. The access to a replica may also trigger its updating to the most recent value. Thus, the replicas are updated on-demand. Usually only a small group of processes is allowed to perform the write operation. It works fine as long as the clients access the same replica all the times. Epidemic protocols are also investigated in [151].

Monotonic Reads   It is defined as follows:

If a process reads a value of a shared data item, then any successive read operation on the same data item by that process will always return the same or a more recent value.

If a system supports monotonic reads, then it guarantees that if a client reads a value from a shared data item, then at no time in the future it can read from that data item a value that is older than the one it has previously read.

Monotonic Writes   It is defined as follows:

A write operation by a process on a shared data item is completed before any successive write operation on that data item by the same process.

The completing of a write operation means that the copy on which the successive write is performed reflects the effects of all previous write operations by that process, no matter where they were issued.

Read Your Writes   This model is defined as follows:

The effect of a write operation by a process on a data item will always be seen by a successive read operation on that data item by that process.

In other words, a write operation is always completed before a successive read operation by the same process, no matter where that read operation takes place, i.e., a process cannot read a value from a shared data item that is older than the one it recently wrote to that data item.

Writes Follow Reads   It is defined as follows:

A write operation by a process on a data item following a previous read operation on this item by the same process is guaranteed to take place on the same or a more recent value of this data item as the read one.

In other words, any successive write operation by a process on a data item will be performed on a copy of that item that is up-to-date with the value most recently read by that process.

2.2.3   Fault tolerance

As the number of nodes in the DSM system grows, the probability that a failure occurs grows as well. The DSM system is a dependable and fault-tolerant distributed system if the system faults are transparent to the applications that use it. The fault-tolerance in the DSM context touches the issues related to correctness and availability of the data, i.e., that the data is never corrupted, that the results of operations on the data regarded as successful are never lost and that the data is available.

The sources of failures can be, e.g., related to the network communication or hardware faults. In [197] the faults are divided in three groups:

- *transient faults*

- *intermittent faults*

- *permanent faults*

There are generally two ways to cope with failures:

- *failure tolerance*

- *failure detection and recovery*

Redundancy, and thus replication of data is one of the methods to make a DSM system failure tolerant. Assuming multiple non-failed data sources the chance to get the correct data increases.

It is very important to recognize that a failure occurred to react accordingly, but in some situations the affected node is not aware of the fact. But, once a failure was detected it is important to bring the system back to the error free state. Checkpointing is one of methods to generate one consistent state of the system to start from in a case of failure. A survey on recovery mechanisms based on checkpointing for DSM systems is presented in [152].

Another method used for recovery in case of failures is using transactions as known from data base systems. In this approach each operation or a set of operations can be regarded as a transaction. As defined in [42], a transaction tr is a program that accesses shared data. During its execution, the transaction reads its *read set* R_{tr} and writes into its *write set* W_{tr} of shared data items. The set of nodes that store the data items from W_{tr} is the *update set* U_{tr}. If the transaction fails before it completes it may happen that only a part of W_{tr} is updated. A recovery is necessary to put the system back in a consistent state.

The distributed coordination of transactions can be realized using two-phase or three-phase commit protocols. A great survey on concurrency control techniques for database systems, including transaction control, is presented in [19].

The transactions can broken down to single data access operations to allow fine grained recovery, but on the other hand this may induce more coordination overhead.

The fault tolerance is an important aspect in the WSN context. Only due to communication issues, like unreliable links and congestion, the failures may occur quite frequently. The main class of failures include not delivered messages, e.g., missing invalidation or update requests causing inconsistent state of the data in the system. In order to cope with this kind of failures it may be necessary to involve a voting system while reading the shared data or direct the query direct to the source of the data. The first solution causes additional communication overhead, the latter puts the replication in question. For some application it may be enough to use the notion of data freshness and to let the application decide if the value of the data is fresh enough, even if it is not the most recent one.

Other failures in WSN include the temporal or permanent unavailability of the nodes. It is already partially covered by the communication issues, but it may be also related to the energy source, i.e., the node may be temporarily or permanently unavailable because its energy source is exhausted, or it may be put in the sleep mode to save energy. It is necessary to integrate the failure tolerance to allow the appearing nodes to integrate back into the system, e.g., they can fetch the new values of all the shared data items they store.

An example of failure detection (and tolerance as well) is a validity period of a shared data item that requires the source to refresh the replicas frequently. If an update is not delivered, the data cannot be read anymore, but a new value can be requested by the source.

2.2.4 Communication Issues

A DSM system is a distributed system and as such requires the nodes to use communication means to exchange the data. Thus, there are several issues related to the communication that can affect the reliability and efficiency of the DSM system.

The update propagation is a central point of every DSM system with replicas. For the consistency model to be supported it may be necessary to assure that the updates are delivered to the replica holders. Regarding the updating process as a transaction, one can expect that it has the features of a transaction, i.e., updating is an atomic process and several updates are realized in an ordered sequence. This can simplify formal definitions, but can also make implementation more complicated.

Not knowing the target group for the update process causes problems with verification if the operation was successful. If the replica holders are a defined group, then an efficient multicast communication mechanism is required. Taking the example of the any-read/all-write combination of operations as presented in Section 2.2.2, one can realize that there are two mechanisms necessary [42]:

- *best-effort multicast*, and

- *reliable multicast*.

The former guarantees that the message is delivered to the reachable and non-faulty nodes from the group defined by its address list. This mechanism can be used to propagate the read requests.

The later, in contrast, guarantees that either, the message is delivered to all nodes from the group defined by the address list, or that the message is delivered to none of them. It is also sometimes referred to as *reliable broadcast* [126, 199, 161].

Another issue in the multicast communication is the ordering of messages. The ideal case is that the messages are delivered without any delay and exactly in the order as they were sent according to a global time. But this is as unrealistic as the atomic consistency in a large system with a huge number of writable replicas.

Thus, according to the needs one of the following multicast ordering can be chosen [42]:

- *FIFO order*–messages from a single node are delivered in the order they were sent.

- *Causal order*–causally related messages from different nodes are delivered in their causal order.

- *Total order*–all messages sent in the group are delivered to all its members in the same order.

A reliable and totally ordered multicast is referred to as *atomic multicast*.

Another issue is to specify the behaviour of the multicast mechanism in case of failures or group changes, i.e., what shall happen when some of the group members fail during the operation, or on the contrary, what shall happen when new nodes join the group [186]. If the change is permanent, i.e., a new node joins the group then it may be added to the list of recipients without problems, but intermittent node failures may cause consistency problems. Thus, it is necessary to agree on the list of group members before the message can be delivered [197]. The group members that are currently not available are excluded from the group. However, it is crucial, that they also know that, i.e., that these excluded group members are aware of the fact and do not use their non-consistent data for further operations.

A failure related extension to the reliable multicast is the virtual synchrony [24, 25]. Virtual synchrony guarantees that a message sent via multicast to a group is delivered to each non-faulty node in this group. But, if the sender of the message fails during the operation, then the message is either delivered to all non-faulty processes or to none.

Usually, the multicast mechanisms are complex and involve exchanging many messages to fulfil their tasks, especially if the number of nodes in the system grows. Research on the optimizations and comparing of approaches in this field are also extensive [39, 168, 134]. The optimizations include, for instance, feedback message suppressing [81].

The invalidation and update request propagation is a crucial mechanism in a DSM implementation for the WSN environment. However, the closed groups mechanisms, like reliable multicast and broadcast, are not really useful in large wireless sensor networks, due to unreliable links and these protocols can cause large delays, huge overhead and scalability issues. Instead, anonymous propagation approaches based on broadcast communication, like delivering the request to a specific number of nodes or to a specified fraction of the nodes available in the network can be used. These approaches are much more efficient and may still be sufficient or combined with appropriate data recovery mechanisms.

2.3 Data sharing and consistency related examples in WSN

This section gives more detailed description of WSN approaches related to data storage or data sharing and to consistency of data that combine these two worlds, i.e., the wireless sensor networks and data sharing.

Trickle Trickle [138] is an interesting protocol that was designed to disseminate code updates in WSNs. It is based on the polite gossip method and provides eventual consistency of the disseminated data.

Each code update is identified by a version number. Trickle realizes the data dissemination by first exchanging the metadata and finally the blocks of data if necessary. The polite gossip is realized by periodic broadcasting of own version number by each nodes. The time is divided into periods and every node can broadcast its version number only once per period. The periods of different nodes do not have to be synchronized. Each node counts the number of received messages that contain the version number equal to its own. If a node receives from other nodes a defined number of such messages, it does not broadcast its own version number in the current period. But if a received message contains a version number that differs from the local one, an data update in up or down direction is triggered, depending on the relation of the versions.

The period length and the number of received packets that cause stopping own broadcast influence the speed and aggressiveness of the dissemination. As already mentioned, the protocol provides eventual consistency of the data. Concurrent writes from two different places of the network cannot be handled, i.e., the protocol is designed to handle a single writer only. But this complies with the initial application of the protocol, the code update propagation, that are usually initiated by a single unit, e.g., a base station.

The algorithm is used to propagate larger pieces of data, but can be also adapted to disseminate small data pieces in an arbitrary group of nodes. If more than one data writer shall be supported an arbitration or serialization of write operations is necessary to order the written data according to the versions. Additionally, the original concept involves a complete code image update, but if incremental code updates are to be supported, then it is not only important to apply the newest update, but also to apply all of these which precede it, before it can be applied. Thus, in such a case additional mechanisms are required to buffer the data and manage sequential data propagation.

Linda Linda is an example of data sharing concept that evolved from large scale workstation networks to wireless sensor networks. The data storage concept is similar to the one proposed in this work, i.e., they both use structured shared data addressed by the content.

Linda was originally designed to support parallel programming and process coordination [8] while supporting the decoupling of processes in time and space. Linda is an abstraction defining an extension to the basis programming language as a set of operations and rules on the shared memory area called tuple space. The tuple space is a collection of tuples, where a tuple is an ordered set (or record) of typed values. A tuple is addressed by its name and content. There can be multiple tuple spaces and an *out(tuple)* operation inserts the given *tuple* into the tuple space, a *rd(pattern)* operation returns a tuple that matches the given *pattern* from the tuple space and an *in(pattern)* operation returns the tuple and removes it from the tuple space. The pattern used by the reading operations can be defined as an incomplete tuple or a tuple with wild cards. The reading operations are blocking and the returned tuple is chosen in an indeterministic way–usually the first that fits. If there is no tuple in the tuple space that matches the pattern then the operation blocks until such tuple appears. There are probe operations *rdp()* and *inp()* that do not block, but fail if there is no tuple that matches the pattern.

The specific features and consistency mechanisms depend on the specific kernel implementations. For instance the hardware features may be used. As mentioned in [8], for the S/Net workstation platform the *out()* does a broadcast and all nodes in the network store a replica of the tuple, thus, each node has a local copy of the tuple space. The *in()* searches in the local copy and broadcasts a delete operation for the matching tuple, that needs to be accepted by the node that is the origin of that tuple. And this acceptance can be given to one requester only. Thus, the *in()* operations are synchronized by the node that issued the tuple. The *rd()* is fast, since it also searches in the local copy, but does not need to update the replicated tuple space.

The kernel for VAX-network works differently. There are no replicas and an *out()* operation creates the tuple in the local storage of the source node. Thus, the write operation is simplified, but the *rd()* and *in()* operations require a broadcast search and may induce lot of traffic, if several nodes have tuples that match the pattern. The blocking of *rd()* and *in()* operations is more complicated as well, i.e, all the nodes store the pattern and the source of the query for a given time, waiting for new tuples to come. After the time elapses, the pattern is removed by these nodes and the requester has to renew the request if it did not get the answer yet. Thus, this implementation is more complex for reading, but does not require hardware support for reliable broadcast and requires less space to store the tuple space on each node.

Another implementation, for the iPSC hypercube hardware, realizes the tuple space as set of tuples, where these tuples are distributed over the network using hash functions. The *out()* operation hashes the tuple to a specific address of a node, where it is then stored.

Linda was generally designed to be applied in a static wired network environment and the above mentioned implementations do not mention failures. The kernel implementation proposed in [211] was designed to provide high availability of the tuple space in presence of failures. To achieve this goal this approach uses replication and consists of two parts, i.e., the operation protocol and the view change algorithm. The operation protocol is the read-one/write-all and in case of failures the view change algorithm is applied to ensure that the new view is consistent. This kernel ensures the correct order of the operations and that the updates survive failures and the processes access a consistent and correct tuple space.

Other papers [33, 72] propose some additions to the abstraction provided by Linda. In [33] the authors add the *collect(ts1, ts2, pattern)* operation that moves the matching tuples from tuple space *ts1* to tuple space *ts2* and returns the number of them. The implementation mentioned in [72] uses two hashing functions to distribute the tuples over a static set of nodes (also referred to as processors or tuple space managers). The first hash function gives the range of nodes based on the type of tuple and the second one chooses a single specific node based on the content of the tuple. Thus, an *out()* operation is simple, because the tuple is transferred to a node defined by these hash functions and stored in its local storage. For an *in()* operation, in case of a pattern with missing fields, the complete set of nodes specified by the first hash function needs to be asked about the pattern. An arbitration is needed to remove only a single tuple.

LIME The next evolution step of the Linda abstraction is LIME (Linda In Mobile Environment) [166, 156, 157]. LIME supports both, agent and host mobility, also referred to as the logical and the physical mobility. The mobility support is provided by the fact that the applications (agents) can move, either in the logical way–the application is migrating between hosts, or physically–the hosts are moving together with the applications installed on them. The devices in use are either mobile devices (like cellphones, PDAs, laptops), or wired computers with mobile agent running on them. LIME assumed that both, the mobile agents and the hosts have globally unique identifiers. Tuple spaces are permanently bounded to mobile agents and mobile hosts and move with them. The memory model is based on data migration.

Due to the characteristic of the environment, the persistence and availability of the global tuple space is unreasonable. In ad-hoc networks partitioning is an usual case, thus, only the tuple spaces available on connected machines are visible and accessible. Thus, in both mobility cases the complete shared memory space is dynamic, consisting of the currently available tuple spaces. The authors call it the transiently shared tuple space. Thus, the term transient sharing is influenced by the connectivity. The notion of connectivity or availability of hosts may depend on variety of factors including, but not limited to, connection cost, quality of service, security consideration, etc.

A mobile agent has access to interface tuple space (ITS) that contains information the agent is willing to share with others. The currently available content of the ITS can be seen as a merge of the all ITSs of the co-located/connected agents on connected hosts. This merging is a dynamic and atomic process that reconfigures the available data on each join (*engagement*) or disconnect (*disengagement*) operation. That is why the tuple space is shared transiently. Actions of becoming connected, merging of ITSs and migration of misplaced tuples take place in a strictly sequential order and are executed as if they were a single atomic operation. The ITS recalculations on engagements and disengagements may become very expensive if the system exposes high dynamics.

An agent can have multiple ITSs and also private tuple spaces, not shared with anyone. To distinguish on which tuple space an operation shall be performed the dot notation is used, e.g., *TS.out()* performs the *out()* operation on tuple space *TS*. So, the tuple spaces are named and only those used by two or more agents together are shared between these agents. All agents use the system tuple space *LimeSystem* that contains system related data, on which the *in()* operation is not allowed.

Agents co-located on the same host create host-level tuple space that can be regarded as the ITS of the host. Connected hosts merge their host level tuple spaces into a federated tuple space. There is no replication of data, thus a tuple in the federated tuple space can be either *local*–stored in the local host storage, or remote–stored in the storage of a remote host that is currently accessible.

LIME provides a location extension to the *out()* operation–the *out[A](tp)* operation stores the tuple *tp* in the chosen tuple space in the local storage and then performs a migration of the tuple to the storage of agent A, if it is connected. If the agent A became disconnected in the meanwhile, the tuple *tp* becomes misplaced and the migration happens as soon as it is connected again and becomes a part of the atomic engagement operation. This extension contradicts a bit with the original decoupling of processes proposed by Linda, since it involves direct interprocess communication. But, here the important question is if the data is used for process coordination, or if the data represents the result of an operation performed for a specific agent and setting the destination in an *out()* operation is used to send the answer back to the initial requester. However, it cannot be guaranteed that the connection will happen again.

LIME provides also location extensions to the *in()* and *rd()* operations–*in[A,B](pt)* and *rd[A,B](pt)* reduce the scope of the operation to the current (A) and destination (B) location of the tuple. The A specifies the current location of the tuple of interest and it may be either an agent or host identifier. If A is unspecified, then the search for a tuple that matches the pattern *pt* will be performed in the complete federated tuple space. The destination location (B) reduces the scope of the operation to tuples with a given location used in the *out()* operation, i.e., it can be used to look explicitly for tuples that were destined to some specific agent. Thus, B can be an agent identifier or may be left unspecified.

Another extension provided by LIME is a mechanism for detecting events. The simplest event detection is an *in()* or *rd()* operation that blocks until a satisfying tuple is available. However, this solution is less efficient if several event notifications are requested, since several threads would be necessary. Linda abstraction forces applications to pull tuples out of the tuple space, but a more flexible solution would be to have a mechanism that pushes the interesting tuples to the application. The *reactTo(s, pt)* operation on a tuple space causes the execution of code block s on detection of a tuple matching the pattern *pt*. A reaction is registered with the given tuple space, it can be also unregistered. During the registration it is specified if the reaction is allowed to execute the code block only once, allowing detecting a single tuple matching the pattern or if it shall execute the block for each tuple matching the pattern. The event detection mechanism evaluates the registered reaction after each regular tuple space operations and if its evaluation is positive the code block s is executed atomically. This procedure is repeated for all registered reactions on that tuple space.

LIME provides also the operation *upon(s,pt)* that reacts asynchronously on availability of a tuple matching the pattern *pt*.

A reaction can be also annotated with the current location of the tuple to be detected and its destination as specified for the *in()* and *rd()* operations–*reactTo[x,y](s,pt)*. However, the current location field (x) must always be specified.

The events notifications only inform about the availability of new tuples, no other arbitrary event detection exists. The implementation mentioned in [166] is built upon IBMs T-Spaces. This implementation assumes full connectivity, thus constrains the idea of dynamic reconnection. The Java implementation mentioned in [156] is further described in [157].

Another publication [167] presents two initial examples of its application. They are games, but use the mechanisms for process coordination, so the solutions can be transferred to similar, more serious applications. The first example is a distributed puzzle game, where the players can choose and reserve the puzzle pieces from the owner machine and then rearrange them even if disconnected. The rearrangements are visible as soon as the player that reserved the puzzles is connected again. The second example is a game where the teams of players explore an unknown terrain. The team members explore the virtually extended real life area and have to find the flag of the other team. The team members share the knowledge about the area (pictures taken by a camera) using the tuple space.

The paper gives some implementation details an code size measures for the Java implementation of LIME. The paper also states that the *reactTo()* is limited to data on the local machine in order to avoid synchronization of reactions over multiple machines, i.e., distributed transactions, maintaining of atomicity and serialization.

Limone Limone [82] is an approach similar to LIME. Limone supports application development over ad-hoc networks consisting of logically mobile agents and physically mobile hosts. It provides an agent centric perspective that allows each agent to create its own acquaintance policy and only agents satisfying this policy are accessed by the operations initiated by that agent. The list of agents satisfying the policy is maintained by the system. This asymmetric style of coordination allows the agent to focus only on relevant peers. In the tuple space point of view, the agent accesses only the tuple spaces owned by the agents from its acquaintance list.

Limone is based on Linda, thus it is kind of LIME competitor that tailors the Linda operations, by removing remote blocking and group operations. It provides timeouts for all distributed operations and reactions.

A profile of an agent is a set of objects that describe its properties. The application may change the engagement policy of an agent to specify which agents are of interest based on their profiles. The policy chooses the nodes in the proximity to be added to the list of agents of interest. It is an alternative solution for the scope of operation provided by LIME. In Limone the agent does not have to know the exact identity of agents it is interested in, but rather specifies the parameters of interest and can access the agents that fit the policy. For each agent the Limone system discovers the agents in its proximity and automatically adds those who fit the policy.

The Limone accepts and acknowledges the unpredictable nature of the wireless link in the ad-hoc networks and its model starts with a promise that a single round trip message exchange is possible. Based on that assumption it provides a precise and reasonable set of functional guarantees. The uncertainty of the system led the Limone developers to restricting the coordination activities to the set of agents included in the acquaintance list of a given agent. Limone system consists of mobile hosts that build up an ad-hoc network, mobile agents that reside on these hosts and data owned by the agents, shared through Linda-like tuple spaces. The agents are able to migrate and the local tuple space of an agent migrates with the agent. Limone uses a beacon-based discovery protocol that notifies each agent on departure and arrival of an agent of interest, according to the engagement policy. Each agent may have a different policy and since each agent has a different neighborhood, the resulting context, the agent operates in, is unique. The authors say that this reduction of set of agents, an agent needs to coordinate with, helps to improve the scalability. This is due to the fact that there is not the case where every agent needs to coordinate with all other agents. But the movements of agents are dynamic as well causing the overhead of creating and updating the discovery, filtering and acquaintance list anyway.

The actual data accesses are realized in this way that an initiating agent requests an agent from its acquaintance list to perform an operation on its tuple space for the initiating agent. Thus, there is no remote access to foreign data. Each agent is thus the manager of its tuple space and the agents may have policies to accept or reject remote access requests. And there is a tuple space for each agent.

The reactive programming feature allows an agent to be notified on appearance of a specific tuple in any tuple space of the remote agents from its acquaintance list. The reference agent registers a reaction in its reaction registry and it is then forwarded by the Limone system to all agents present in its acquaintance list. Each agent from the list decides if it accepts or rejects the reaction to be placed in its tuple space. When the tuple space of a remote agent contains a tuple that fires a reaction, a copy of the tuple is sent to the requesting agent together with the identifier of the reaction. The receiving agent executes the action associated with that reaction atomically. The authors say that this method provides reactions to state, rather than to data operations. For instance, if a new agent is added to the acquaintance list its tuples may generate a firing of a reaction that corresponds to its state. So it is not a pure publish/subscribe mechanism.

The discovery mechanism is based on beacons. Each Limone server broadcasts a beacon with the profiles of agents running on top of it. Other Limone servers forward these profiles to their agents. A profile is a set of tuples, each of a form *(name, type, value)*. Two system defined entries contain the host identification and an unique agent identity. The application can add other entries. Each agent passes the profiles to its engagement policy handler, which decides which agents are of interest and will be added to the acquaintance list. Once an agent is added to the list, the handler monitors its profile and updates the list if needed. If the profile changes and do not fit the policy or is not received for a defined period of time, the agent is removed from the list. Once an agent is added to the list, the reactions of the owner of the list are forwarded to it. The new agent decides if it wants to install it.

All application data is stored in individually owned tuple spaces. The tuple structure is the same for all tuples (*(name, type, value)*). The authors say that this helps to improve the expressiveness of the tuple space matching. All local operations are performed locally on the local tuple space. Thus, since they do not require transactions with remote agents, they can be executed atomically. The local operations include: *out()*, *in()*, *inp()*, *ing()*, *ingp()*, *rd()*, *rdp()*, *rdg()* and *rdgp()*. The operations take the template as the parameter. The remote operations are performed as follows; the requester sends a request to the owner agent, starts a timer and waits for what comes first, either the timeout or the answer. The remote operations include: *out()*, *inp()*, *ingp()*, *rdp()* and *rdgp()*. They take the agent identifier and the template as parameters. Each request has its identifier, to distinguish the responses.

The reactions are a mechanism that informs that the initiating agent is interested in a particular type of tuples. As soon as such a tuple appears in a tuple space of any agent in the acquaintance list the initiating agent is notified and executes an application defined call back function. A reaction consists of a reactive pattern and a call back function. The acquaintance list of the initiating agent specifies a list of agents the reaction shall be propagated to. Once such a tuple appears, its copy is sent to the initiating agent together with the reaction identifier and the call back function is executed. There are no transactions while sending the reaction notification, so there is no guarantee that the function will be executed even if the tuple that matches the reactive template was found. If the initiating agent receives the notification message the reaction code is executed atomically. To avoid deadlocks the functions cannot use blocking operations. There are two types of reactions regarding their lifetime; *ONCE* and *MULTIPLE*. There is no history of registered reactions. *ONCE* reactions are unregistered as soon as they fire, *MULTIPLE* reactions stay registered for ever. Reactions registry stores the reactions of a single agent and is used by the Limone to propagate the reactions to the agents on the acquaintance list. The reaction list contains all the reaction patterns registered on the agent tuple space together with the identity of initiating agent that needs to be notified.

The agents may migrate between hosts. In the case of an agent migration, the Limone system automatically updates its context and reactions. The acquaintance list is updated and the reactions are forwarded to all the agents on that list. The reaction list is maintained with the help of the discovery mechanism. Agent mobility is based on Code. Code servers run on the hosts and each agent provides a method *go()* that takes the reference to the new server as parameter and moves the agent to the new host. Prior to its migration, the agent first unregisters all of its reactive patterns from remote agents and removes its profile from the beacon of the old host/server. On the new host the agent adds its profile to the beacon and collects new agents of interests. Limone is implemented in Java.

TinyLIME The next step in the evolution of the Linda abstraction is the integration of wireless sensor nodes into the system. In [62] the authors propose an extension of the LIME middleware to enable this integration. On top of LIME, they have built a client application (the TinyLIME) that accesses data from the sensor network (or actually from single sensors) and makes this data available in the shared tuple space available for the other mobile devices in the mobile ad-hoc network (MANET). Unfortunately, the sensor nodes cannot be regarded as a network, because they do not communicate with each other. They only communicate with a gateway mobile device that is currently in their vicinity. Due to that, the authors claim that their approach provides context-awareness, since the device, and thus the person holding it, gets information from the sensors located nearby.

The sensor nodes connected to the mobile device are visible in the ITS of the device. Thus, specifying the scope of the read operation the application can get local values from the surrounding. The sensor data are read only, i.e., they can be only accessed using *rd()* operation or reactions and the *in()* operation is not available. The time is divided into epochs and the measurements are identified by the epoch they were taken. The duration of an epoch is deployment specific. Epoch counter on each sensor node works independent and there is no synchronization. This causes shifts of epochs on different nodes.

Setting the parameters of the sensor nodes is more complicated. A specified set of these has been defined and can be set using functions provided by the main class of TinyLIME. However, even though these functions generate tuples inserted into the tuple space, the actual access to the sensor nodes is done using the client application that reads the sensor nodes and orders the measurements in behalf of other processes on the mobile device. The operations on nodes include reading, setting a reaction (periodic reading with transfer on a specified condition), aborting an operation and setting a parameter. The TinyLIME specifies how often the data shall be read from sensor nodes and defines freshness of data. It also keeps historical data, but using a different tuple template. The reactions support more sophisticated conditions on data, e.g., a range check. The actions to be triggered on the mobile devices are fixed and represented by functions. LIME and Linda provide only template based reactions, thus an equal condition.

Obtaining the data from sensors on demand is not optimal, i.e., all the mobile devices broadcast the request for the data and the nodes nearby respond, what this can be quite expensive and without a guarantee of success. If a *rd()* was issued and no sensor node replies, the mobile device retries the sending and blocks the processing until an answer comes.

In [61] the authors extend the description of TinyLIME by the aggregation and energy saving capabilities. TinyLIME supports temporal and spatial aggregation. Spatial aggregation is realized on mobile devices, where the *rdg()* operation returns all collected measurements of the same parameter and then the aggregation operation can be applied. The temporal aggregation is realized on the sensor nodes, i.e., the client application orders a given number of measurements (one per epoch) of a chosen parameter and requests preparing an aggregate over these measurements.

To save energy, the sensor nodes sleep during the *sleeping time* and are awake for the *nominal awake time*. The burden of communication is put on the mobile devices, which repeat sending a message to ensure its delivery. Knowing the *sleeping time* the mobile device can send the message for a little bit longer and then it is sure that all sensor nodes receive it.

In [154] some example applications of TinyLIME are given. These examples are computer games that involve sensor measurements–pervasive games.

TeenyLIME The last step on the evolution of the Linda concept is the TeenyLIME middleware [56, 57], which runs on wireless sensor nodes. Thus, compared to TinyLime the TeenyLime provides the tuple space abstraction directly to the nodes, not to mobile devices like PDAs or laptops. More details on the implementation are given in [55].

The TeenyLIME focuses on the following high level challenges:

- localized computations–the computations are performed as close to the sensing/acting area as possible,
- multiple tasks in parallel–several control loops running in parallel using the same shared data,
- statefull coordination–using a shared piece of data as state (requires reliability),
- reactive interactions–reactions to external conditions still require proactive interactions, like reading the sensor values.

The applications of TeenyLime focus on sense-and-react scenarios and as an example an air conditioning and fire detecting system is given. The TeenyLime concept is as follows. Each node owns a tuple space that it shares with other nodes within the direct (one-hop) communication range. In this context the sharing means that a node views its local tuple space as a sum of its own data and the data contained in the local tuple spaces of its direct neighbors. The access operations include *out()*, *in()*, *rd()*, *ing()* and *rdg()*. TeenyLIME also provides operations to add and remove a reaction. None of these operations is blocking. The TeenyLime is implemented in TinyOS and implements these data access functions as split-phase operations. The access functions return an operation identifier that allows combining the answer provided by the *tupleReady()* TinyOS event with the request.

Except the tuple or pattern the parameters of these access functions allow specifying the scope of the operation and the desired reliability level. The scope can be either limited to the local tuple space of the node, the shared tuple space of the neighborhood or to the tuple space of a specific node from the neighborhood. The reliability has two levels; a lightweight form of best-effort communication or stronger guarantees for applications requiring statefull interactions.

The names of tuples are replaced by integer identifiers, thus the flexibility of the approach is reduced compared to Lime and others for more powerful devices. This causes also that the Teenylime is actually configured at compile time. However the integer identifiers are not fixed in a sense of their amount, but care shall be taken to avoid collisions of tuple identifiers.

The TeenyLime tuple matching extends the standard Linda patterns by allowing range matching, i.e., defining that the requested value in the tuple shall be greater or smaller than a given value. The patterns are created using predefined compare functions that take two values as parameters and return a Boolean result of the comparison. The patterns include the index of the compare function and the value to be compared with the value in the tuple. It is possible to create user-defined compare functions.

In TeenyLime the time is divided into epochs and every data tuple is stamped with the epoch number. This field of the tuple can be accessed with the provided helper functions. The *setFreshness(pattern, freshness)* adds the freshness condition to the pattern and a tuple older that the requested number of epochs is not interesting anymore. The *getFreshness(tuple)* returns the number of epochs that elapsed since the tuple in question was created. And the *setExpireIn(tuple, expiration)* specifies the number of epochs the tuple will stay in the tuple space. After that it will be automatically removed.

The TeenyLime was designed to allow easy extension and customization of the middleware. In order to make this possible the local and distributed processing as well as the communication are fully decoupled processes. Thus, any of these aspects can be modified without influencing the others.

The remote reactions are periodically refreshed on the remote nodes. Each node periodically transmits reactions to be installed on its neighbors and they restart a timeout timer on reception of such a request. If the timer expires the reaction is removed. This solution works well with disappearing nodes, i.e., the reaction of a dead node is removed automatically and the resources are saved. If a node does not need a reaction anymore it simply stops propagating the reaction request.

Each node informs its neighbors about its capabilities. To show what kind of data the node is able to produce, it issues a capability tuple, which is actually a pattern. The node appends this tuple describing itself to every outgoing message and the neighbors overhear it and add to their tuple spaces, if it is not already there. The capability tuple of a neighbor node is inserted into the local tuple space with an expire period. Thus, if the neighbor disappears and does not resend its capability tuple, it is automatically removed. This is a form of neighbor discovery realized using the capability tuples also referred to as *NodeTuples*. In order to enable this mechanism TeenyLime requires from the communication layer the ability to overhear transmitted packets.

Thus, the tuple space of each node contains the tuples describing its neighbors. If an *in()* or *rd()* operation matching a capability tuple is issued, the TeenyLime middleware signals the *reifyNodeTuple()* (TinyOS) event allowing the programmer to generate the application specific data on demand. This is a very interesting feature that allows taking measurements only when necessary. This can also be used to trigger any action, e.g., computing an average of measurements taken before.

In case a node issues a request that matches a capability tuple of another node it is necessary to keep track of the query to deliver the tuple with the answer to the requester after the tuple containing the measurement is inserted into the tuple space. In order to realize that the TeenyLime automatically installs a reaction on the node whose capability tuple matches the query and as soon as the tuple with the measurement is available, the reaction fires, provides the requester with the data and is automatically removed.

In [55] more details on the reliability levels of the operations are given. The reliability is based on an atomic protocol (reliable and ordered message delivery) for both, unicast and broadcast. This protocol works for the defined group of neighbors. And since the Teenylime uses one-hop neighborhoods, this group of nodes is the one-hop radio range group. The protocol requires the sender to repeat sending of the message until all the intended recipients have received it. To avoid the traffic overhead caused by per message acknowledgments, it requires the recipients to attach the acknowledgments to other outgoing messages. The protocol assumes that a broadcast-based communication is available where all nodes receive all messages, i.e., no address filtering in the radio module.

The key task of the protocol is to maintain a table that contains the most recent sequence numbers of the messages sent to each neighbour as well as the sequence numbers of messages most recently received from each neighbor. Each sender generates the message sequence numbers for each recipient separately and each message contains a sequence number for each recipient. This means that a recipient only needs to check if the sequence numbers of the messages it has received from a single sender are continuous. This simplifies the task of the protocol, but causes the approach to send very large data packets, if the number of neighbors grows.

To acknowledge phase is realized as follows. Each node attaches the list of sequence numbers of messages received from all its neighbors to every outgoing message. And since all communication is overheard by all nodes, each sender verifies its corresponding sequence numbers and checks if it has to resend messages to that node. Again, if the number of neighbors grows, the messages can become very big.

The approach requires actually also a buffer for messages, which need to be saved for the sake of retransmission. With each buffered message its list of intended recipients is stored as well. On a reception of an acknowledgment a recipient is removed from the list. If no recipients are left on the list the message is said to be delivered and is removed from the retransmission buffer.

If a recipient receives a message with a sequence number which says that there are some missing messages between the most recently received one and the current one, the recipient ignores the current message and sends a dummy message containing only its list of received sequence numbers to indicate that the sender needs to retransmit some messages. The sender resends the messages starting from the oldest one. Since the acknowledgments are piggybacked, it is possible that the sender may wait long for them, if a receiver does not currently need to send any message. To avoid this and to ensure a predicable maximum delay each receiver starts a timer after receiving every message and if the node does not need to send any own message in that period, it sends a dummy message containing only the sequence numbers of the messages it received from its neighbors, i.e., the acknowledgments.

If a message was lost on the way to the recipients or the message with acknowledgments was not received by the sender, there is no feedback to the sender to remove the message from the buffer. Thus, in order to avoid stalling messages in the buffer, the sending node retransmits periodically the messages not acknowledged yet, to increase the chance to reach the recipients.

The piggybacked acknowledgments are also used by the neighbor discovery mechanism. Receiving capability tuple of a new node (A) does not mean that the link is bidirectional. Thus, before the receiving node (B) puts the received capability tuple into its tuple space, it includes the node (A) into the message sequence number list, indicating that no message has been received from that node yet. If the link is bidirectional, the node A receives this message and is sure that link between it and node B is bidirectional and adds node B to its own list of neighbors, i.e., put the capability tuple of node B into the local tuple space. This causes that the node B will also be included in the acknowledgment part of messages send by node A and as a result, node B adds the capability tuple of node A to the local tuple space.

The protocol sounds reasonable, but may have scalability problems. For several nodes it may work fine, but as the density of the network grows the messages grow very fast. The piggybacked part of the message may become very large. Each message contains the capability tuple of the sender node as well as the list of most recent sequence numbers of messages the node received from its neighbors. Additionally, every message has a complete list of recipients and an individual sequence number for each. In a standard WSN hardware restricted messages the amount of data may be an overkill.

In [57] the authors state the code size requirements of TeenyLime based exemplary application implemented in nesC for Mica2 to be 80-90kB. Without TeenyLime the same functionality (fire detection and air conditioning) requires 69-72kB.

In [37] the authors present an application example of the Teenylime middleware. This deployment requires long term operation, and thus, low energy consumption. The authors claim to be the first who applied a middleware for a real world scenario and not used an application on top of an operating system. The middleware is responsible for application logic as well as for providing lower level services as data collection, data dissemination and time synchronization, what they claim to be new as well.

Using Teenylime as the bounding block of all of the other components allows shorter development times, higher reusability and less testing time. The authors implemented a transport protocol on top of Teenylime to transmit the data from the nodes to the sink. The protocol supports hop-by-hop retransmissions if the parent node in the routing tree discovers a missing packet from its child. The only situation where packet losses are envisioned are connected to tree reconstructions, where the new parent may do not have the complete history of child data. Due to that, for high reliability traffic the tree reconstruction is temporary switched off until the transmission completes. Time synchronization is also based on a hierarchical construct (tree) of nodes, where the children synchronize with the parent, etc., up to the root. The timestamping is not really optimized, but the system achieves the requested time difference of less than one ms.

The deployment requires a partial reconfiguration of acquisition rates and intervals. The reconfiguration must be reliable and the data needs to be eventually consistent in the network. The eventually consistent delivery of data is realized by an implementation of the Trickle algorithm using Teenylime. Since in the deployment there is only one sink, and thus, only one source of configuration tuples, there are no write conflicts. The configuration parameters are combined in one tuple what easies the handling of multi parameter configurations–they are all delivered in one piece.

The application scenario induces several changes in the basic Teenylime. The authors introduced typed tuples, the developer specifies the types of tuples and a preprocessor constructs optimized data structures for storing and searching the data based on all kind of tuples used in the system. This solution causes the approach to be more space efficient, but less flexible, since all nodes need to be reprogrammed in case of changes in the tuples. The storage of the tuples is realized in chunks. Applying these two techniques saved about 80% of allocated memory.

The authors mention also automatic data fields, e.g., link quality indicator (LQI) that are filled automatically and are available via the tuple space. The low power operations are supported by the low power listening and timeouts for remote requests.

Hood Hood [210] proposes a neighborhood abstraction layer for TinyOS. It is an interesting approach to manage the groups in the WSN in an abstract way. Hood provides a discovery mechanism to manage the list of neighbors based on a set of defined attributes and allows read access to these.

The neighborhood is defined as a set of criteria to choose nodes that become neighbors and a set of variables to be shared in that neighborhood. These neighborhoods may be asymmetric, i.e., one node can belong to a neighborhood of a second one, but it does not mean that the second belongs to the neighborhood of the first one. Thus, to distinguish the nodes regarding this asymmetry, the following naming of nodes is used.

The nodes that belong to a neighborhood of a node are its neighbors, but the nodes to whose neighborhood a node belongs are its co-neighbors. If a node is a neighbor and at the same time a co-neighbor of another node, then their relation is symmetric.

The defined set of variables specifies the shared data. The default setting is, that these variables are broadcast and each recipient decides, based on the defined criteria, if the sender should be added to its list of neighbors. This decision is recipient's own and the sender does not know to whose neighborhoods it belongs. This means that a node knows its *neighbors*, but it is not aware of its *co-neighbors*.

The process of choosing the neighbors is called filtering. Since the size of the neighborhood list is predefined, if a node A has already a full list of neighbors and receives a message form a node B who is not on the list, node A has to evaluate the node B according to the defined criteria for the neighborhood. If node B is better suited than some of the nodes already included in the list, then node A has to remove the least suited node from its neighborhood list. At some point in time, node A may also decide to remove node B from its neighbors list, if node B does not meet the criteria anymore.

The list of the neighbors includes the data about each neighbor node, i.e., its identity and the mirror (cache) of its variables defined for this neighborhood. Additionally, it may include data about the neighbor that are derived locally, e.g., the LQI or a distance estimate. The cached variables are called *reflections* and the locally derived data items are called *scribbles*. The scribbles are set in the filtering phase. Own variables are called *attributes*. Thus, the attributes become reflections on remote nodes. The Hood is a simple reflective memory with no consistency, or, according to the authors it is related to eventual consistency. The reflections reflect the most recent value of the attribute, there is no support for history.

The way the attributes are broadcast, i.e., on every change or periodic or not at all, is defined by the push policy. As already mentioned, by default, it is broadcast on every change. The push policy can be specified and implemented by the application designer. It may specify how frequent the data shall be sent and in which chunks, since several attributes can be sent in one packet, what is especially important if the filtering is based on multiple attributes.

The data access is realized as follows. Every node is able to read and write its own attributes. A co-neighbor can only read the reflections, and read and write its local scribbles related to a neighbour. In a setting where the push policy is configured not to send the data at all, the node interested in data uses the *bootstrap()* command, provided by the main Hood interface, to trigger all potential neighbors to send their attributes. A specific node, already included in the neighbor list, can be asked about the current values of its attributes using the *pull()* command provided by the reflection interface.

The implementations of the specific neighborhoods are generated using a precompiler that parameterizes the module and connects the push policy and filter algorithms.

The Hood is a lightweight framework that provides a simple abstraction, but the most of the work needs to be done by the application developer. It is implemented in a modular way and adapting the modules the user can adapt the behavior to her needs. These adaptations include the examples mentioned by the authors like multi-hop neighborhoods or bidirectional, reliable neighborhoods, but are not limited to.

In Hood the mirrors on different co-neighbors may have different content. There is no notion for data versions, thus the values of reflections are those received at some point of time and recognized as interesting. If consistency mechanisms are required, they have to be implemented within the push policy. The simplest realizations are, e.g., sending a burst of packets to increase the robustness of delivery. Acknowledgments have to be realized by the application on top of Hood.

Mechanisms to support data reliability have to be implemented by the application designer as well. If a neighbor runs out of battery and stops sending its attributes and no better neighbour appears to replace it in the list, the most recent values of its attributes may be used even if they are not relevant anymore. In this case the dead node will not even respond to neither *bootstrap()* nor *pull()*. This information may be used to remove the node from the list. If may be also realized by a periodic check of the nodes in the list.

On the other hand, the lists of neighbors can be quite dynamic. If the filter looks for neighbors with some attribute higher than a given threshold and a node sends values about the threshold but once smaller and the other time larger, then it is repeatedly added and removed. Thus, there is no consistent view on the data, since the data is only a trigger that influences the group creation process. The data is interesting if it satisfies some condition, and a node that sent that data is considered interesting as well. The single attribute scenario can be extended to a filter that checks several attributes together with some locally derived scribbles, like RSSI, LQI or distance estimate. Anyway, the data or parameters specify if the node is currently interesting enough to be added to the neighbour list.

Restricting the size of the neighbor list helps to manage the memory and the filtering chooses the most suitable nodes to be included on the list in order to save the space available. Thus, Hood is a management framework for the dynamic (due to space limitations) neighbor list. And the membership is based on the relevance of the data the node delivers.

Abstract Regions In [207] the authors present an abstraction for building groups of nodes in a WSN that offers an interface to control the communication costs and accuracy. It is a framework that was designed mainly to support in-network processing and also to provide data sharing facilities. It is also a communication abstraction intended to simplify the development of applications. It hides the details on data dissemination and aggregation within predefined regions. The regions may be defined based on radio connectivity, geographical location or other properties of the nodes. Examples are *the set of nodes within N-hops* or *the set of nodes within distance d*.

The Abstract Region abstraction supports the identification (discovery) of neighbors, data sharing and data reduction (aggregation). These operations were inspired by Hood and its idea of group management. However, in Abstract Regions the focus is quite different, i.e., it focuses on the topology of the network, and thus, on the communication aspects.

The neighbor discovery procedure dependent on the definition of the region, but it is based on the exchange of data between nodes that has the goal to inform the node performing the discovery about the other nodes. In contrast to Hood, the discovery is not data related and is thus not an integral part of the data dissemination, but it is an individual process that may be continuous or repeated if the node wants to capture the changes in the region. The discovery process returns a metric to measure the accuracy of the discovery, such as percentage of potential neighbors that responded to the discovery request.

After the initial discovery, each node may enumerate the region, e.g., in order to address the nodes for direct communication. Additional information like the locations of the nodes can be accessed as well.

The data sharing is realized using key/value pairs representing the shared variables. The operators to access the variables allow to read local and remote variables and to write local variables. The simple implementation may cause a read to fetch the variable from the source. More sophisticated may one use caches on remote nodes and cause a write to broadcast or gossip new values.

The reduction operator is used to perform an aggregation operation like sum, maximum or minimum across the region. It takes the key of the desired variable and the operation to be performed. The result is stored in another shared variable. The reduction may be implemented in a number of ways, like collecting all the values locally or forming a spanning tree and performing the reduction operation on each level. The Abstract Regions hide these details of the realization from the application programmer.

The Abstract Regions provide an unified interface regardless from the definition of the underlying region. Thus, once implemented, a higher level application may be used on top of different regions.

Actually, an implementation of a region is very specific and can be very application dependent. It defines the way the read and write operations work and specifies the costs of the operations with respect to communication. The specific region implementations can be realized as a library of region definitions.

The Abstract Regions framework provides feedback to the application to indicate the accuracy (or completeness) of the performed operation. In the most cases the measure is presented as a percentage of nodes that were involved in the operation, e.g., in an aggregation. The application may use this feedback to affect the resource consumption using a tuning interface that allows specifying low level details like the number of message broadcasts or the number of candidate nodes to consider during the creation of the region. The set of parameters to tune is said to be region definition specific, what sounds reasonable, since the definitions differ quite strong and it is not easy to provide an generalized set of low-level parameters for a variety or region definitions.

Compared to Hood, where the data sharing was the center of operation and actually defined the neighborhood creation, the Abstract Regions abstraction is rather focusing on the building of the neighborhood and the actual data sharing plays a background role.

MacroLab In [94] the authors propose a data-centric macroprogramming system for WSN. The most interesting part of the approach is the definition of the shared data space. The framework is a high-level abstraction and the underlying software implementation is based on tinyOS.

The application developer writes a single program for the entire network and the system decomposes it into microprograms that are loaded onto each node in the network. The decomposition is realized deployment dependent and its main aspect is the data handling.

The data in the system is represented by a *vector* also referred to as *matrix*, where the first dimension is always the set of node identities. Thus, these vectors are actually arrays (or maps) that map the node identifiers to the data sets corresponding to each node. The authors call this data representation a *macrovector*. The data set per each node is global for all the nodes in the network, what is the natural consequence of the array data representation in the system.

These are several possibilities to physically distribute the data stored in a vector over the nodes in the network. It may be stored in a *centralized* storage, i.e., on a single node, it may use a *distributed* storage, where each node stores its own data set from the vector, or a *replicated* storage, where each node stores a complete copy of the entire vector.

Standard vector operations such as addition, subtraction, cross-product, find, maximum and minimum can be applied on the vectors. Additionally, the authors propose a way of indexing the elements in the vector, i.e., the dot-product index. Depending on the representation the vector operations induce different costs. The distributed representation, where each node holds only own data causes the binary operations, like addition or subtraction to be very efficient, i.e., the vector elements identified by the same node identities are combined together. On the other hand, the intra-row operations, like maximum, minimum or find are most efficient in the centralized representation, since all the data is available at the central node and no message exchange is necessary. The replicated representation, where all nodes have all data, combines the feature of both, the distributed and centralized representation, i.e., the entire data is available on each node. However, for the replicated representation, the maintaining of changes is expensive since every change needs to be propagated to all the other nodes.

Thus, based on the input from the application developer regarding communication costs and possible communication patterns (unicast or broadcast) and depending on the kind of computations, to be realized on the data by the application, the cost estimator estimates the optimal distribution of the data choosing one from these three data distributions (also referred to as partitioning). The authors call this approach an deployment-specific code decomposition. The goal of the decomposition is to preserve the semantic of the macroprogram, while providing an efficient way for a distributed execution.

The run-time system (RTS) component is responsible for the run-time analysis of the system. And if it discovers that the choice on the data partitioning was wrong, because of changing environment conditions or because of incorrect input data from the application developer, then it may initiate a change of the data partitioning to a more appropriate one. However, this causes the state to be lost since the nodes are simply reprogrammed with a new version of software and reset.

Only the owner is allowed to write its corresponding element in the macrovector. In distributed representation there are no message exchanges on write, in centralized, the central node has to be updated and in the replicated all other nodes need to be updated. The implementations of the access operations are taken from the template library, depending on the data representation.

The run-time system delivers several management functions for coordinating the processes on different nodes. The inter-node coordination in MacroLab is based on synchronizations based on the current position in the code represented by the address in the program counter (PC). The *owner(PC, M)* function returns the identification of the requester node at the given value of the program counter that wants to access the vector M. The functions *wait(PC, list)* and *notify(PC, list)* synchronize all nodes represented by the given *list* of identities, so they reach the same point in the macroprogram (PC). The *wait()* waits until all nodes from the list notify and the *notify()* waits until all the nodes on the list reach *wait()*. The synchronization of execution is used to keep the data consistent and to preserve the semantic of the original macro code, but it causes lot of message exchange. And, since there are applications that do not need such a strict synchronization, every vector operation has an unsynchronized equivalent. Thus, the synchronization can be relaxed for some applications, but then there is no coordination anymore and the dynamic network links can make some trouble.

The cost analyzer described in the paper uses only one cost parameter, i.e., the messaging cost. The application developer has to provide the description of the network, what is not really precise and quite fuzzy. The static cost analyzer needs to know the topology to estimate the number of messages exchanged between nodes. This approach is quite simple and static, but provides the initial comparison of the different data partitioning. The runtime cost analyzer simply logs the numbers of sent messages and the estimated numbers of messages that would be sent in the other decompositions. These numbers are compared and may trigger the reprogramming of the nodes.

The compilation process is quite complicated and involves several steps. The microprogram generated by the decomposer is written in Embedded Matlab and it is compiled to C by the compiler provided by MathWorks. This C code is then compiled together with the RTS module and other tinyOS modules using the nesC compiler.

As an evaluation the authors provide the number of lines of code for standard applications. One of them is Surge, which generates data and forwards it to the sink. The MacroLab code (7 lines) is compared with the tinyOS implementation (100 lines). This comparison is not really fair, since in case of MacroLab there is much code hidden in the RTS extensions that need to be provided by the application developer. However, if the hidden part is configured and does not need to be changed, the development time is much shorter.

Second part of the evaluation compares several versions of an application for bus tracking, using either the centralized or the distributed vector representation. The compared scenarios are evaluated regarding the amount of exchanged messages while performing the same task. This evaluation is very interesting, because it shows how the centralized approach behaves compared to the distributed logic and data handling. Additionally in one of these test scenarios, a high gain antenna is attached to the base station reducing the cost of the communication link between the base station and the nodes. In this case, the total cost of the centralized approach was smaller compared to the distributed one. These results show, that the way the data is distributed in the network, as well as the network parameters play an important role in the costs of the application execution. These evaluation results are general and applicable not only for the system presented in the paper.

Data Consistency in WSN There is also research on different aspects of data consistency in WSN. Some of these approaches regard these consistency issues only theoretically, other provide some data quality requirements of specific applications and try to measure them with a kind of data consistency.

In [188] the authors propose to use data consistency as a metric to evaluate the quality of data in a WSN. They consider three perspectives of consistency: temporal, numerical and frequency (consistency). And these for both, individual data pieces and data streams. The authors say that the success of the WSN applications depends on their ability to deliver high quality data streams over a long period of time and they argue that the quality of data should be a basic metric for the performance evaluation of protocols as the energy efficiency does.

The authors present a mixture of the parameters of the data (data handling) and the network parameters. The temporal consistency presents the temporal description how long should it take to transport the data to the sink (or destination). The numerical consistency represents the error by the measurement, so it already touches the content of the data. Going even further, the frequency consistency controls how often a dramatic change in the stream of data may appear. The dramatic change includes, e.g., a measurement out of the allowed range. Thus, the authors go here into plausibility check of the data and specify the largest delay allowed to transport the data items.

The focus is on the consistency of the data values. In general the consistency is specified for a specific scenario, i.e., the measurements are taken and are transported towards the sink. The nodes on the way have their old cached values and they do the checks for the new coming data from the stream. The semantic is checked hop-by-hop, for the hop consistency to keep the data consistent. End-to-end consistency is checked either using the single-path consistency or multi-path consistency. The difference between these two is that either a single copy or multiple copies arrive at the sink depending on the underlying protocols. Regardless of the scope of the check (hop or end-to-end) the procedure is the same, the difference between the new and the old cached value is checked, if it is as required and the data item is still fresh and consistent.

There are the two consistencies; numerical and temporal. The multipath check also allows to check if at least k-copies of the same item arrived at the sink. The authors say that using this feature can help to detect and filter out fake measurements.

The stream consistency models, proposed by the authors, focus on the delivery of the stream elements while fulfilling the semantic of the numerical consistency. The models include the strict consistency, the α-loss consistency, the partial consistency, the trend consistency, the range frequency consistency and the change frequency consistency.

The strict consistency requires that all the items are delivered in time (the temporal aspect) and the numerical consistency is maintained. The temporal strict consistency requires a good transport protocol that guarantees that all packets are delivered. Additionally, the temporal character of this consistency model requires that the protocol needs to guarantee the maximum delay, and thus supports quality of service. The numerical aspect of the model is depending on the content of the stream.

The α-loss consistency model allows that $\alpha\%$ of the data items can be lost during the transmission. The partial consistency relaxes the temporal requirements of the α-loss consistency. Like the α-loss consistency, it allows $\alpha\%$ of data items to be lost, but additionally, it allows the data items to be delivered out-dated, but not more than specified by a given parameter.

Trend consistency relaxes the numerical consistency in a sense that it checks if the trend of the data items in the stream is maintained.

The last two models focus entirely on the frequency of abnormal effects in the readings in the data stream, thus they are purely data plausibility check based. In cases where it is known a priori which values are allowed for the data items in the stream, then the values can be checked against these rules. The range frequency consistency checks, if the defined allowed number of readings that are out of range, is not exceeded. The change frequency consistency checks the changes between the following data items in the stream and checks if the defined changes, e.g., larger than a given parameter, do not appear too frequent and their number exceeds some allowed threshold.

These consistency models mix the quality of the data storage and actually delivery with some data monitoring. The mix here under the name of consistency is like putting all the functionality on one box. Further, the authors present the open issues in their opinion. The first issue is the lack of an adapting protocol that can improve the data quality and take the advantage of the data consistency by considering data dynamics. Here they say that models for data dynamics are required. Of course every kind of data to be measured has a different characteristic, thus, doing something like that to fit all the needs is not trivial. Another issue is the intelligent data management algorithm that can reduce the amount of data by filtering the unnecessary data.

The paper uses a quite high level of abstraction. It provides ideas, but looks at the applications as at monolithic blocks. These ideas do not look like they were implemented, because the paper only presents the ideas and not the ways how to implement these.

Another interesting data consistency related work is presented in [194]. The paper describes the spatio-temporal consistency in a network of sensor nodes equipped with cameras. The authors mention two application scenarios, the coast observation and parking space finder. In both scenarios, a set of nodes delivers pictures that shall be composed in a large picture that is temporally consistent, i.e., the pictures used shall be taken in approximately the same time. It presents a mechanism to ensure that the collected pictures from all the space correlated nodes are composed correctly.

The temporal consistency is realized as a mechanism that responses to a query that specifies the maximum age for the complete composed picture. The response is a temporary consistent set of pictures. Since the nodes take the pictures asynchronously the set consists of pictures that are taken at different points of time, anyway. The maximum allowed time difference is specified in the query as well. Thus, the response to the query shall return the most recent set of pictures with a defined maximum age and a defined maximum time difference between the individual pictures.

Since the images can be large, the mechanism is realized as a two stage approach, i.e., the metadata is collected first, and finally the actual data is delivered to the requester. The nodes collect two arrays, one with the picture data and one with their corresponding time stamps at which the pictures were taken. Thus, the nodes need appropriate time synchronization available is in order to achieve the required temporal resolution.

The process of response creation uses the tree topology of the network and requires that each parent node in the tree knows the timestamps of its direct children. The result in a form of a set of timestamp pairs traverses up the tree and then, the pictures of the most appropriate set are requested by the root of the tree by specifying the range that suits the query the most.

Since the cameras may observe the same area but at a different angle it is necessary to provide the spatial consistency, or the way the pictures are composed together. This process is based on landmarks, i.e., known positions are mapped to the appropriate pixels on the pictures taken on each camera and as the pictures overlap, these positions are used to stitch the pictures together after transforming to fix the angles. But this part is rather done on a central processing unit with more computation power.

This paper proposes an interesting mechanism to provide a temporary consistent multi-part reply to a query. It requires a specific static topology of the network with the appropriate distribution of the knowledge within it, but it is feasible to design a similar dynamic mechanism based on a spanning tree created on demand and rooted at a node that received the query from a mobile client.

Another paper [71] proposes a cache coherency protocol, which distinguishes the importance of the nodes in the network and combines push and pull accesses to the data to achieve its goals.

There are three kinds of active nodes in the network; the source of the data, the mediators and the caching nodes. The source node pushes the changes of its data to the mediator nodes and the caching nodes pull it from the mediators. The caching nodes can reply to queries of nodes not involved in the caching of that particular data. The pushed update and invalidate messages are broadcast in a limited region defined by a TTL parameter and all the nodes selected as mediators for that data cache it. A node that is located further in the network and wants to read the data has to send a query to the source, but if a mediator receives that query it can also answer it, what can reduce the communication costs as well as latency.

Thus, the importance of the nodes is based on a metric called centrality index.

This metric is calculated for the whole network at the application start and is assumed to be static. The index is the ratio of all shortest paths containing the node under investigation to the total number of shortest paths between all the nodes in the network. The nodes that are present in the largest number of all the paths are considered as more important and they are more desired to become mediators.

Such an approach causes the set of nodes that have the highest centrality indices and are thus the most attractive as mediators, to become overwhelmed with data caching and eventually may use their energy faster. The approach is described in a formal way, but the real world applicability of the concept may be poor, due to a number of assumptions it uses.

One of the assumptions is that each node broadcasts a beacon message containing the list of its neighbors and thus, every node is aware of a two-hop neighborhood. Every node calculates the index of importance for its one-hop neighbors and chooses the ones that are best suited to be mediators. The minimum set of nodes with the largest indices that cover the two-hop neighbourhood of the node become the mediator set of that node. This actually fixes the replication range to two hops.

With a system defined period DUI (data update interval) each source node sends invalidation messages. Each message contains the *dataID* that identifies the data item, the data item itself or NULL if the data did not change, the time to live (TTL) and a version number of the data item. If the data was changed during the DUI, the source node issues an update message to its mediators. The update message is identical with the invalidation message, but it always contains the data item. The mediators rebroadcast the update and invalidation messages and also use them to check and update their cached data.

The nodes that take active part in the caching of a data item maintain its dataID, the data it stores, the size of the data and the version number. The mediators cache the pushed data and answer the queries forwarded by caching nodes issued by the client nodes. A caching node can store the data it was asked and forwarded a reply for. If a caching node receives a query about the same data item, it can answer it based on its local copy, or forward the query to the mediator. The mediator answers the query or forwards it directly to the source. These steps depend on the local availability and the freshness of the locally available data.

Another work [28] proposes a mechanism that allows the nodes in the network to agree on a single value of a taken measurements in order to obtain the data consistency, i.e., a consistent view on the measured data in presence of corrupted nodes.

All these above mentioned approaches either touch the distributed shared memory area, or the data consistency issues. They do not cover all the aspects of consistency that one can imagine, but provide an overview. In this work, the main aspect of data consistency is the coherency of the multiple copies of replicated data items.

Chapter 3

The WSN related aspects of a DSM realization

This chapter discusses the mechanisms and principles that allow the application engineers to adjust a DSM system for WSN to their needs. As already mentioned in Section 2.2, there are several aspects of a DSM realization. Some of them specify the different ways to reach one chosen goal, like the implementation level, other define the set of provided features. These parameters or design choices need to be evaluated regarding feasibility and the best suitable ones from the given set need to be chosen.

Here, the initial evaluation of the design choices from Section 2.2.1 is summarized into a theoretical DSM framework for WSN that is used for the further discussion in this chapter. Thus, the most suited DSM system for wireless sensor networks is fine granular, preferably with replicated shared data items that can be also referred to as *shared variables*, or simply, variables.

Scalability is also very important, thus, memory management algorithms based on a master copy are preferable. The master copy can be either located at a fixed node or can be able to migrate. Distributed ownership management is preferable to cope with disappearing nodes. Both, write-invalidate and write-update coherence protocols can be applied. However, from the (data) reliability point of view, the write-update protocols are preferred. Ideally, the nodes should not remove any data, since it is stored and distributed to increase the robustness of the storage. To extend that statement, the nodes can even support historical data storage, i.e., each new value written to the shared data item creates a new *instance* of this data item that is uniquely identified either by a version number or a timestamp. Following this idea, the data replacement strategies can be applied to clean the storage from the least recent instances.

The implementation layer is most probably software, e.g., realized as a middleware layer. The WSNs can consist of different nodes that differ in used hardware and software, thus, heterogeneity should be addressed. In this chapter the individual mechanisms that can help to optimize and apply the distributed shared memory abstraction in the area of wireless sensor networks will be examined together with the ways the DSM system can support heterogeneity and the ways this abstraction can be provided to an application. These mechanisms can be parameterized in order to allow their use in applications with different requirements.

First, the scalability related issues and mechanisms are presented. The following section proposes a scalable and lightweight broadcast mechanism that combines the best effort costs with message serialization. Then, the ways to describe both, the replication goal and the replication strategy to fulfil this goal are presented. These allow detailed definition of the system behaviour and thus, tuning the DSM according to the needs. The following sections present another two message oriented mechanisms; the master copy discovery and the migration of the master copy. Then, the instance filtering is introduced It is a mechanism that reduces the processing effort by extracting the information out of the data. Instance filtering helps to cut the storage requirements and the costs of updating the replicas to the minimum and to further increase the scalability.

Then, the sections on heterogeneity issues and on the ways to provide the abstraction to the application follow. First, the access possibilities and the level of the access transparency that can be ensured by both compile-time and run-time tools are discussed. Then, the heterogeneity issues are elaborated and a software adapter system is proposed to allow executing a single DSM setup on different hardware-software platform combinations. The final section of the chapter discusses the principle DSM issues related to the span of data access operations, i.e., it analyses the possible ways to define the start and the end of these access operations in the WSN context.

3.1 Request forwarding

The requests messages represent the desire of one node to perform an operation on another one, thus the requests have to be propagated from one node to another. The following forwarding mechanism combines the best effort broadcast mechanism in a specified region with message serialization features. It allows defining how far each request will be forwarded in the network and thus, helps reducing the global range of the operations increasing the scalability of the system. It has very low memory requirements, independent from the size of the network and the forwarding distance. Each forwarding node stores only the forwarded request together with the address of the immediate message source, for a relatively short time.

Each request is identified by the address of its source node and a sequence number for the requests generated at that node–the *request number*. Combination of these

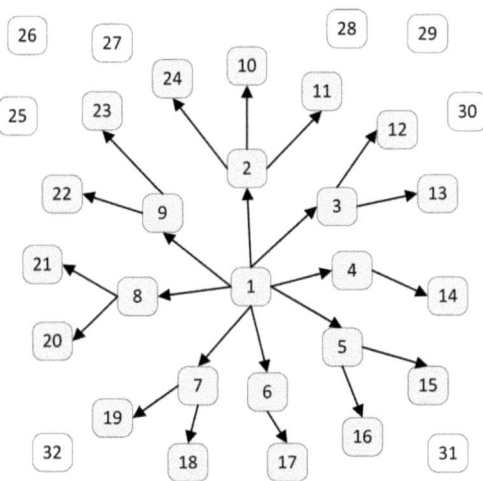

Figure 3.1: An example of a request forward tree

two allows distinguishing between any two requests sourced from any node. It also allows ordering the requests sourced from a single node. Since the request number is a counter, it can make a cycle. Thus, depending on the frequency of request generation, it is necessary to choose the size of the request number properly, to avoid the possibility of having two requests issued by one node with the same request number, in a specific time window.

During the forwarding of a request a controlled flooding of the network is realized, i.e., a directed tree rooted at the source node is created. This process is dynamic and repeated for every new request. The height of the tree is controlled by the source node, who specifies it by setting an appropriate value as the desired *hops count* in the original request message. This value is decreased by the other nodes on reception of the message. The nodes, for which the hops count reaches zero become leafs in the tree and do not forward the request any further.

Each node stores the received request together with the address of the node it directly received the request from in its local request buffer, i.e., each node stores the request together with the reference to its parent in the tree. But, before storing the request, the node checks if the request is not already stored, based on the address of the source node and the request number. The received request is ignored if it is already present in the local request buffer. This helps avoiding loops and propagating the same request multiple times. An example of a network with a request propagation tree is shown in Figure 3.1. The source of the request is the node number one and the number of hops is set to two.

The lifetime of the forwarding tree is limited to the lifetime of the corresponding request. The forwarded request is stored on each node until it is replied by its children nodes (which are not known until then) or until the request times out. The timeout is based on the *request timeout* value specified for the requests on the shared variable and is used to avoid stalled requests that block the buffer. If the request requires a reply, then the standard timeout is multiplied by the value of the hops count, taken from the request message, increased by one. Thus, in this case the timeout period on each node depends on its distance from the root and the total height of the tree, in order to allow all the answers to be handled on all levels of the tree. If the forwarded request does not require a reply, it is stored for a single request timeout period, only to avoid loops and forwarding the same request multiple times.

The nodes send the replies to their parent nodes in the tree and these collect them and forward them to their parents in the direction of the root node–the source of the request. Depending on the kind of the request there are different ways to handle the replies. If the request requires a single reply message, e.g., it is a read or write request sent to a single (but unknown) distant node, then this reply message is simply forwarded back up the tree to the request issuer. In such a case the replying node sets the hops count in the reply message to zero and the value is incremented by every forwarding node on reception, what allows the issuer of the original request to get the information on the distance to the node that replied to the request, e.g., the source of a particular data.

But, if the request requires multiple replies, then it is necessary to combine the replies coming from the children nodes, i.e., the parent nodes have to perform some aggregation of these replies. For instance, if the original request is a quorum read operation, a parent node chooses the most frequently received answer. Similar, to find the most recent value of the data item, the parent node can choose the answer identified by the most recent timestamp or version number, i.e., in this case a *survey convergecast* over the neighboring nodes is performed. Similar, for a replica update or invalidate request, the replies may contain the result of the operation and each parent node may count the numbers of positive and negative acknowledgments received from its children.

3.2 Replication strategy

The replication related mechanisms presented in this section take into account the specific kind of the network the DSM system shall work in. The WSN nodes are considered rather as data carriers and the main goal can be seen as following a strategy to keep the data in the network available and still consistent. This section proposes a way to describe the desired goal to be achieved and a mechanism that applies a strategy to achieve this goal. Both are parameterized and allow the application engineer to adjust the features of the system to the application needs and according to the allowed costs.

An important aspect of the replication strategy is the definition of the replication goal, which is defined individually for each shared data item using spatial and quantitative parameters. The *replication range* (RR) specifies the area of replication as the maximum number of hops the replica update requests issued by the owner of the master copy can travel through the network. Thus, the replication area is defined as a given subset of nodes in the network with the master copy owner in the center of this area. This is an important factor from the scalability point of view that takes the advantage of the usual locality of data in WSN and reduces the global character of the replication. The quantitative parameters are defined by the desired *replication density* (RD) of the replicas over the replication area or by the desired total number of *replicated copies* (RC) in the area. The replication density is specified as an array of values, one for every hop distance within the replication range. These values specify the desired density of the replicas in the given distance from the owner, i.e., the percentage of nodes that shall ideally store a replica of the data item.

The replication goal is a static definition. The actual replication is a dynamic process that operates on that target and provides the replica holders with the new data as the master copy changes. And, this dynamic process needs to operate within the defined boundaries in order to satisfy the replication goal at every point in time and still be energy efficient.

In an ideal case the data replication should be realized by performing an atomic update for every change of the shared data item. Such an approach is very expensive and relaxing this update requirement allows reducing the resource consumption, e.g., the replica update requests can be propagated using the request forwarding mechanism presented in Section 3.1, but sacrifices the consistency.

The proposed replication strategy mechanism distinguishes between four types of update requests. They differ in the operations they trigger, as well as in the costs they induce. Their common feature is that they all contain the new instance of the shared data item and the recipients that already store a replica of the item are asked to update their replicas.

Advertisement Update Request With the *advertisement update* request the owner of the master copy additionally announces that it is looking for new replica holders, i.e., the owner asks the recipients of the request to decide if they want to replicate the data item, if they are not, already. The replication decision is made according to the following condition:

$$random(100) < RD[hops] \qquad (3.1)$$

Where:
random(100)–is a function returning a random value between 0 and 100,
RD–is the array representing the replication density parameter for the shared data item,
hops–denotes the distance from the owner node in hops.

Verified Update Request With the *verified update* request the owner of the master copy asks the recipients of the request to reply with the result of the update operation. Having the information, the owner is able to check it against the replication goal, to verify if it is fulfilled.

Depending on the way the replication goal is defined, the recipients reply to the request either only in case they store a replica of the data by sending a positive acknowledgment (ACK) or they are also requested to provide the owner with a negative acknowledgment (NACK) if they do not store a replica of the item. If the replication goal is defined by specifying the number of replicated copies, then only positive acknowledgments are necessary to count the total number of replicas in the network. Thus, if the number of replicated copies is defined, the verification condition is as follows:

$$\#ACK \geq RC \qquad (3.2)$$

Where:
$\#ACK$–is the number of positive acknowledgments received by the owner,
RC–is the value defined for the variable as the desired number of replicated copies.

Both, positive and negative acknowledgment are requested if the replication goal is defined by specifying the replication density only. In this case the master copy owner needs the information on the total number of nodes and the number of replicas to compute the achieved density and to verify the achievement of the replication goal using the following equation:

$$\frac{\#ACK}{\#ACK + \#NACK} \geq avg(RD) \qquad (3.3)$$

Where:
$\#ACK$ and $\#NACK$–are the numbers of positive and negative acknowledgments,
$avg(RD)$–is the average of the values defined as the desired replication density for the

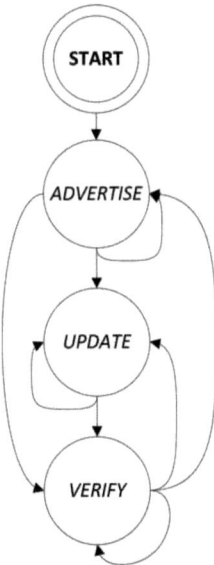

Figure 3.2: The state diagram of the proposed replication strategy

shared data item.

Verified Advertisement Update Request The *verified advertisement update* request combines the features of the two above mentioned types, i.e., the node that owns the master copy asks the recipients to decide if they want to join the group of replica holders of the given data item and, additionally, it asks the recipients to reply with the result of the update operation to verify, if the replication goal is achieved.

Plain Update Request The last, fourth type of update request is the *plain update* request, which does not require any additional action except of updating the replica of the data item.

Specifying a replication strategy that defines the combination of these request types allows controlling the trade-off between the control over the content of the replicated data in the system and the resources needed for that.

The replication involves up to three phases: *ADVERTISE*, *UPDATE* and *VERIFY* and follows the algorithm presented in Figure 3.2. These phases use the different types of the update requests. The transitions between these phases occur as indicated by the arrows synchronously with the issuing of the requests to update the replicas of the data item. Thus, they are triggered by each new value written to the master copy of the data item.

The replication strategy is defined by the *update pattern* (UP), a triple, whose values describe the sequence of the different update requests. The first value in the triple defines the maximum number of repetitions in the *ADVERTISE* phase. The second defines the number of repetitions in the *UPDATE* phase and the third, again the maximum number of repetitions in the *VERIFY* phase. If any of these numbers is zero, the corresponding phase is disabled. The following paragraphs describe how the update pattern influences the replication process.

The replication process always starts with the *ADVERTISE* phase, even if it is disabled by the update pattern. In this phase the owner node announces that there is a new shared data item available in the network. It sends the advertisement update requests or verified advertisement update requests if the *VERIFY* phase is enabled.

In the *ADVERTISE* phase the advertising is repeated for the successive instances until the maximum allowed number of advertisement repetitions defined by the update pattern is reached or the verification result is a success. Then, if the *UPDATE* phase is enabled, a transition into the *UPDATE* phase occurs, otherwise into *VERIFY*. Shall the *VERIFY* phase be disabled as well, the replication remains in the *ADVERTISE* phase.

In the *UPDATE* phase the plain update requests are sent, i.e., the replica updating is performed only on nodes, which have already decided to replicate the data item and other sensor nodes just ignore these requests. In this phase the source node is not informed about the result of the replication. The sending of the plain update requests is repeated for the successive instances, until the number of repetitions defined by the update pattern is reached, what is followed by a transition to the *VERIFY* phase. Shall the *VERIFY* phase be disabled, the replication remains in the *UPDATE* phase.

In the *VERIFY* phase the owner of the master copy of the data item wants to investigate how many replicas of the item are available in the network, without asking new nodes to hold a replica. To do so, the owner node sends the verified update requests. In this phase, the owner repeats the verification for the successive instances of the data item, either until the maximum allowed number of repetitions, as defined by the update pattern, is reached, or the result of the replication goal verification is a success. If the verification fails, a transition to the *ADVERTISE* phase occurs, otherwise, the mechanism proceeds with the *UPDATE* phase. If the target phase is disabled, the mechanism remains in the *VERIFY* phase.

The update pattern allows skipping the phases by setting the corresponding value in the array to zero. However, some of the combinations with zeros are disallowed and induce a change in the setting. For instance, if all the values are set to zero, then the *ADVERTISE* phase is enabled automatically. In such a setting only the advertisement

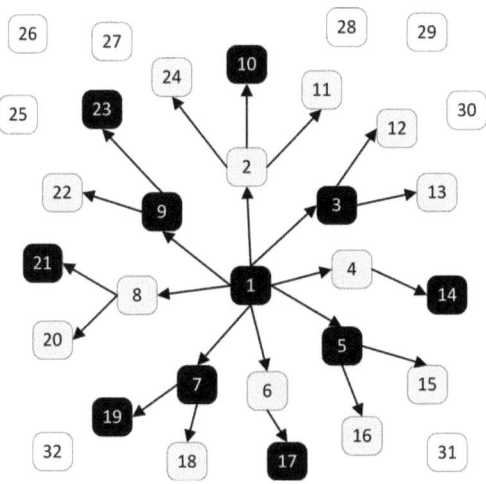

Figure 3.3: Update request forwarding tree–independent forwarding

update requests are sent and no acknowledgments are provided. Thus, it results in the eventual replication density reaching 100 per cent for the chosen replication range.

3.3 Dependent request forwarding

The forwarding of requests can significantly influence the total energy consumption of the system, since the requests can be issued very frequently. Thus, the request forwarding mechanism introduced in Section 3.1 can be optimized in order to reduce its costs. The dependent request forwarding assumes that not all of the nodes are holding the replicas of all the shared data items and tries to take advantage of that fact. In such a case the request forwarding tree can be limited to nodes that hold a replica of the data item the request is about, i.e., only nodes that hold a replica of the data item process and forward the request. Thus, the forwarding depends on the content of the local memory of the nodes. However, this cost reduction comes at the price of reduced penetration scope.

The mechanism will be explained taking as an example the replica update propagation in a system where the nodes decide if they want to store a replica of a data item, as described in Section 3.2. The group of replica holders is further the target of the update requests that contain the new instances of the data item. In order to reduce the cost of the message forwarding, it may be reasonable to reduce the span of the forwarding tree to the replica holders only. In contrast to the standard approach described in Section 3.1, further referred to as *independent forwarding*, the *dependent*

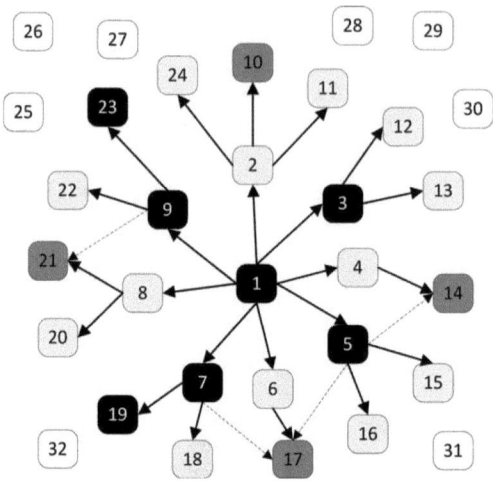

Figure 3.4: Update request forwarding tree–dependent forwarding

forwarding is realized by allowing only the replica holders to take an active part in processing of requests on the given data item and all other nodes ignore these request messages. Hence, the forwarding tree includes only branches that consist entirely of replica holders.

The clear disadvantage of the dependent forwarding approach is that it requires replica holders on every level of the forwarding tree, i.e., the forwarding is not possible if the desired *replication density* parameter describing the replication goal, contains zeros. Similar, defining very small values for the replication density for closer distances from the master copy owner, followed by higher densities at further distances, will cause trouble in achieving this replication goal or will deform the actual result. Figure 3.3 shows an example of independent update request forwarding for the forwarding tree presented in Figure 3.1, where the black shapes represent the replica holders. In contrast, Figure 3.4 presents an example of the dependent update forwarding. Again, the black shapes represent the replica holders. The dark grey shapes represent the nodes that are not reachable by the update requests, in the example tree, due to the lack of replica holders in their branches. Even if the most of them can still be reached by alternative paths represented by the dashed arrows, there are nodes that cannot be reached anymore, like node 10 in Figure 3.4.

Additionally, if a forwarding replica holder disappears, the nodes further in the branch may lose the connectivity as well. Anyway, the dependent forwarding of update requests may reduce the number of sent and received messages, and thus, the total cost of the update request propagation. The choosing between independent and dependent forwarding of update requests allows optimization of the forwarding mechanism following the requirements of the application. The dependent request forwarding cannot be used for every kind of replica update requests, e.g., those with the advertise function, since they have to reach new replica holders.

The dependent request forwarding mechanism can be also used for quorum read operations. Since in such case, the nodes of interest are anyway those, who are holding a replica of the data item in question, the advantage is clear.

3.4 Master copy discovery

The master copy is the only writable replica of the given data item in the system. In a system without replicas, the master copy is the only copy of the data item. If a shared data item does not have an a priori fixed owner of its master copy, then, as the system starts, the holder of the master copy of the data item is undefined. Then, the node that performs the first write operation on that data item, becomes the owner of the master copy. Thus, if a node wants to perform the write operation on the data item, it needs to check if the master copy of the data item exists, or more specific, the node checks if it has the knowledge on the location of the master copy. If the owner of the master copy is defined, then the write request is sent to the owner, but if the knowledge is not available, then the node assumes that the master copy is not created yet, so it creates it and appoints itself as its owner. Of course, this can lead to inconsistencies in the global view on the data item.

In order to avoid such a situation, the node can issue an master copy discovery request on the data item before writing to it. This discovery request is forwarded using the request forward mechanism described in Section 3.1 and it is parameterized by the maximum hop distance for the request to be forwarded by setting the hops count in the request message. The timeout for the reply is defined based on the *request timeout* value.

The shared data items may be initialized during their definition. In such a case, the value is set and thus, the local copy is available for a read request, but the owner remains undefined. In order to provide more flexibility to the application, a read operation can be realized as an explicit read from the local replica that only returns the value, or as a standard read operation that returns the complete set of informations on the data item, i.e., together with the address of the owner of the master copy. Thus, the latter requires the knowledge on the owner of the master copy and performs the owner discovery, if this information is not available in the local replica.

If the data item was not initialized and its value was not written so far, then the explicit read operation from the local replica returns an error. The standard read

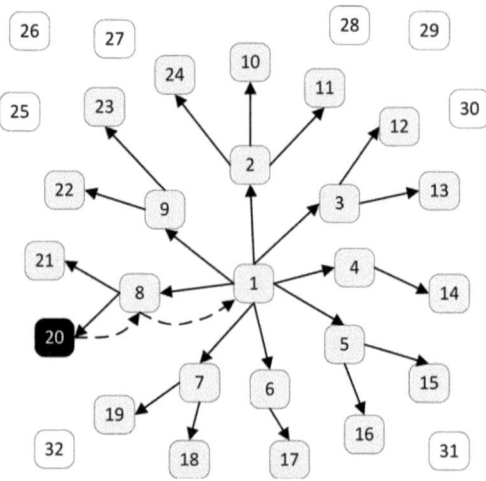

Figure 3.5: The ownership discovery mechanism

operation is then necessary to perform the discovery, in order to find out both, the value and the owner of the master copy.

If the master copy discovery returns with an error, i.e., no reply to the request arrives, then the node assumes that the master copy is not defined, so it can perform the write operation and appoint itself as the owner of the master copy.

Figure 3.5 shows an example flow of the master copy discovery mechanism. Node one initiates the discovery and specifies the maximum forwarding distance to equal to two. In this example scenario, node 20 holds the master copy and thus, it sends a reply message to the requester as indicated by the dashed arrows. The reply is forwarded up the tree towards the node one. The forwarding nodes, in the other branches of the tree, keep the forwarded request in their buffers, until the timeout period elapses.

Integrating the master copy discovery mechanism into the write operation could be an option, but it would make the write operation more complex. The discovery mechanism fits naturally to the scope of the read operation. Providing the discovery as a separate kind of request allows flexible creating of different types of read and write operations according to the needs of the application.

3.5 Master copy migration

As already mentioned, a shared data item does not have an a priori fixed owner of the master copy and the node that performs the first write operation on the data item, creates the master copy. However, it may also happen that the first node that

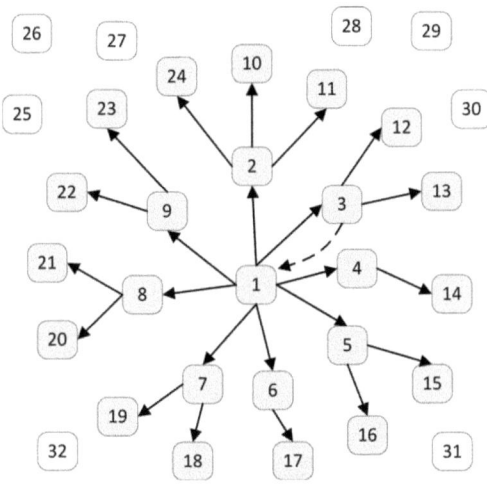

Figure 3.6: Master copy migration–updating the replicas

writes the data item does it only once and the further write operations are issued by other nodes. If a sequence of the write requests is sourced from a single node, it may be reasonable to allow transferring the master copy of the shared data item to that node, to save the costs of sending the write requests to the owner. This solution also significantly improves the flexibility of the system.

The master copy migration mechanism is parameterized by the number of consecutive write requests from a single node that shall trigger the migration and is realized as an extension to the update request processing. Figure 3.6 shows a write request issued from node number three represented by the dashed arrow. It is followed by the propagation of the update request in the replication area in the example network. The update request is triggered by the write request and thus, the address of node number three, which initiated the write request, is contained in the request message, as the actual source of the request. If the migration of the master copy shall occur, its current owner (node one) indicates in the update request message that it asks the replica holders to update the location of the master copy of the data item together with its value. Thus, from now on, these nodes regard the node number three as the owner of the master copy of the data item and all write requests are now sent to that node. The new owner of the master copy is also responsible for issuing the replica update requests after each write operation. And since the defined replication range for the data item does not change, after the migration of the master copy, the replication area may differ from the previous one, as depicted in Figure 3.7, where the nodes represented by black shapes join the replication area and the ones represented by gray checked shapes are

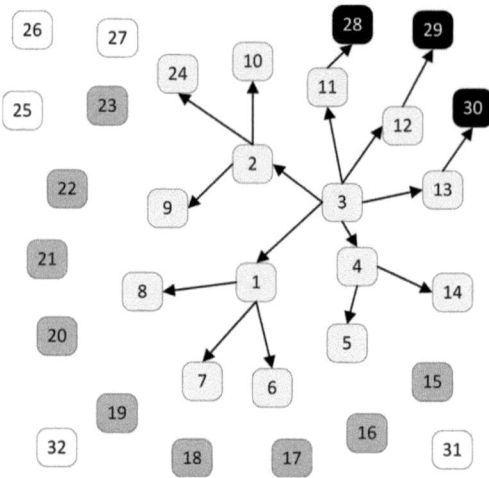

Figure 3.7: Master copy migration–the new replication area

excluded from it.

The above example shows that having a relatively small replication area in a large network with frequent master copy migrations can cause the replication area to involve different nodes every time the master copy migrates. To avoid this, the replication range shall be chosen adequately for the size of the network or even cover the complete network, if it is small. Additionally, to avoid a Ping-Pong effect, the value of the parameter that controls the number of consecutive write operations from a single node that trigger the migration shall not be too small. The optimal value for the parameter is application and deployment specific.

3.6 Instance filtering

A write operation on a shared data item can occur very frequently. Since the application is interested in important information only, frequent updates of unchanged data items, e.g., measurements are an unnecessary burden for the whole system. So reducing the number of write operations can be done without loosing information. The instance filtering mechanisms can be applied on the node that owns the master copy to virtually reduce the amount of write accesses and, as a result, to reduce the required nonvolatile storage for the historical data and the costs of updating the replicas of the data item on the remote nodes, by filtering out data that is redundant or of lower relevance. These two cost factors, i.e., storing the historical values and updating the replicas can be controlled independent from each other and individually for each shared data item.

Thus, the instance filtering allows reducing the resource consumption by reducing the processing to the most relevant data only. It can be seen as a reduction of the storage reliability, since it excludes some information from being replicated and stored in a permanent storage. However, it helps to dramatically reduce the resource consumption, especially for the sending of replica update requests. Additionally, the most recently written value is still available in the master copy.

There are two dimensions used to filter the instances of a data item, i.e., they can be filtered in the temporal, as well as in the value domain. The temporal dispersion allows creating a sequence of instances with a maximum frequency of occurrence. It is realized by specifying a *minimum delta time* (MDT) parameter. The *minimum store delta time* (MSDT) and *minimum update delta time* (MUDT) parameters allow specifying the minimum time difference between two consecutive accesses to the historical storage to store an instance of the item and between two consecutive propagations of the requests to update the replicas of the data item, respectively. If the filter is enabled, the respective operation is allowed only if the following condition is fulfilled:

$$CT \geq LT + MDT \qquad (3.4)$$

Where:
CT–is the timestamp of the current instance to check,
LT–is the timestamp of the instance for which the last operation was performed,
MDT–is the minimum delta time defined for the data item

Filtering the instances only by specifying the minimum time difference between two stored or replicated instances may cause that the storage on the master copy owner node and the replicas on the other nodes miss some important and critical data from the value perspective. In order to cope with that issue the second filter that takes the changes of the value between consecutive instances into account can be applied.

Defining a *minimum delta value* (MDV) parameter allows specifying a boundary within which the values of the newly written data do not trigger the operation, i.e., that can be seen as a hysteresis for the input values. The *minimum store delta value* (MSDV) and *minimum update delta value* (MUDV) parameters specify the minimum difference required between the values of two consecutive instances to be stored in the historical storage and to issue a request to update the replicas, respectively.

The filtering of the instances regarding the value difference may be realized in two ways, i.e., the minimum difference may be defined either as an absolute value or it may be defined by a per mille ratio. Enabling the value based instance filtering with per mille difference check causes the respective operation to be allowed if the following condition is fulfilled:

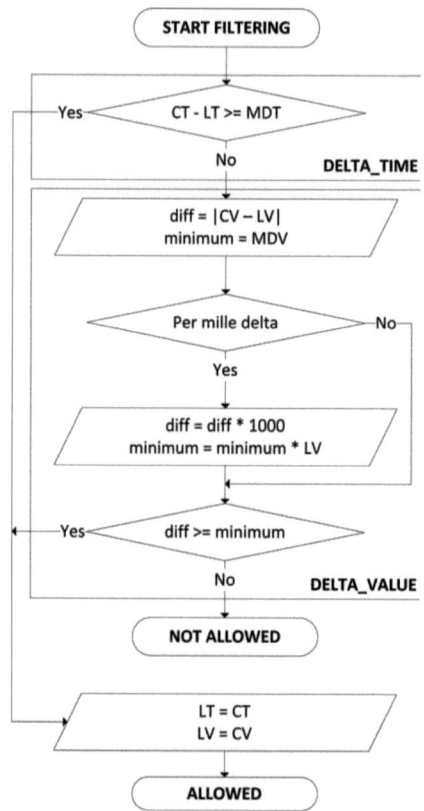

Figure 3.8: The algorithm of filtering the instances to reduce the frequency of storing and update requests

$$\left|\frac{CV}{LV} - 1\right| * 1000 \geq MDV \tag{3.5}$$

In contrast, enabling the absolute value difference check causes the condition to be as follows:

$$|CV - LV| \geq MDV \tag{3.6}$$

Where:
CV–is the value of the current instance to check,
LV–is the value of the instance for which the last operation was performed,
MDV–is the minimum delta value defined for the data item

Again, applying only the value based instance filtering may cause that no operations on the data are performed for a long time due to small value changes. In order to achieve value based filtering with a specified frequency of operation executions, these two proposed filtering approaches may be combined. If both, value and time difference filters are enabled, then the operation is performed if it is allowed by any of the filters. The combined filtering algorithm is presented in Figure 3.8.

The instance filtering mechanism is especially interesting for periodically written data items, e.g., those storing measurement results. Additionally, it is reasonable to define the sequence of instances that are stored by the master copy owner in its historical storage to be a superset of the sequence of instances to be replicated, or at least to have these two sequences equal. In such a setting the master copy holder has more detailed information on the data item available locally.

3.7 The access transparency

An important aspect of the DSM system is that its services shall be transparent to the applications that are using it. An application issues read and write requests and the way these requests are identified in the application source code depends on the level of access transparency provided by the DSM system. The application engineer can either apply the accesses to the shared data in a specific way or use automatic tools that support the application development in the pre-compilation phase. This section analyses the required pre-compilation steps needed to be applied, depending on the support provided by the operating system.

Any read or write operation involving a shared data item that is not exclusively available locally implies waiting for the result. And since the actual realization of the data access can differ for different hardware and software platforms, the issue becomes important for heterogeneity support.

Suppose the following operation in the application code:

$$a = b \qquad (3.7)$$

Where both, a and b are shared data items. This operation can be expressed as the following function calls, with the naive assumption that an operation is always successful and returns immediately with the result.

$$write(a, read(b)) \qquad (3.8)$$

A simplified and idealized flow of the operation is shown in Figure 3.9. Depending on the capabilities of the operating system there are three main possibilities for the DSM system to handle it:

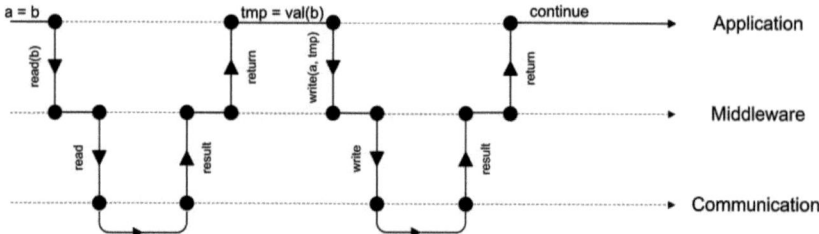

Figure 3.9: An idealized flow of a distributed operation

- *block*–the thread is blocked by a wait-loop, until the result can be delivered.

- *freeze*–the current context is frozen until the result is available and, if there are other tasks in the scheduler list, the CPU control is given to these, otherwise the CPU is idle or can be put into sleep mode.

- *split-phase*–the operation is broken into requests and result handler routines, i.e., the flow is not kept inside one function or instruction block.

The TinyOS operating system is generally based on the split-phase manner, but providing a blocking functionality as an artificial construct is possible in this WSN operating system. Similar applies to the IHPOS system. In Contiki and Reflex it is possible to freeze the current context and yield the control to one of the other scheduled threads. Since the network communication is always a split-phase process, freezing and blocking can actually only represent more or less efficient ways to adapt the data accesses to a non-split-phase manner.

Both, freezing and blocking fit best the non-distributed way of thinking while programming, i.e., accessing a variable results either in its value or a change of its value, right now and right here–without significant delays. In case of distributed operations, delays have to be considered, but both freezing and blocking cause the control related to the current thread to stay at the point where the request was issued and proceed further from that point as soon as the result is available. The difference between these two handling solutions is the way the control is kept at the request issuing point, i.e., the continue condition *the result is available* is either checked in the wait-loop inside the DSM system or in the scheduler of the operating system, because the thread related to the access operation yielded the control. The blocking is easy to implement, but usually implies energy wasting. On the other hand, the freezing is more energy efficient, but requires support from the operating system, causing the operating system to be more complex.

For both freezing and blocking the abstraction of the access to a variable is as simple as a function call. This does not require significant changes to the program flow, i.e.,

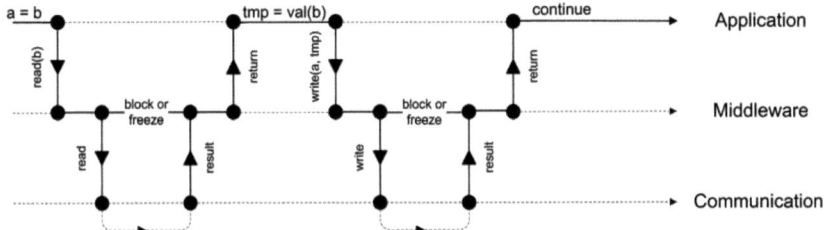

Figure 3.10: The blocking flow of a distributed operation

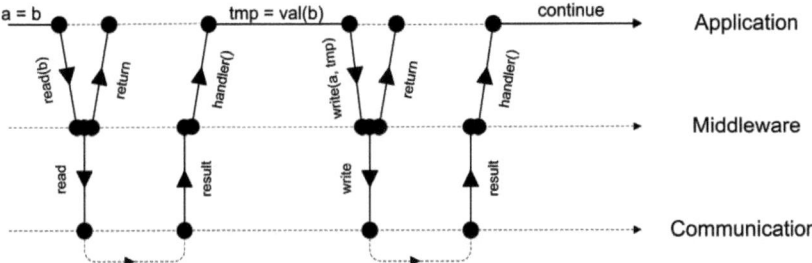

Figure 3.11: The split-phase flow of a distributed operation

the read and write operations are transparently exchanged by appropriate function calls. This simplifies the task of the supporting tools, since the flow in that case (see Figure 3.10) does not differ much from the idealized one presented in Figure 3.9.

In contrast, the split-phase is a more natural way to handle a distributed operation, i.e., the request is issued, the control is given away and the incoming result triggers a handler routine that takes care of the correct interpretation of the result. Such a request-response manner is also similar to the way hardware works, making it suitable for embedded systems, where any kind of no-operation loop implies waste of energy. Keeping the operation abstraction to be as simple as a function call, is not that easy anymore. The split-phase flow is presented in Figure 3.11. The disadvantage here is that the DSM system needs to store the context information by itself to be able to link the result with the request and to continue the application code starting from the right point.

The different ways of handling a distributed operation influence the changes in the original source code needed to keep the original flow of the application. The following paragraphs discuss the required modifications of the original code and show pseudo code snippets for the above mentioned handling options. Taking an example operation, which reads a value from one shared data item and stores it in a second one, and extending it by operations that precede and follow it, results in the following pseudo code snippet that represents the original operation with its context used for the further analysis.

```
(...)
preceding operations;
a = b;
following operations;
(...)
```

The handling of distributed operation that involves blocking or freezing in the access functions results in the following code snippet.

```
(...)
preceding operations;
write(a, read(b));
following operations;
(...)
```

What is important, this code modification is independent of the location in the original application source code. Thus, the DSM layer may be realized really transparent to the application and does not require dramatic changes in the program flow.

For the split-phase approach the original code results in the following representation.

```
start(){
  (...)
  preceding operations;
  read(b);
}

//handler for the read() function
readHandler(valB){
  write(a, valB);
}

//handler for the write() function
writeHandler(){
  following operations;
  (...)
}
```

This shows that the mapping of operations is not easy anymore, and the task of pre-compilation may become tricky, especially for applications with many accesses to the shared data items. Additionally, if multiple threads are allowed, the task of binding handler calls with requests requires storing the context from which the request was called to continue with the right operations.

There are two solutions to the problem of flow control in case of the split-phase operation handling; either to decompose the application in the pre-compilation phase to a state machine, or to require the application engineer to think in the split-phase way and provide a split-phase interface between application and the DSM system. The following section describes the latter option.

3.8 The operating system adaptation layer

If the tool support for the automatic data access identification and pre-compilation is too expensive or too complicated, then there still exists the option to require the application engineer to use a provided application programming interface (API). This solution sacrifices the transparency to some extent, but simplifies the required tool chain and actually gives more control to the application engineer. And as long as the functionality behind this API is consistent for diverse platforms, the heterogeneity can still be supported, i.e., the DSM system can be applied in systems composed of diverse nodes.

Since different operating systems usually provide different application programming frameworks, a single application level API for the DSM system cannot be applied for all of them. Thus, in order to simplify the support for application development on each platform, it is necessary to decompose the DSM system into two parts–the interfacing part and the logic part. The DSM logic is shared between platforms and provides a single interface. It is encapsulated in the DSM interfacing part. The interface provided by the DSM logic core can also be used by the automatic tool chain to support the application development.

In order to allow the use of the DSM logic on different operating systems or platforms there is a need to provide an individual interfacing part for each of the supported operating systems or platforms, i.e., a platform specific adaptation layer has to be provided. This layer adapts the interface of the DSM system logic to the programming framework provided by each operating system, i.e., it translates the services of the DSM system to the programming convention of the operating system, so they can be used by the applications. The adaptation layer also supports the reverse direction, i.e., it translates the services of the operating system, so they can be used by the DSM system. Thus, the interfacing part provides a single API of the DSM system for a given operating system. This API can be used by all applications implemented for this operating system.

The separation of logic and interface parts helps to simplify the porting of the DSM

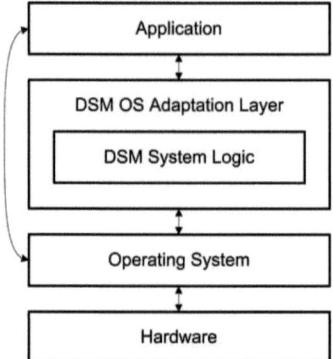

Figure 3.12: An architecture including the operating system independent DSM system

system on different platforms. Reimplementing the complete DSM system, including the core logic, for each operating system may be error prone and increases development time. Additionally, it may cause inconsistencies between the versions of the DSM logic for different platforms and as a result, disables heterogeneity. However, this solution assumes that the logic of the DSM system is implemented in a programming language, which can be included in every of the operating systems to be supported. It also requires that the core DSM logic uses only services provided by all of the supported operating systems. An architecture of a system that uses the proposed operating system adaptation layer to integrate the universal DSM logic is presented in Figure 3.12. It is worth to mention that the *Application*, as well as the *DSM OS Adaptation Layer* are both software modules developed within the programming framework provided by the given operating system.

A question that arises here, is the additional cost of the adaptation. Depending on the complexity of the adaptation layer this additional processing cost may differ, but it is usually in acceptable, or even negligible range [32].

3.9 The operation span

One of the characteristics of a WSN deployment is the size of the network. And since the sending power determines the transmission range, the size of the network, besides of its spatial dimensions, is usually specified in the number of hops (forwarding operations) needed to reach the nodes in the network. An arbitrary size of the network together with the unreliable characteristics of the links between the nodes, results in an unpredictable transmission delay. Thus, from the scalability reasons, it is crucial to specify the start and the end of a data access operation, to avoid access conflicts.

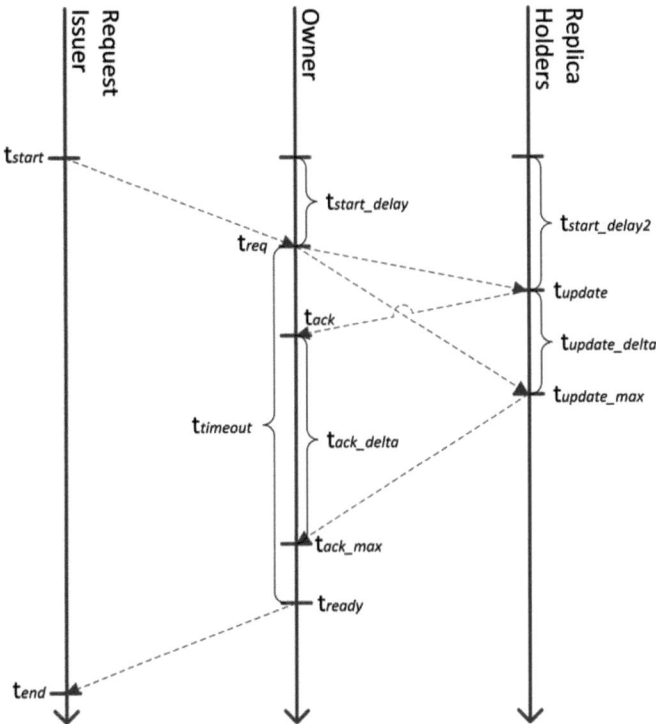

Figure 3.13: The flow of a write operation in a system with replicas

Figure 3.13 presents the flow of an example write operation in a DSM system with replicas. The diagram takes the delays into account and presents the different points in time that can indicate the progress and state of the operation. The operation is initiated at t_{start}, the owner of the master copy (or short, the owner) of the data item receives the request at t_{req} and starts the replica update mechanism. Due to different delays on the path the replica holders receive the update request at different points in time, i.e., between t_{update} and t_{update_max}. The replica holders reply with acknowledgments that again arrive at the owner of the data item at different points in time, i.e., between t_{ack} and t_{ack_max}. In the presented diagram the owner of the master copy uses a request timeout ($t_{timeout}$) to specify the time it waits for the acknowledgment messages. After this time period elapses at t_{ready}, the owner replies to the issuer node with the result of the complete operation. This reply arrives at the issuer at t_{end}.

The fundamental kind of conflict is the write-write conflict. In this case the set of conflicting operations can be extended to include all those that modify the state of the data, e.g., the migration of the master copy of the data item. These operations,

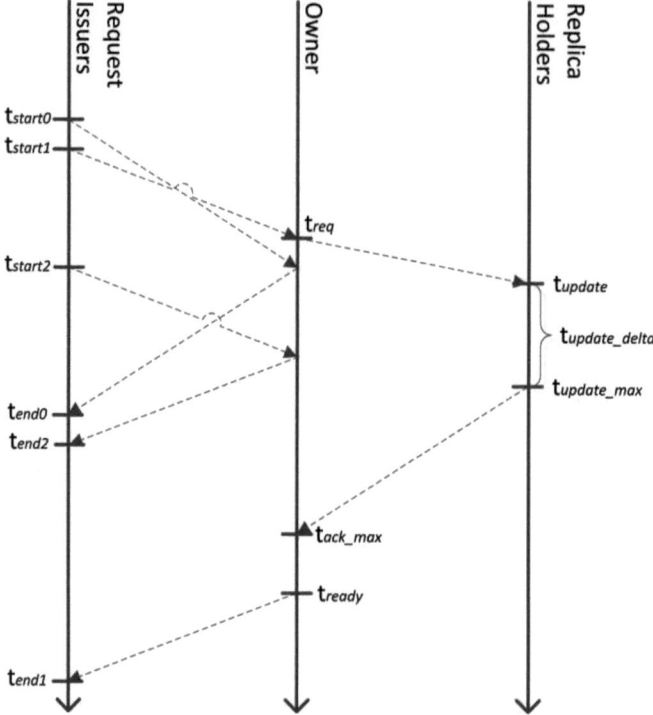

Figure 3.14: Write-write access conflict example flow

if applied in parallel may cause serialization issues and result in inconsistencies in the global view on the data item. An example of such a conflict is a write operation issued from multiple distant nodes at about the same time (see Figure 3.14). These requests are delivered with some delay since they may require different amount of hops to reach the owner. In the example diagram presented in Figure 3.14, the request that arrives at the owner as the first one, is executed and the other two issuers receive replies that their requests failed. This already indicates the first problem in the case of write-write conflicts, i.e., it is necessary to specify what to do with write requests that are received by the owner of the data while another write operation is executed. In general there are three options; the received requests can be either regarded as failed, they may be executed in parallel or they may be queued for execution after the current access request is processed.

This is also related to the request ordering problem. In an ideal shared memory system the data access operations shall be ordered and executed in the order they were issued, thus based on the t_{start} of each request. However, this solution requires global time synchronization and sending the t_{start} in each request. Additionally, in the WSN environment with its unpredictable delays this requirement to order the requests regarding their initialization time induces another issue, i.e., handling of request issued before the requests that were already executed. Here, in the ideal case the requests that were already executed shall be invalidated, the older request shall be executed and followed by the execution of all the invalidated requests. Such a solution is very expensive and rather not affordable in the WSN environment. Another solution is to execute the missed request and inform all the replica holders about that missing value, but this requires these to store an access history to check which read accesses have to be invalidated, making this solution even more expensive than the previous one. A more optimal option is to regard this outdated request as failed, and thus, to request the issuer to retry the operation.

Usually, none of the issuing nodes is aware of the fact that another node issued a request as well. Global synchronization of requests on the issuer level, e.g., by informing all other nodes about the intention, would require a huge communication overhead and the scalability would suffer.

Thus, it is reasonable to define the start of a write as the point in time where the access request arrives at the owner of the master copy (t_{req}). In such a setting, requests under delivery are not regarded as started yet.

In a DSM system with replicated data it is also important to cope with the write-read conflicts. As shown in Figure 3.13, the new value of the data item is available at the owner for reading not before t_{req}, so t_{start_delay} later. And since the owner is also not aware that a node issued a write request until it arrives read operations between t_{start} and t_{req} result in incorrect value if operation initialization time is regarded as operation start.

Additionally, at any replica holder the new value is not available before t_{update}, thus t_{start_delay2} after the t_{start}. This causes an additional problem, because regarding the t_{req} as the operation start also does not protect against incorrect read operations from replicas in the time between t_{req} and t_{update} (or even t_{update_max}). A currently written data item can be read after the start of a write operation, but before the actual updating of the accessed replica. This issue touches the memory consistency model features and realization problems that are further investigated in Chapter 5. But, generalizing, in order to be sure that the read value is the most recent at any time it would be necessary to use the t_{req} as the operation start and to issue the read requests direct to the owner of the data item, i.e., to abandon the use of replicas for reading. This would result in the central server memory management and all the advantages of the data replication would be lost.

From the perspective of an ideal operation span, a write operation shall be regarded as completed as soon as all the replicas are up-to-date. However, due to temporary

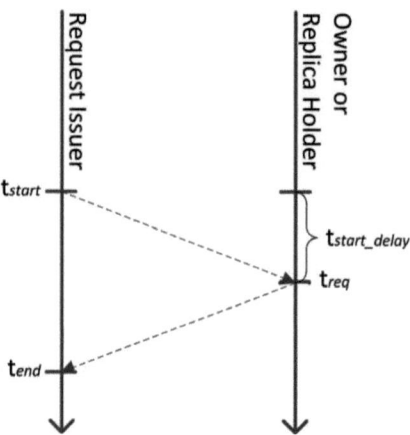

Figure 3.15: A time flow of master-read and any-read operations

node unavailability and to reduce the operation costs, the result of the operation can also be represented as the result of the replication goal achievement (see Section 3.2). The owner of the master copy of the shared data item responds to the node that issued the write request as soon as it knows if the replication goal was achieved and this point of time represents the completeness of the write operation. The write operation is also completed after it is regarded as failed, i.e., it actually does not change the state of the data.

The definition of the span in case of a read operation is much simpler, but also not trivial. The operation request is issued at t_{start} and is handled until t_{end} by the owner of the master copy (*master-read*) or any of the replica holders (*any-read*), as presented in Figure 3.15, or it is sent into the network for processing, e.g., in order to trigger voting (*quorum-read*), as shown in Figure 3.16.

For the first two types of a read operation (master-read and any-read) the request can be even handled locally if a replica (or master copy) of the data item is available locally on the requester node. In such a case the differences between t_{start} and t_{req} as well as between t_{req} and t_{end} can be neglected. In case of the quorum-read (see Figure 3.16), the requests are delivered to the replica holders at different points in time (between t_{req} and t_{req_max}) and the answers from individual replica holders arrive at the requester node between t_{ans} and t_{ans_max}. The $t_{timeout}$ is defined to specify the maximum processing time of the read operation. If an answer arrives at the request issuer after that period, it is not considered for the result.

The span of the read operation on the nodes processing the read request is also clearly defined by its function, i.e., a version of the data item is read from the replica and delivered to the requester, what completes the operation. The choice of the ver-

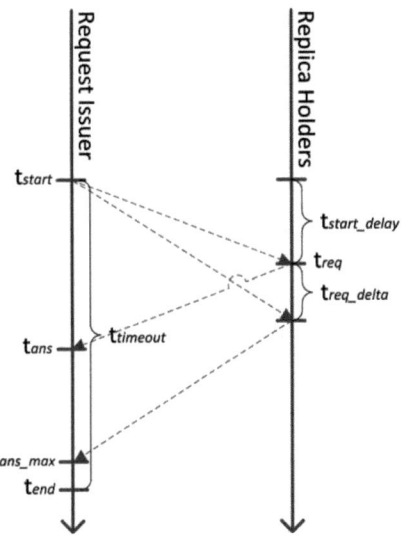

Figure 3.16: A time flow of a quorum-read operation

sion to include in the answer is defined by the way the start of the read operation is defined. Similar to the write operation, it can be either the t_{start} or t_{req}. The first option requires the read requests to be timestamped and, assumes the availability of mechanisms for time synchronization, as well as the historical values of the data item. The processing nodes answer with the correct value of the data item, according to the request initialization time. Regarding the t_{req} as the start of the read operation simplifies the system, i.e., the replica holders store only the most recent value of the data item and they always use this value to answer the read requests. Additionally, the t_{start} does not need to be transmitted together with the read request.

Chapter 4

The tinyDSM Middleware

This chapter introduces the tinyDSM middleware [170] that was designed within this work, to provide the *practical* framework for the proof of concept. The term practical means that the main aim of the middleware is to be useful for a number of applications in the wireless sensor network area, so it should not only be a theoretical deliberation. It should be also easy to use and efficient. Thus, this chapter starts with some discussion on the main features the middleware should provide, i.e., the way of providing the distributed shared memory abstraction and supporting the application developer, taking into consideration the specific environment it should work within–the wireless sensor network.

After discussing the set of functions the middleware provides (the shared memory abstraction; compile time event definition and runtime detection; data replication to improve the robustness; compile time definition of system behaviour using policies) and its interfaces, the details on the realization of the middleware are provided together with the methodology how to use it.

The detailed description of the middleware provided here, allows further use of the tinyDSM as a fundamental building block for the implementation of the consistency models, without explaining the way it works.

4.1 The goals

Before specifying the goals, it is necessary to think about the application environment– the wireless sensor network. As already mentioned, this environment can be classified as a loosely coupled multiprocessor system with a potentially great number of nodes, each equipped with own memory. However, in that kind of system, there are several limitations that need to be taken into account. Regarding the nodes themselves, they have rather constrained resources, i.e., their computation power and the amount of available memory are quite limited. Taking the network as a whole, the connection means between the nodes are limited as well, i.e., the transmission speed and the link reliability are quite poor. The available energy is a limited resource as well, causing a trade-off between the lifetime of the desired system and the allowed power to be consumed by the nodes. All these constraints combined with the fact that the network is not always static, since nodes may disappear or new nodes may appear, cause the programming of wireless sensor network applications to be a very interesting, but challenging, task.

Wireless sensor networks are considered to be the key enabling technology for a large variety of innovative applications. But still, the majority of applications is using the wireless sensor networks in a passive way, i.e., the sensor network is used to measure and store data that is then requested by an external application, which sends queries into the WSN, whenever it needs the data. This type of data storage and query technique is quite well researched. Prominent concepts are tinyDB [147], cougar [212], tinyPEDS [88]. There are several other middleware approaches that are the result of research in the distributed computation and data storage domain [146], [56], [2] and [91], just to mention a few. The tinyDSM approach differs from those by being the first one that aims at providing really DSM like data storage.

But in order to use the potential of a wireless sensor network it is necessary to exploit its power that is the ability of cooperative problem solving due to the high parallelism. However, the main advantage of parallel computing in sensor networks is not the increase of the total computation power. Even if it may be of some importance for specific solutions, it is rather more interesting to go in the direction of distributed thinking or reasoning based on global or distributed knowledge. In such applications it is important to have the possibility to use some shared memory abstraction.

There is also a class of applications that require the sensor nodes in the network to become active in a certain situation. Health care and homeland security applications are the prominent examples where the sensing extended by detection provides the most advantages. Detection of some predefined situation can change the behaviour of the network or part of it, e.g., causing changing the sampling rate or sending the latest measurements to a predefined sink. Such applications will profit from the ability to be automatically notified about specific changes in the data storage.

The tinyDSM middleware was designed to support both these classes of applications. The goal was to provide a distributed shared memory abstraction with configurable replication and consistency parameters as a basic data storage concept on top of which an event detection mechanism is realized as well. The benefit of this solution is that a certain part of the network can change its behaviour simultaneously due to the common knowledge on the changes in the shared measured parameters or state data. Thus, events can be defined on a more abstract level. And doing this using an event definition language is much easier and faster compared to hardcoding certain behaviour into sensor node applications and wiring it to deployed protocols.

Another goal was to make the application development easier but without taking the complete control from the application engineer. She needs to know what happens in the system, at least to a certain extent. It is currently a trend to provide tools that allow anyone to automatically generate application code based only on some simplified description. However, in the area of sensor networks this is not optimal and having at least basic knowledge is absolutely necessary to be able to estimate the results of own requirements. Anyway, a middleware that provides a clear interface and is built using a pre-defined set of functional blocks that are composed together and configured according to the requirements can greatly reduce the application development time, simplify the testing and can also provide reusability of code and configuration.

Additionally, in order to support the heterogeneity of possible deployments, the tinyDSM middleware is designed to be hardware and software platform independent. This goal was achieved by a pure C programming language implementation of the main logic blocks and a set of adapters that allow using the middleware in different hardware and software configurations.

This solution has the advantage that it can be applied in any environment where the C module can be compiled together with the application code or used as an external library. The most of the operating systems used in the wireless sensor network area, like tinyOS [137], Contiki [74] and Reflex [206] are C++ or C-based, but it is also possible to use tinyDSM in Java for the Sun SPOT nodes [105], using the Java Native Interface (JNI).

4.2 The architecture and services

This section discusses the architecture of a system that uses the tinyDSM middleware and the services the middleware provides. These services include those provided in the on-line phase, as well as those provided at the compilation time.

Figure 4.1 presents the placement of the tinyDSM middleware in an application for a given platform. As already mentioned, the core of the tinyDSM middleware is implemented in C programming language and is compiled together with the application logic. It uses the services provided by the target platform, but different target systems provide services like timers; interrupt handling and communication means, differently. Thus, it is necessary to provide an adapter–the OS adaptation layer that adapts these services to the needs of the tinyDSM middleware core (see Section 3.8). This layer needs to be provided once for each new platform and can be reused for all tinyDSM applications for that platform. Additionally, if the services of the operating system are provided in a hardware independent way, then the adaptation layer can be used on

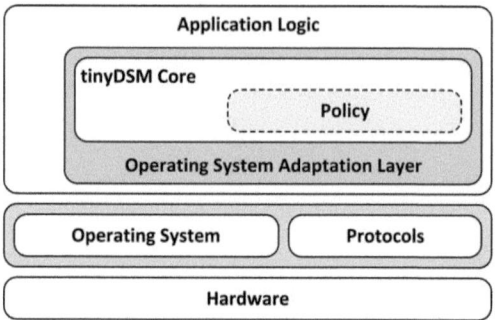

Figure 4.1: The architecture of a system based on the tinyDSM middleware

every hardware platform supported by that operating system. The adaptation layer enables the tinyDSM middleware to be used in heterogeneous systems and the main logic of the middleware can stay unchanged.

Since the adaptation layer encapsulates the tinyDSM middleware, it specifies the interface actually provided to the application logic. Depending on the programming convention required by the operating system, the original interfaces of the middleware can be almost freely adapted, so they can be used by the application logic on any hardware and software platform.

The tasks of the modules presented in Figure 4.1 are as follows:

- **Application Logic** controls the behaviour of the nodes that build up the global application; it defines the sources of data and behaviour in case of event detections. It can read and write the shared data from the middleware.

- **OS Adaptation Layer** maps the services of the platform (or operating system) to the functionality needed by the middleware and also specifies the final tinyDSM interface available to the application logic.

- **tinyDSM Core** represents the logic of the tinyDSM middleware.

- **Policy** is a virtual component that is actually compiled into the tinyDSM Core and determines the instantiation of the tinyDSM during the implementation phase and configures its behaviour.

- **Operating System, Protocols** and **Hardware** constitute the target system where the application is deployed. The specific combination of these can be also referred to as the platform. The hardware influences the physical features that can be provided. The operating system defines the programming language and convention. And the protocols are a library of available modules for the given operating system and hardware.

Figure 4.2: The internal architecture of the tinyDSM Core

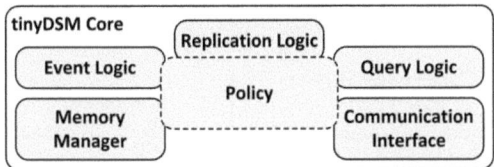

Figure 4.3: The logical division of the tinyDSM Core

Internally, the tinyDSM core is built as presented in Figure 4.2. It consists of the fixed, application independent core logic and the application specific logic, generated for a given application and configured by the policy settings. The logical division of the tinyDSM core is presented in Figure 4.3.

The tasks of the modules presented in Figure 4.3 are as follows:

- **Event Logic** is responsible for detecting the events and notifying the application.

- **Replication Logic** takes the decision on the replication of data, storage of new data and controls the data locating.

- **Query Logic** is responsible for interpreting incoming messages (queries or requests) and building results into answer messages. It may also allow the use of complex database-like queries issued by the user.

- **Memory Manager** controls the physical data storage structures on the node.

- **Communication Interface** handles the communication with other nodes. It may also include security functionality like encryption or integrity tests of the data.

The main diversification of the services, the tinyDSM middleware provides, is regarding the phase of application life. The middleware supports the application development in the off-line phase and provides the on-line functionality to the application during run-time. The following paragraphs describe the middleware interface delivered to the running application and then the services of the off-line phase to show how they help the realization of the former ones.

Figure 4.4 shows the interfaces the middleware provides during the run-time. There is a differentiation between the part of the application that resides locally on the nodes

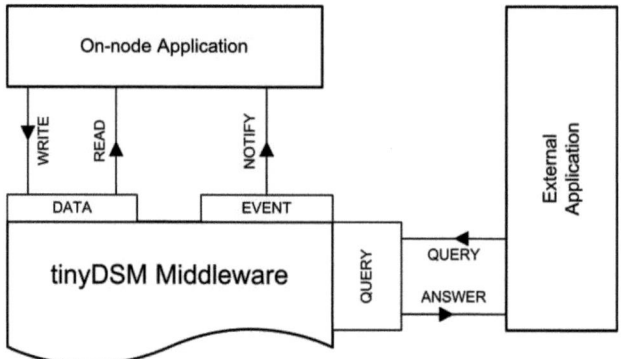

Figure 4.4: The tinyDSM interfaces

and the external application, represented, e.g., by the end-user devices. The part of the application that resides on the nodes uses the *DATA* and the *EVENT* interfaces. The *DATA* interface provides access to the shared data, allowing reading and writing. Using the *EVENT* interface the application is notified about the occurrences of the pre-defined events. These events definitions are based on the values of the shared data items.

For the external application, the tinyDSM provides the *QUERY* interface. Currently, it only supports read and write operations similar to those provided by the *DATA* interface, but it can be extended to answer more complicated queries than those supported by the *DATA* interface, e.g., SQL like ones.

Thus, from the application perspective the middleware provides the following services in the on-line phase:

- WRITING the shared data,

- READING the shared data,

- NOTIFICATION in case a defined state of the data is reached,

- Answering external QUERIES based on the content of the memory.

In order to provide the desired services to the application the tinyDSM middleware needs to be configured properly in the off-line phase. Since there is no single solution that fits all requirements of all possible applications, there is a need to adjust the middleware. In the off-line phase the application engineer is able to parameterize the middleware to the application needs. This is realized using a specified set of keywords that are inserted in the application code to define the set of shared data items and to specify the desired behaviour of the distributed shared memory middleware

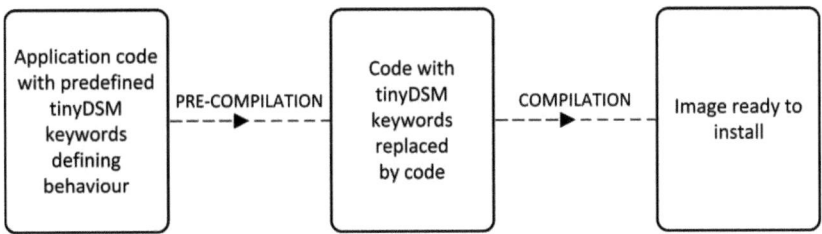

Figure 4.5: The two-step compilation approach

while handling these variables. A pre-compiler tool translates these keywords producing middleware source code that is ready for compilation, after which the application containing the middleware is ready for installing on nodes (see Figure 4.5).

4.3 The distributed shared memory abstraction

The basic concept behind the tinyDSM middleware is to provide means that allow sensor nodes to share their data in an application defined way following the concept of distributed shared memory as close as possible.

In order to define the shared memory space the application developer specifies a set of shared data items that are foreseen to be used by the application and are to be managed by the tinyDSM. Each data item in this set has a specified type and the desired way it shall be handled, defined using the policy parameters. These definitions are common for the network covered by the application and the identities of these data items, as well as the handling they require, are known to all the nodes in this network. Again, these shared data items are also referred to as *shared variables*, or simply *variables*.

A shared variable can be defined either as a *global variable* or as an *array variable*, where the latter is the default setting. In case of a global variable there exists only one single entity of this variable in the network and one of the nodes manages it. In contrast, in case of an array variable, there exist as many entities as many nodes are in the network, i.e., each node manages its own entity of that variable. The entities of a variable are logically independent shared data items, they store different values and are handled separately, e.g., replicated independent from each other, but according to the same rules defined for the variable. These two different ways to define a shared variable allow generating either a single shared data item for the whole network, or an array of shared data items, one for each node, independent of the size of the network. The latter is similar to the definition of a vector proposed in [94].

To help understanding the concept of array and global variables an example of each will be given. An array variable *temperature* can be used to store the temperature measurements taken by each node. Each entity of the variable is independent and there are as many of them as many nodes are in the network. Every node writes its measurements into its own entity. On the other hand, a global variable *period* can control the period between each measurement. There is only one entity of the variable in the network, relevant for all the nodes.

As mentioned above, each entity of a shared variable has its *manager* also referred to as the *owner*. The owner is the only node that is allowed to directly write this entity of the variable, i.e., it owns the master copy of the entity. When the owner writes to the entity, the written value is further handled in the middleware as the *instance* of the entity of the variable, or simply, the instance of the variable. An instance is represented by a tuple consisting of address and data fields (see Figure 4.6). Each instance is unique and the content of the tuple allows distinguishing between any two instances. The *VariableID* specifies the variable, and thus, the data type and the required handling. The identity of the node *(NodeID)* specifies the manager of the entity, i.e., the address of the node holding the master copy. The *Timestamp* (or version number) allows distinguishing any two instances of the same entity. These addressing fields are completed by the *Value*.

Thus, the shared memory space consists of a set of instances of the defined variables. It can be seen as a tuple space, but it can be also seen as a distributed database with a single table, whose records are defined by the structure of the above mentioned tuple. An instance can be added to the shared memory space, but it cannot be explicitly removed or changed. It can be discarded due to its expiration or it can be lost if the node that stores it disappears.

Multiple instances of an entity can be present in the shared memory space, e.g., if the configuration of the variable enables history. These instances are chronologically ordered by the timestamp (or version number) and create a log of value changes in the entity of the variable. If no historical storage is defined for that variable, then the previous instance expires as soon as a new one is created.

In order to address the data items in the shared memory space the identity of the variable is used as the primary part of the address. It reduces the set of instances to those containing the values of the chosen variable. For an array variable it needs to be extended by the identity of the owner to point out the entity of interest. For a global variable the middleware will automatically locate the current owner of the single entity. If the current configuration for the variable allows storing historical data and

| VariableID | NodeID | Timestamp | Value |

Figure 4.6: The structure of an instance of a variable

	Variable	Entity	Instance	
	VariableID	NodeID	Timestamp	Value
	0	1	1	1
	0	1	2	2
	0	2	1	3
	0	2	2	4
	1	1	1	5
	1	1	2	6
	1	2	1	7
	1	2	2	8
	2	1	1	9
	2	1	2	10
	2	2	1	11
	2	2	2	12

Two instances of one entity (rows 1-2). Four instances of two entities of one variable (rows 1-4).

Figure 4.7: Addressing of the data in the tinyDSM middleware

the desired item is not the most recent one, then the timestamp or version number can be specified as well, to choose a specific instance (see Figure 4.7).

In order to ease the access to the data in the shared memory space and to increase the robustness of the storage, the instances of the entities can be replicated on nodes other than the owner. The policy chosen for the variable controls the way the replica holders are chosen from the nodes in the vicinity of the owner. The nodes can be obligated to store the replica, or they can for instance decide on a random basis if they want to store it. The decision is taken per entity and is obligatory. If the policy for a variable enables replication, then an owner broadcasts the newly created instances of entities of the variable after the write operations. The nodes in the vicinity can use these updates to refresh their replicas of the entity.

The replication can be adjusted regarding several aspects. If it is enabled in the policy, the replication can be configured regarding range (spatial limitation), saturation and frequency (see Section 3.2 and Section 3.6). The replication in tinyDSM is based on updates, since due to the small sizes of the shared data items, updating is of advantage compared to invalidation. The concept of nodes in the vicinity is similar to those presented by Hood [210] and Abstract Regions [207]–in tinyDSM it is based on the communication means, i.e., n-hop broadcast. The replication of the data allows any of the replica holders to perform a read operation on the replica. This reduces the delay of the read operation and decreases the communication costs in applications where the number of read operations is larger than the number of write operations. Additionally,

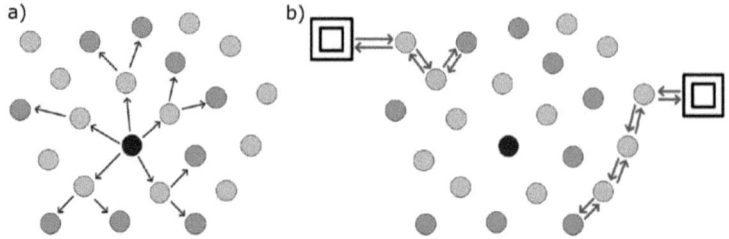

Figure 4.8: Replication of data in the tinyDSM middleware

such a node is able to answer queries for which it has the appropriate data stored, without the need of forwarding the query to the owner node. It is also of advantage, if the changes of the value of an entity that belongs to one node influence the behaviour of the nodes in its vicinity. An additional important feature of data replication is that it assures the information to be available even if some nodes are exhausted or in sleep mode. Figure 4.8 shows the idea of spatially limited replication (a) and its advantage in case of a remote read operation (b).

The middleware is designed to provide controlled replication of the data that is stored in it in order to increase the reliability and availability of the data. The primary concept was to allow specifying an area of replication that surrounds the owner of the data and within this area it has to be possible to distribute the copies of the instances of the variables in a random way, to achieve an equal distribution of these.

As already mentioned, the owner is the only node able to directly write its entity of a variable. Any other node willing to write this entity needs to send a write request to the owner, who performs then a local write operation and sends an acknowledgment to the requesting node. This solution has been chosen because of the spatial focus of the replication, i.e., the write request may come from any node in the network, even a very distant one, but since the replication area is the vicinity of the owner, this is the best node to initiate the update of the replicas. But an even more important reason is to keep the right order of the write operations needed for the consistency model research. This choice may cause the owner to become a bottleneck, but the complexity of the system would suffer from extending the write operation to allow all the copies to be writeable.

The tinyDSM supports the multiple readers and single writer (MRSW) access pattern. But the write operation limitation is mitigated by the possibility given to all the nodes to issue a write request to the node able to write the given entity. For global variables this limitation can be soften by enabling the migration of ownership, e.g., to cope with dying nodes, or by distributed ownership to distribute the tasks of the owner over some redundant group of nodes (especially interesting in dense networks) or combination of both. These options are especially interesting for global variables, since the ownership binding for entities of array variables is fixed by definition.

The event mechanism available in the tinyDSM middleware allows monitoring the values in the variables. It is based on compile time definitions, to reduce the complexity of the evaluation logic. An event is defined as a logic equation with the shared variables in its terms. Such an event equation is evaluated each time a variable, present in it, changes its value. The result of this evaluation is stored in a special *event variable*, associated to each event. These variables are shared as well, but they are read-only for the application and their type is fixed to Boolean. Except of that, they are like standard shared variables. An event variable can be used in terms of other event definitions, but not in the one it is associated to. Depending on the definition of the event, the application is notified either about every evaluation, about the change of the evaluation result or is not notified at all. The last option can be used to support sub-events, used in equations of other events.

Following the concept of event variables that store the result of the evaluation of a defined expression, the basic functionality of shared variables is extended as well. It is possible to define a variable that automatically derives its value from an expression with other variables as terms. In this case it is also forbidden to create mutually dependent variables, i.e., two variables cannot derive their values from each other. The expression is re-evaluated every time any of its terms changes its value.

The definitions of shared variables and events are provided by the application engineer in a configuration file and are used by the tinyDSM pre-compiler to adapt the middleware to the needs of the application. The desired handling of the instances of a given variable in the system is specified using the chosen policy parameters. The policy parameters can be set one-by-one or as pre-defined policy sets, provided in a policy file, that can be used to simplify the definition and increase its readability. The currently supported policy parameters are presented in Section 4.4. The syntax of the definitions of a shared variable and an event are as follows:

distributed [**global**] [policy parameters] type **name**[=value or {expression, trigger}];

event [**global**] [policy parameters] **name** = {expression, trigger};

Array is the default setting for the kind of a variable and if a variable shall be defined as a global one, it has to be explicitly stated in the definition by using the **global** keyword. Actually, this is one of the policy parameters, since it controls the handling of the instances of the variable, but due to its importance and for the sake of clarity it is provided separately in the above definitions.

The specification of the policy parameters is a space separated list. Depending on the kind of the parameter, it is either an appearance of the parameter name in case of switching parameters or the name followed by the values that quantify the parameter. A parameter set can be defined as a macro with a defined number of values.

After specifying the policy parameters, it is necessary to specify the name of the variable or event. In case of a variable it is also necessary to specify its type, which can be any standard C programming language type.

In contrast to an event the entities of a variable can be initialized during the definition. If no initial value is given all the entities of the variable are marked as unset, what is the default case for the entities of an event variable. Such an unset entity cannot be read and remains in this state until it is written for the first time, either by the application or as a result of the evaluation of the associated expression.

```
enum triggers {
  FTR_NC   = 0x0,  // event() not called—default
  FTR_OC   = 0x1,  // event() called on change
  FTR_ET   = 0x2,  // event() called everytime
  FTR_MASK = 0x3,  // event() Function TRigger mask
  STR_OC   = 0x0,  // value set on change—default
  STR_ET   = 0x4,  // value set everytime
  STR_MASK = 0x4   // value Set TRigger mask
};
```

Listing 4.1: The constants defined for the trigger parameter

The *trigger* parameter specifies the condition, the result of the evaluation of the associated expression need to satisfy, to update the value of the variable and, in case of an event, to notify the application. The variable can be set after every evaluation of the expression or, per default, only if the result differs from the current value stored in the variable. Similar applies to notifying the application about the result of the evaluation, but the notification can be also switched off completely, what is the default setting if no trigger parameter is provided. The value of the trigger parameter is set using one or a combination of the defined constants (see Listing 4.1).

4.4 The policy parameters

The policy parameters are used in the definition of each variable and specify the behaviour of the tinyDSM middleware while handling the instances of the particular variable. They control, for instance, the mechanisms described in the previous chapter. The tinyDSM compiler uses the list of parameters defined for each variable to generate the data structures and a set of functions that control the behavior of the middleware. This section describes the individual policy parameters, their interdependencies and mentions the functions they influence. These functions are, in most of the cases, part of the *replication logic* module that is explained in detail in Section 4.5.4.

The syntax of a policy parameter in the definition depends on the kind of information the policy parameter takes as input. The parameter can either be used as a switch, can take one value or can take an array of values. In case of a switch parameter the occurrence of the parameter in the definition of the variable turns on a specific functionality, which is switched off by default. Parameter that needs specifying a value or an array of values as input, appears in the definition followed by the colon sign (":") and the value or the comma separated values inside curly brackets. In case of an array input, if the parameter requires more values than specified, the last one is duplicated to extend the array to the required size. If there are too many values provided, only the required number of these is taken into account.

Regarding the character of the controlled functionality, the policy parameters can be grouped in the following classes:

- Identification,
- Replication,
- Reliability,
- Optimization,
- Access rights.

The following subsections describe the parameters that are defined for the current version of the tinyDSM middleware.

4.4.1 Identification policy parameters

The policy parameters from this group define the way the instances of the variables are addressable. These parameters allow the choice between defining a variable as a global one or as an array, as well as the choice between identifying each instance of the variable using a timestamp or a version number. Thus, these parameters cover the entity identification as well as the instance identification choices. Additionally, they control the request identification.

The **global** parameter (see Table A.1) is used to indicate that the variable is a global one. If it is not enabled the variable is an array variable. The **migration** parameter (see Table A.2) enables the migration of the ownership of the entity of a global variable. The parameter specifies the number of required consecutive write operations from a single external node to the entity that trigger the migration of the ownership. If the parameter is set to zero or not defined the migration is disabled.

The **timestamp** parameter (see Table A.3) enables choosing between time-stamping and versioning the instances of the variable. This parameter defines the actual meaning of the value in the *timestamp* field of each instance of the variable. Versioning is the default option. The following two parameters are independent from the actual content of the *timestamp* field - **timestamp_size** (see Table A.4) and **timestamp_tolerance** (see Table A.5) specify the minimum required size of the *timestamp* field in bytes and the maximum allowed difference between the timestamp of the instance stored in the tinyDSM middeware and the timestamp specified by a read request to be able to answer the request with the stored instance.

The **request_number_size** parameter (see Table A.6) specifies the size of the data type required to store the request sequence number for the given variable.

4.4.2 Replication policy parameters

The parameters from this group specify the features of the replication for all the entities of the variable. They control the replication strategy mechanism and the forwarding of the update messages introduced in Section 3.2 and Section 3.1, respectively. The **replication_range** parameter (see Table B.1) specifies the maximum distance from the source node in hops within which the instances of the variable can be replicated. Thus, this parameter specifies the potential copy holders of the data. If the **replication_range** is set to zero, then the replication area is unlimited, i.e., the variable will be replicated in the whole network. Leaving it undefined disables the replication for the variable.

The **replication_density** parameter (see Table B.2) specifies the desired density of the replicas in the network depending on the distance from the owner of the master copy. The size of the input array is defined by the **replication_range** parameter. These values specify in per cent how many of the nodes at each hop shall store replicas for the variable. The first value in the array (index zero) represents the owner of the master copy and is always regarded as equal to one hundred.

The **replication_copies** parameter (see Table B.3) defines the desired number of replicas in the part of the network defined by the **replication_range** with the distribution defined by the **replication_density**. As mentioned in Section 3.2, if this parameter is set, then only the nodes that store the replicas send the acknowledgment messages. Thus, it may reduce the network traffic compared to the verification in the pure density based approach. However, it requires a priori knowledge on the amount of nodes in the network, to avoid specifying the number of copies to a value that cannot be achieved.

The **update_pattern** parameter (see Table B.4) is used to specify the replication strategy (see Section 3.2) for the entities of the variable. It takes as input three integer values that parameterize the phases of the replication. The first value specifies the maximum number of advertisement repetitions in the *ADVERTISE* phase if the replication goal is not reached. The second value specifies the number of successive update requests in the UPDATE phase that do not require any acknowledgments that are sent until the *VERIFY* phase is applied. The third number specifies the maximum number of verified update requests, if they repeatedely state that the replication goal is not reached. If any of the values is set to zero, the corresponding phase of the replication is not executed.

The **replication_history** parameter (see Table B.5) defines the number of the historical instances to be stored on the remote nodes that store the replicas of the entity of the variable, depending on the distance from the owner node. The size of the input array is defined by the **replication_range** parameter and its values are influenced by the **replication_density** input, i.e., if any of the values in the **replication_density** is set to zero, then the corresponding value in the **replication_history** array is set to zero as well. The first value in the array represents the source node itself, i.e., it defines the size of the history on the owner node.

By default, the dependent forwarding of update requests is used (see Section 3.3). The **independent_update_forward** parameter (see Table B.6) enables forwarding of the update requests even if the forwarding node does not store the data contained in the message. This allows increasing the penetration strength of the update requests and reaching nodes that are hidden to the update mechanism by the neighbors that decided not to store the replica. It allows achieving an equal distribution of the replicas in the replication range. However, this is combined with increased communication costs. If the **replication_density** array contains any zero followed by a non-zero value, then the **independent_update_forwarding** is enabled automatically. If the **replication_range** parameter is set to one, then the **independent_update_forwarding** is disabled.

4.4.3 Reliability policy parameters

Parameters from this group control the reliability of the data storage in a broad meaning of the term.

The **permanent** parameter (see Table C.1) indicates that the local copy of the most recent instance of the variable shall be stored in a non-volatile storage. This ensures that the most recently written value will be available even if the node experiences problems that caused hardware reset and the content of the RAM memory is lost. It influences the implementation of the functions to access the storage where the local copies are stored (see Section 4.5.2).

The **variable_timeout** parameter (see Table C.2) enables a different kind of reliability–the data reliability, i.e., it specifies the period the instance is valid after it is stored in the local storage. This ensures that, in case the source of the data is not on-line anymore, the out-dated data is not used and increases the quality of the data storage.

The **answer_not_local_gets** parameter (see Table C.3) allows the nodes to respond to remote read requests about entities that do not belong to them. On one hand, this increases the reliability of the system by increasing the chance to get the data, but on the other hand, it induces additional resource consumption. The default setting is that a node answers only requests about its own data.

4.4.4 Optimization policy parameters

In general, the policy parameters from this group allow enabling and controlling mechanisms to save resource consumption. These resources include memory, transmission and processing time. The parameters from this group can also influence the reliability of the system by controlling the use of these resources.

In order to reduce the chance of keeping stalled requests that will never be handled and block the resources to handle new ones, a timeout period for a request can be defined. After this time elapses the request is marked as failed due to timeout and a notification is sent to the source of the request. The timeout period can be set depending on the source of the request using the **local_request_timeout** and **external_request_timeout** parameters (see Table D.1 and Table D.2). Setting the timeout parameters to zero disables the timeout mechanism for the particular variable.

The **local_request_retries** and **external_request_retries** parameters (see Table D.3 and Table D.4) specify the maximal number of delivery retries for requests in order to reduce the chance of storing requests for which the delivery fails forever. Setting any of the parameters to zero disables the limitation of the number of delivery approaches, i.e., it will be retried until the delivery is successful.

The **fifo_processing** parameter (see Table D.5) indicates that the variable requires that the requests on its entities are processed by each node in the sequence they were delivered to that node.

The **discovery_hops** parameter (see Table D.6) specifies the maximum height of the request forwarding tree for the master copy discovery described in Section 3.4. Setting the parameter to zero disables the discovery mechanism for the variable. This is also the default setting.

The following paragraphs present the parameters that control the instance filtering mechanism as described in Section 3.6. They control the behaviour of the master copy owner. The replica holders are not affected by these settings, they only replicate the data that is sent to them.

The **min_store_delta_time** (see Table D.7) and **min_update_delta_time** (see

Table D.10) parameters allow specifying the minimum time difference between two consecutive accesses to store the instance of the variable in the history storage and between two consecutive replica update requests for the instances of the entity, respectively. Setting to zero disables the filter.

The replica update requests are issued by the owner only for instances that it stores in its local history storage, so the value specified for the **min_store_delta_time** also applies for the **min_update_delta_time**, if the value defined for the latter is smaller.

The **min_store_delta_value** (see Table D.8) and **min_update_delta_value** (see Table D.11) parameters specify the minimum allowed difference between the values of two consecutive instances to store in the history storage and to issue a replica update request, respectively. Setting the parameters to zero disables the filter.

The minimum value difference may be defined either as an absolute value or it may be defined by per mille ratio. Setting the **permille_store_delta_value** (see Table D.9) or **permille_update_delta_value** (see Table D.12) enables the per mille ratio for the respective filter. By default the minimum delta value is provided as an absolute value (see Section 3.6 for details).

Again, the filter specified for the storing of the instances in the history storage may also apply for the replica update request issuing, if the filter of the latter is stricter. However, a direct comparing of these two filters is only possible if the minimum difference for both is defined in the same way, i.e., either they are both defined as absolute or they are both defined as per mille delta.

4.4.5 Access rights policy parameters

The access rights policy parameters specify the allowed operations to be performed by the local node on its own entity of the given variable (see Table E.1) and on an entity that belongs to another node (see Table E.2).

4.5 The implementation details

This section presents the details on the implementation of the tinyDSM middleware. It starts with the interface description and goes into details of the internal data structures, logic and processes.

The source code of the tinyDSM middleware can be split into two parts; the fixed part and the application specific part. Figure 4.9 presents the content of the two directories with the source files for each part. The *tinyDSMCore* directory contains the fixed part, the *tinyDSMConf* directory contains the source files generated for the specific application. The content and functionality implemented in the most important of these files are explained in detail in the following sections.

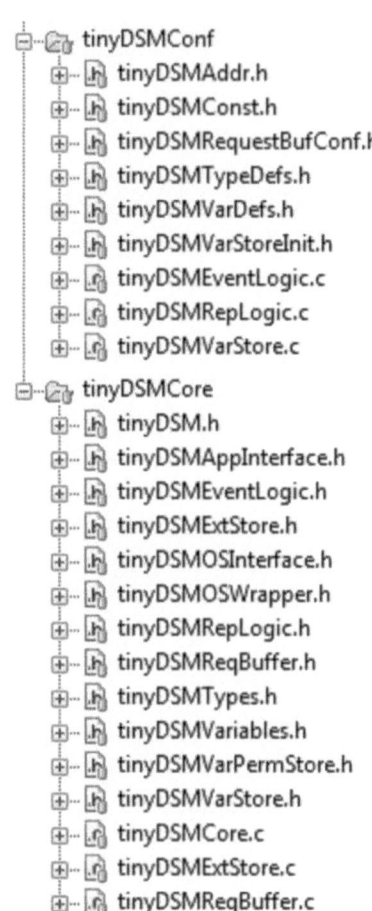

Figure 4.9: The structure of the source folders of the tinyDSM middleware

4.5.1 The functional interface

The core of the tinyDSM middleware has clearly defined interfaces that specify the functionality the middleware provides to the application, as well as the functionality it uses from the operating system. As already mentioned, the core of the tinyDSM middleware is implemented in the C programming language, thus, its interfaces are described by a set of type definitions, constants and functions collected in header files.

On the operating system layer level, there is no common and unambiguous interface that provides the functions of an operating system. And thus, as already mentioned, in order to support the operating system independence of the middleware, it was necessary to specify a minimum and consistent set of the needed functionality. This essential interface can be adapted to any operating system, if the operating system only provides the necessary functionality in some way. This adaption is realized by the operating system adaptation layer that actually encapsulates the tinyDSM middleware (see Section 3.8). This approach allows using the middleware in many environments, and thus, supports heterogeneity. An advantage of the operating system abstraction layer is also the separation of the middleware and the lower layer (operating system and hardware) details.

If the target environment is based on the C programming language, then the original application interface provided by the tinyDSM can be directly used (pass-through) by the upper layer (application), located on top of the middleware. But, this interface can be also adapted by the adaptation layer, for example to encapsulate the tinyDSM in an object to be used in a C++ based environment.

A very important feature of separating the original application interface by the adaptation layer is the possibility to change the way it works, e.g., the split-phase character can be adapted to blocking (or freezing) the context, so the request functions do not return until the request is fulfilled or times out (see Section 3.7).

```
#include "tinyDSMTypes.h"

void    tinyDSM_init(node_addr_t addr);
reqno_t tinyDSM_get(var_id_t var_id, node_addr_t *addr,
            ts_t *timestamp);
reqno_t tinyDSM_set(var_id_t var_id, value_t value,
            node_addr_t *addr);
error_t tinyDSM_getLocal(var_id_t var_id, value_t *value,
            ts_t *timestamp);

void    tinyDSM_registerEventHandler(error_t (*tinyDSM_event)
            (var_id_t event_id, bool evalue, var_id_t var_id,
            value_t value, node_addr_t addr, ts_t timestamp));
void    tinyDSM_registerGetDone(error_t (*tinyDSM_getDone)
            (reqno_t reqno, var_id_t var_id, value_t value,
            node_addr_t addr, ts_t timestamp, error_t res));
void    tinyDSM_registerSetDone(error_t (*tinyDSM_setDone)
            (reqno_t reqno, var_id_t var_id, value_t value,
            node_addr_t addr, ts_t timestamp, error_t res));
```

Listing 4.2: The tinyDSMAppInterface.h header file

The interface originally provided by the tinyDSM middleware to the application is described by the *tinyDSMAppInterface.h* header file (see Listing 4.2). It consists of seven functions that are the essence of the tinyDSM functionality in the on-line phase. The *tinyDSM_init()* function is used to initialize the middleware. The *tinyDSM_get()*

and *tinyDSM_set()* functions allow the application to issue a read or write request on a specified entity of a variable. These functions return a non-zero *request number* used to identify each request or zero if the issuing of the request failed. Both these requests are realized in the split-phase manner. If the request issuing was successful then the application is notified on the actual result of the operation using an appropriate callback function with the correct request identifier.

In contrast, the *tinyDSM_getLocal()* function allows direct reading of a local copy of a global variable or an own entity of an array variable. Thus, if the entity is set and available locally, then the function returns the value and its corresponding timestamp immediately.

Using the *tinyDSM_registerEventHandler()* function the application registers the callback function used by the middleware to notify the application on detection of any of the predefined events. The *tinyDSM_registerGetDone()* and *tinyDSM_registerSetDone()* functions allow binding the callback functions that are used to notify the application logic on the completion of a read or write operation, respectively. If these functions are not registered, then the tinyDSM middleware skips this step and does not inform the application about this.

The *tinyDSMAppInterface.h* file includes also the definitions of all types used by all these functions provided by the *tinyDSMTypes.h* header file. These types are explained in Section 4.5.2.

The application interface is completed by the *tinyDSMVariables.h* header file which provides the definitions of constants used as the identifiers of the variables in the application code to simplify it and increase the code readability.

The minimum set of operating system functionality needed to fulfil the tasks of the tinyDSM middleware is described by the *tinyDSMOSInterface.h* header file (see Listing 4.3). This interface consists of functions that need to be provided by the operating system layer (OSLayer), as well as functions provided by the tinyDSM middleware. The latter are simply fixed callback functions, to be called from the OSLayer and these are marked with the *extern* keyword.

The operating system layer related functions can be divided into five categories. The first category is related to task scheduling. The task defined in the middleware by the *tinyDSM_processingTask()* function has to be scheduled for execution using the *OSLayer_postProcessing()* function, provided by the operating system layer. A requirement to the scheduler is that it has to allow scheduling the task from the task itself. It is not necessary to count the number of posts and to run the task exactly that number of times. It is sufficient to execute the task once and it will reschedule itself, if necessary.

The second category is the timer related functionality. It includes reading the current timestamp with the *OSLayer_getCurrentTime()* function and initiating a periodic triggering of the *tinyDSM_timerFired()* function, available in the middleware, using the *OSLayer_startPeriodic()*, provided by the operating system layer.

Both, the third and the fourth category are communication related and involve the radio and the serial port functionality. They are similar, the *OSLayer_radioBusy()* and the *OSLayer_serialBusy()* functions provide the information on the availability of the respective communication module. The data can be transmitted using the functions *OSLayer_radioSend()* or *OSLayer_serialSend()* and the completeness of the operation is acknowledged using *tinyDSM_radioSendDone()* or *tinyDSM_serialSendDone()*, respectively. On the reception of a packet destined to the tinyDSM, the middleware it is notified using the *tinyDSM_radioReceive()* or the *tinyDSM_serialReceive()*. The tinyDSM is using these communication modules, but is not directly aware about their capabilities, like the bitrate or the used medium access control (MAC) protocol, in case of radio module. The communication interfaces and the data types they use are further described in Section 4.5.3.

The last category is related to the permanent data storage functionality. The flash access requests from the middleware are triggered using the *OSLayer_writeFlash()*, the *OSLayer_readFlash()* or the *OSLayer_eraseFlash()* function, respectively and are realized in the split-phase manner, i.e., acknowledged using the relevant callback functions (*tinyDSM_writeFlashDone()*, *tinyDSM_readFlashDone()*, *tinyDSM_eraseFlashDone()*), provided in the middleware. In order to support multiple flash storage units or blocks differentiated based on their content, it is of advantage, if the functions providing flash access allow specifying a device for each request. These devices can be either physical memory chips or virtual partitions on these. The implementation details are operating system and hardware platform dependent and hidden from the middleware. The flash memory manager module in the tinyDSM middleware needs to have a specification of the available devices on the target platform. This specification includes the data about the size of each device, possibly together with the erase block sizes it supports. This data is used at compile time to influence the internal functions of the flash memory manager in the middleware.

The *tinyDSMOSInterface.h* interface is completed by the definitions of all the types used by the above mentioned functions provided by the *tinyDSM.h* header file. These types are explained in detail in Section 4.5.2 and in Section 4.5.3.

Figure 4.10 shows the location and interfaces of the operating system adaptation layer. In this Figure the adaptation layer encapsulates the tinyDSM middleware, completely separating its original interfaces from both, the application logic and the operating system interfaces.

The adaptation layer can be reused between different tinyDSM based applications that use the same software and hardware platform. This is due to the fact that the interfaces of the tinyDSM middleware core are fixed. This reusability improves the

```c
#include "tinyDSM.h"
error_t OSLayer_postProcessing(void);
extern void tinyDSM_processingTask(void);

uint32_t OSLayer_getCurrentTime(void);
error_t OSLayer_startPeriodic(uint32_t millis);
extern void tinyDSM_timerFired(void);

bool OSLayer_radioBusy(void);
error_t OSLayer_radioSend(radiodata_t *data,
        node_addr_t to);
extern void tinyDSM_radioSendDone(radiodata_t *data,
        node_addr_t to, error_t result);
extern error_t tinyDSM_radioReceive(radiodata_t *data,
        node_addr_t from);

bool OSLayer_serialBusy(void);
error_t OSLayer_serialSend(serialdata_t *data);
extern void tinyDSM_serialSendDone(serialdata_t *data,
        error_t result);
extern error_t tinyDSM_serialReceive(serialdata_t *data);

error_t OSLayer_writeFlash(uint8_t devID, uint32_t address,
        uint8_t *buffer, uint16_t length);
error_t OSLayer_readFlash(uint8_t devID, uint32_t address,
        uint8_t *buffer, uint16_t length);
error_t OSLayer_eraseFlash(uint8_t devID, uint32_t address,
        uint8_t blockSize);

extern void tinyDSM_writeFlashDone(uint8_t devID,
        uint32_t address, uint8_t *buffer,
        uint16_t length);
extern void tinyDSM_readFlashDone(uint8_t devID,
        uint32_t address, uint8_t *buffer,
        uint16_t length);
extern void tinyDSM_eraseFlashDone(uint8_t devID,
        uint32_t address, uint8_t blockSize);
```

Listing 4.3: The tinyDSMOSInterface.h header file

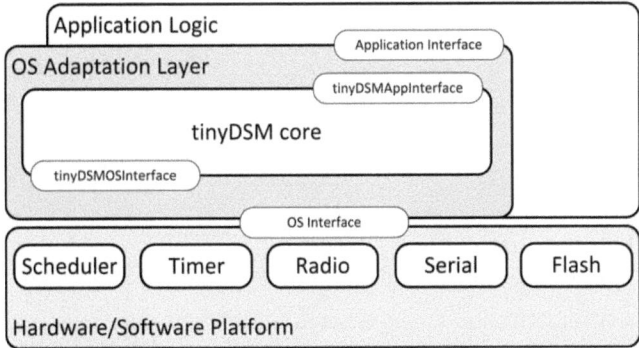

Figure 4.10: The Operating System adaptation layer–its location and interfaces in a tinyDSM based system

application development time.

4.5.2 The data structures

The tinyDSM middleware uses internally three main data structures. These structures are used by the internal processes to store the data temporary for processing or permanent, depending on the structure. These three structures are also called data storage modules due to their logical independence. They are the *request buffer*, the *local variables and metadata* and the *external variables and history data*. The *request buffer* stores the currently processed requests, until they are processed and the requesters are notified about the results. The *local variables and metadata* contains the values of local entities of array variables and the values of global variables, as well as the configuration data for all the variables. The *external variables and history* contains the values of foreign array variables and historical values of both, own and foreign variables.

The definitions of these structures are generated by the tinyDSM pre-compiler and are application dependent. They also include mechanisms to protect the data, they store, from concurrent modifications. Each of these data structures can be described as a database table, with a defined record structure and a primary key.

Figure 4.11 shows the data structures and the tinyDSM processes that use them. A solid line arrow indicates data flow or influencing the data. A dashed line arrow indicates triggering or scheduling of a process. Processes not included in tinyDSM are represented by dashed shapes. A request can be issued by the *Application Logic* on the node or from an external node, using the *Communication Interface*. In both cases it reaches at the *Query Logic*, where the request is parsed, inserted into the *request buffer* and the *main process* is scheduled. The main process uses the two other data structures to answer the query with the locally available knowledge. If the request

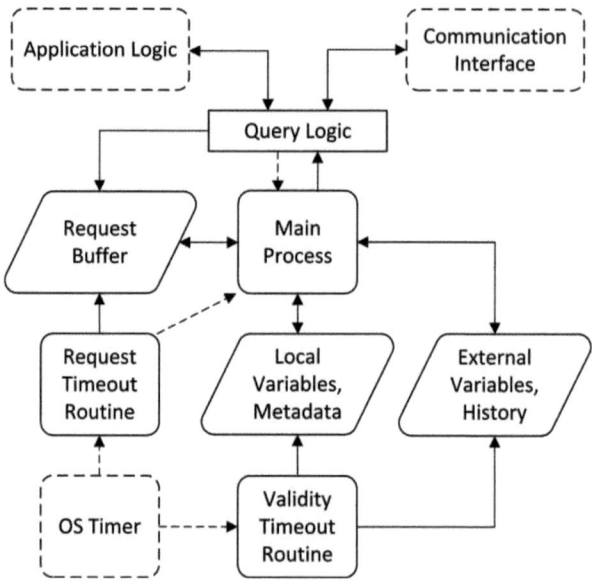

Figure 4.11: Data structures and processes in tinyDSM

cannot be answered based on local knowledge, the *main process* sends an external request via the *Query Logic* and finally via the *Communication Interface*.

The data stored in the data structures is additionally influenced by timeout routines triggered by the timer process from the operating system. In order to avoid wasting the storage space for stalled requests and out-of-date data, it is possible to define the corresponding timeout periods. These are set using the **variable_timeout** policy parameter for the instances of variables and using **local_request_timeout** or **external_request_timeout** for requests. The *request timeout routine* looks for out-dated requests in the *request buffer*, marks these accordingly and triggers the *main process* to notify the requester. The *validity timeout* routine looks for out-dated instances of variables in both data structures containing the values and invalidates them.

The request buffer

As already mentioned, the *request buffer* stores the currently processed requests, until the requested information is available or the request times out. In any of these two cases, the request is transformed into a reply and the data is forwarded to the source of the request, either to the local application logic or to the application logic on another node. Thus, the *request buffer* is a temporary storage for the data needed for request processing and collected during the processing.

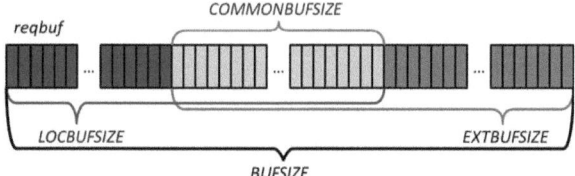

Figure 4.12: The request buffer

Since the simple platforms do not support dynamic memory allocation, or using this functionality can be very error prone, the *request buffer* is realized as a statically defined array of *request_t* structures (see Listing 4.7). In order to use the available memory with care, there are several data types defined by the tinyDSM pre-compiler especially for the particular application, based on the information provided by the application engineer.

A new request cannot be handled if there is no room in the *request buffer*. In order to provide a kind of quality of service, the *request buffer* can be split into two parts, one for the requests from the local application logic, the second for external requests. This ensures that the local requests can be handled even if there is a huge amount of external requests, and vice versa. The constants that define the sizes of these two parts of the *request buffer* are provided by the application engineer. The constants *LOCBUFSIZE* and *EXTBUFSIZE* specify the amount of buffer elements allocated for local and external requests, respectively. These two parts of the *request buffer* can overlap, creating a part of the *request buffer* that can be used for both kinds of requests, independent from their source. The constant *COMMONBUFSIZE* specifies the size of this common part of the buffer. The *BUFSIZE* constant is the actual size of the *request buffer* (see Figure 4.12) and is defined at compile time based on the three other constants as shown in Listing 4.4. These settings influence the way the requests are handled, e.g., setting the size of the request buffer to one causes pure sequential processing without buffering.

```
#define BUFSIZE (LOCBUFSIZE + EXTBUFSIZE − COMMONBUFSIZE)
request_t reqbuf[BUFSIZE];
```

Listing 4.4: The definition of the request buffer

As a new request is issued or received, the middleware tries to allocate storage for it in the common part of the buffer and, if it is full, in the part of the request buffer adequate to the source of the request. If both these parts of the buffer are full, the request cannot be handled.

In order to provide its functionality to the core DSM logic module that is application independent, the *request buffer* is managed by a software module that provides a fixed functional interface independent from the internal configuration of the buffer.

The functional interface to the *request buffer* is provided in Listing 4.5. The function *reqBuf_init()* allows initializing (and clearing) the *request buffer*. A buffer element for a new request is allocated using the *reqBuf_allocateElement()* function, which distinguished between local and external requests and returns NULL if there is no space left in the buffer for the requests of the given type. As soon as the request is handled and the requester is notified, the buffer element can be freed using the *reqBuf_releaseElement()* function. The *reqBuf_isRequestInBuffer()* function allows checking if a given request identified by its source, operation and request number is already present in the *request buffer*. The main process traverses trough the allocated elements in the *request buffer* using the *reqBuf_getNextElement()* function that returns the pointer to the element that follows the one identified by the *current* parameter or returns NULL, if there are no more elements. If the *current* parameter is equal to NULL, then the function returns the first element in the *request buffer*. The *lock* parameter enables the locking of elements to protect their content. The *reqBuf_timeoutFired()* function checks the timeout counters of all the allocated buffer elements. It returns *true* if any of the elements in the buffer was out-dated, or *false*, otherwise. These functions have to support the FIFO queue of requests, if the **fifo_processing** policy parameter is defined for any of the variables.

```
void reqBuf_init(void);
request_t *reqBuf_allocateElement(bool localRequest);
bool reqBuf_isRequestInBuffer(uint8_t operation,
        node_addr_t reqSrcAddr, reqno_t reqno);
void reqBuf_releaseElement(request_t *data);
request_t *reqBuf_getNextElement(request_t *current,
        bool lock);
bool reqBuf_timeoutFired(void);
```

Listing 4.5: The functional interface to the request buffer

A simplified SQL database like description of the *request buffer* is presented in Listing 4.6. The kind of the request is stored in the *operation* field, the source of the request in the *reqSrcAddr* field and the unique request identifier, for this source node, is stored in the *reqno* field. These three fields constitute the primary key of the *request buffer*. The *var_id* field is the identifier of the variable the request is about and it is required to be set for every valid request. The remaining fields contain the data required to specify and process the request and to store the requested information collected during the request processing. A request is actually represented as a *request_t* structure (see Listing 4.7), containing the fields from the above mentioned database record. The final set of these fields for a specific application and their optimal order in the structure according to their types is generated by the tinyDSM pre-compiler. These fields will be explained in detail.

```
CREATE TABLE request_buffer(
    operation    INTEGER NOT NULL,
    reqSrcAddr   INTEGER NOT NULL,
    reqno        INTEGER NOT NULL,
    var\_id      INTEGER NOT NULL,
    addr         INTEGER,
    timestamp    INTEGER,
    value        INTEGER,
    result       INTEGER,
    timeout      INTEGER,
    retries      INTEGER,
    hops         INTEGER,
    opflags      INTEGER,
    intflags     INTEGER,
    reqstate     INTEGER,
    msgSrcAddr   INTEGER,
    noACKS       INTEGER,
    noNACKS      INTEGER,

    PRIMARY KEY (operation, reqSrcAddr, reqno)
);
```

Listing 4.6: A SQL like description of the request buffer

The *operation* field specifies the type of the request stored in this *request_t* structure. The operations are identified by constants, defined as shown in Listing 4.8. The *GET* and *SET* operations represent the read and write requests. The *UPDATE* operation represents a middleware internal request issued by the owner node after a write operation on the owner's entity and sent to the nodes that store or may be willing to store replicas of this entity to update their storage. If the *REPDIFF* flag is set in the operation field, then the structure contains a reply for the request of the specified type, i.e., an *ANSWER* reply for a *GET* request, an *UACK* acknowledgment for an *UPDATE* request or a *SACK* acknowledgment for a *SET* request.

An operation can be enhanced using the *opflags* (operation flags) field. The length of the field is adapted according to the requirements of the policies applied to the defined variables. If none of these policies requires operation enhancements the field is removed from the definition of the *request_t* structure.

Example definitions of operation flags that specify additional features of *UPDATE* requests are presented in Listing 4.9. In combination with a specific policy for a variable, these flags can trigger a specific behaviour different to the standard one. For

```
typedef struct request_t{
  uint8_t operation:3;
  uint8_t opflags:3;
  uint8_t intflags:2;
  var_id_t var_id;
  node_addr_t addr;
  ts_t timestamp;
  value_t value;
  node_addr_t reqSrcAddr;
  reqno_t reqno;
  uint8_t bufstate:2;
  uint8_t reqstate:6;
  error_t result;
  timeout_t timeout;
  uint8_t retries;
  bufsize_t prev;
  bufsize_t next;
  hops_t hops;
  node_addr_t msgSrcAddr;
  node_no_t noACKS;
  node_no_t noNACKS;
} request_t;
```

Listing 4.7: The definition of the *request_t* structure

```
enum operations{
  GET    = 1,
  SET    = 2,
  UPDATE       = 3,
  REPDIFF = 4, // the reply flag
  ANSWER       = GET | REPDIFF,
  SACK   = SET | REPDIFF,
  UACK   = UPDATE | REPDIFF
};
```

Listing 4.8: The tinyDSM operation constants

instance, the *UPD_ADVERTISE* flag, if set, indicates the additional information to the recipient of an *UPDATE* that it can decide to hold a copy of the entity of a variable in question. In other words, the owner advertises its data. On the other hand, if the flag is not set only the nodes that already decided to hold a copy of the entity use the data in the request and update their storage. This feature gives the owner the control over the number of copies of its data. This can be further optimized by reducing the number of update acknowledgment *(UACK)* messages sent from the nodes as the result of an *UPDATE* request. If the *UPD_VERIFY* flag is set in the *opflags* field of an *UPDATE* request, the owner of the data indicates that it is interested in getting the *UACK* messages for that particular request. Collecting these, the owner of the data can get the information on the current number of copies independent from the advertisement of the data and can even decide to trigger the advertisement, if the number of copies dropped below a defined threshold. These two flags are used by the replication strategy mechanism described in Section 3.2.

```
enum opflags {
  UPD_ADVERTISE = 0x01 ,
  UPD_VERIFY    = 0x02 ,
  UPD_MIGRATION = 0x04
};
```

Listing 4.9: The example constants for the operation flags

The third example is the *UPD_MIGRATION* flag. It applies to global variables with the support for ownership migration in their policies. If set, the flag indicates that the current owner requests that all the copies are updated not only regarding the value, but also regarding the owner. The new owner is identified by the request source address (*reqSrcAddr*) in the *request_t* structure. This mechanism is described in detail in Section 3.5.

```
enum intflags {
  IFLAG_FROM_SERIAL = 0x01 ,
  IFLAG_INTERESTING = 0x02
};
```

Listing 4.10: The example constants for internal request flags

The *opflags* field is transmitted between nodes to provide additional information needed to process the request. To store additional information used during the request processing, but relevant only for the local node, a second flag field is used–the *intflags* (internal flags) field. This field is also used to change the standard behaviour of the middleware while processing a particular request, but the content of this field is not transported between the nodes together with the request. It remains a private knowledge of the processing node. The example definitions of internal flags are shown in Listing 4.10. The *IFLAG_FROM_SERIAL* flag indicates that the *GET* or *SET* request was not issued by the local application logic, but it was generated by an external device using the serial port of the node (see Section 4.5.3). Thus, the reply needs to be sent via the serial port back to the device and not to the local application logic, although the local node is the source of the request. The *IFLAG_INTERESTING* flag, if set, indicates that the data in the request was recognized as interesting during the event evaluation. This fact can, for instance, influence the decision process regarding creating a local copy of the data.

The length of the *intflags* field is adapted according to requirements of the policies applied to the defined variables as well as to the requirements specified by global settings, like the ability to issue requests from devices attached to the nodes. In general, the *intflags* field contains helper data for the local processing and handling of the particular requests, but, what is important, it is not the state of the request processing.

The identity of the variable (*var_id*), the address of the owner (*addr*), the *timestamp* and the *value* fields can store any instance of any variable from the shared memory space. These fields are thus a mixture of address and data fields. Depending on the value in the *operation* field, these fields are used to create a new instance, to create copies of an instance or to locate an existing instance of a variable.

The different operations require different fields to have defined values. The *var_id* field specifies the variable and has to be set for all the operations. The *GET* and *SET* requests require the *addr* field only for an array variable, for global variables, this field is set with the address of the owner of the variable or with the address of the requester node if the owner is not known to the requester. For the *SET* request, the *timestamp* field does not matter and is ignored, if set. For the *GET* request, the *timestamp* field can be left empty to get the most recent instance or can specify the timestamp of interest with the tolerance specified by the **timestamp_tolerance** policy parameter. A *SET* request requires the *value* field to be set. If the request was successful, the correct values of the *addr*, *value* and *timestamp* fields are available in the *ANSWER* or *SET* acknowledgment (*SACK*) message.

The *UPDATE* request has to have all the four fields set with the correct values. This request is an informational request, and thus, its result is not the data, but a success or a failure of its processing on each single node and a combination of these individual results according to the replication strategy, as defined by the policy chosen for the variable. However, an extension to such a policy that maintains a list of copy holders is possible.

The data types for these four fields are defined by the tinyDSM pre-compiler. The *var_id_t* type is specified by the number of variables defined in the system. Currently, the variables are identified by their indices according to the definition order, thus, the *var_id_t* type is defined as the smallest type that can store the largest index. Extensions that allow predefined identifiers for variables are possible. Such a solution could help combining several tinyDSM based applications with different configurations into one working system without conflicts in the variables domain.

The *node_addr_t* type is defined by the application engineer, based on the addressing supported by the communication module. Additionally, the physical addresses can be broken into two logical parts, i.e., the node and the network address parts, using the *TINYDSM_NETWORK_MASK* constant that allows defining this splitting bitwise. Defining a nonzero value for the *TINYDSM_NETWORK_MASK* creates logically separated sub-networks. In order to issue a request that reaches nodes independent from their network addresses, the broadcast network address, defined by the *TINYDSM_NETWORK_BROADCAST* constant, can be used. These three address related settings are defined in the *tinyDSMAddr.h* header file.

The *ts_t* type is derived from the definitions of all the variables. In a definition of each variable the application engineer specifies, if the instances of the variable are to be differentiated by timestamps or version numbers. An option to choose both is currently not supported, but is a possible extension. The timestamps and version numbers of different variables can have diverse sizes specified by the **timestamp_size** policy parameter and the *ts_t* type is defined by the tinyDSM pre-compiler to be the smallest type able to store the timestamps or versions for each of all the defined variables.

For each defined shared variable the application engineer also specifies its storage type. The *value_t* type is defined by the tinyDSM pre-compiler to be the smallest type able to store the value of each of all the defined variables.

The request source address (*reqSrcAddr*) and the request number (*reqno*) fields allow distinguishing between any two requests, by identifying the node that is the source of the request and the sequence number of the request on that node. The request source address is of the *node_addr_t* type. The *reqno_t* is defined by the tinyDSM pre-compiler as the smallest integer type capable to store any request sequence number for all the defined variables. The requested size of the request number is defined by the **request_number_size** policy parameter for each variable. If it is of advantage to choose a small type for the request numbers, then in order to extend the amount of distinguishable requests issued by one node, the nodes can use two separate sequences, one for *GET* and a second for *SET* requests. This separation is enabled by defining the *SEPARATEREQNOS* constant. An *UPDATE* request is triggered by a *SET* request and thus, uses the same request number as the original *SET* request.

In case of an *UPDATE* request the meaning of the *reqSrcAddr* is slightly different. Due to the fact that an *UPDATE* is actually a part of a *SET* request, the *reqSrcAddr* field indicates the node that triggered the *SET* request. The source of the *UPDATE* request is the owner of the entity identified by the *addr* field. This is the natural consequence of using the *UPDATE* requests that are triggered by the *SET* requests and provides the complete set of information to the processing nodes.

The buffer element state (*bufstate*) and the request state (*reqstate*) fields describe the current state of the *request_t* structure and the request it contains, respectively. The states are based on flags and the currently defined ones are shown in Listing 4.11, for the buffer element state and in Listing 4.12, for the request state. Similar to the internal flags in the *intflags* field, both these state fields are not transported outside the processing node.

```
enum buffer_states {
    REQBUF_FREE       = 0x00,
    REQBUF_ALLOCATED  = 0x01,
    REQBUF_LOCKED     = 0x02
};
```

Listing 4.11: The definitions of the buffer element state flags

If the *bufstate* field is cleared, and thus, equal to *REQBUF_FREE* (see Listing 4.11), then the buffer does not contain any request and can be allocated to store a new one. Once the buffer element is allocated, the *REQBUF_ALLOCATED* flag is set and blocks the access to the buffer element for the allocation procedure. An allocated buffer element can be further locked by a process, using the *REQBUF_LOCKED* flag, to protect the content of the buffer from modifications done by some other processes that may pre-empt it.

```
enum request_states {
    REQBUF_WAIT4NOTIFY   = 0x00,
    REQBUF_WAIT4INIT     = 0x01,
    REQBUF_WAIT4STOR     = 0x02,
    REQBUF_WAIT4STORREP  = 0x04,
    REQBUF_WAIT4SEND     = 0x08,
    REQBUF_WAIT4SENDREP  = 0x10,
    REQBUF_WAIT4RELEASE  = 0x20
};
```

Listing 4.12: The definitions of request state flags

The flags in the *reqstate* field (see Listing 4.12) represent the processing steps that the request is waiting for and thus, describe its state from initialization to completeness. Once the buffer element is allocated and the request data is copied into it, the *reqstate* is set to *REQBUF_WAIT4INIT*, i.e., the request is waiting for the initial processing. In this initial processing phase, the *REQBUF_WAIT4INIT* flag is cleared, but other flags can be set, based on the request type and the availability of the data. Accesses to *local variables and metadata* are realized during the initial processing, as necessary and without delay, since they are available in the RAM memory. If the request requires access to data, which is either in the storage for *external variables and history* or on another node, then the processing of the request needs to be paused until the access can be realized. Since these accesses are usually split phase and potentially block the resource, like a radio module or a flash memory chip, the realization needs to be split into two steps. First, the request waits for the access to the resource (indicated by the *REQBUF_WAIT4STOR* or the *REQBUF_WAIT4SEND* flag set) and then waits for the reply from it (the *REQBUF_WAIT4STORREP* or the *REQBUF_WAIT4SENDREP* flag, respectively). Radio modules and flash memory chips expose this behaviour, but in a slightly different manner. Both these resources have limited ability for parallelized processing. However, a radio module is blocked only during sending and receiving and is able to send multiple requests, without waiting for the replies. In contrast, a flash chip is usually blocked during the whole time it needs for processing the request. Due to that, the *REQBUF_WAIT4SEND* flag can be also used to send a request without waiting for the reply, e.g., in case of an *UPDATE* without acknowledgments or while sending a reply.

If a processing step completes and the request is not waiting for any other steps, i.e., the *reqstate* field is cleared, then the request is in the *REQBUF_WAIT4NOTIFY* state, meaning that it is actually waiting for the final processing step–the notification of the requester. The *reqstate* field is also cleared if the request times out. In this case, the result field is set accordingly.

After a successful notification, the *REQBUF_WAIT4RELEASE* flag is set in the *reqstate* field, to indicate that the request buffer element can be released and can be further used for new requests.

The *result* field specifies the result of the request processing. Example definitions of constants used as results of the tinyDSM request processing are presented in Listing 4.13. The *error_t* type is defined to be the smallest type able to store all the possible result values.

The *timeout* field is the counter for the request timeout routine. Based on the timeout settings for the requests defined by the **local_request_timeout** and **external_request_timeout** policy parameters chosen for all the variables, the common timeout unit (CTU), equal to the greatest common divisor of all timeout periods, is calculated. The *timeout* field of a request buffer element is set after the request data is copied into it. The value represents the amount of CTUs and is set according to the above mentioned policy parameters for the variable the request is about. The request timer routine is triggered every CTU and decrements the counters of all not out-dated requests. If the routine detects that the allowed number of units elapsed, it clears

```
enum errorcodes{
  SUCCESS = 0,     // success
  FAILED,          // general, failed
  EBUSY,           // busy
  EINVAL,          // invalid parameter
  ESIZE,           // wrong size
  EBUFFERFULL,     // request buffer full
  ENOTALLOWED,     // operation not allowed
  ENOTREPLICATED,  // data was not replicated on the node
  EWRONGADDR,      // wrong address in the request
  EVARNA,          // variable not available
  ENOSPACE,        // no space to store the variable
  ETIMEOUT,        // timeout
  ESENDFAIL,       // sending failed
  EALREADYTHERE    // the request is already in the buffer
};
```

Listing 4.13: Definitions of the result constants

the *reqstate* field, sets the result field to *ETIMEOUT* and triggers the main process to notify the requester (see Figure 4.11). For requests without time limitations the *timeout* field is cleared at the initialization time.

The tinyDSM middleware manages the retransmissions of requests. The *retries* field is used to specify the number of unsuccessful sending approaches needed to define a request as failed. The value is specified by the **local_request_retries** or **external_request_retries** policy parameters chosen for the variable, depending on the source of the request. If the number of retransmissions is not limited, the *retries* field is cleared.

The *timeout* and the *retries* fields can be omitted if none of the policies chosen for the used variables defines the respective restrictions.

The *request buffer* can be configured to implement a FIFO queue to order the requests according to the time they were inserted into the request buffer. The requests are then processed according to the order. The *prev* and *next* fields are used to store the indices of the preceding and the following element in the queue created using the static elements of the request buffer. The *bufsize_t* type is defined to be the smallest type able to store the indices. Thus, it is influenced by the value of the *BUFSIZE* constant.

The **fifo_processing** policy parameter, defined for a given variable, specifies that the requests require FIFO queue for their processing. If any of the defined variables requires the FIFO queue, it is applied for the complete request buffer.

If any of the defined variables requires tinyDSM middleware layer request forwarding mechanism presented in Section 3.1, then the *hops* and the *msgSrcAddr* fields are required in the *request_t* structure, as well. The *hops* field stores the current level and the *msgSrcAddr* field the address of the parent node in the request forwarding tree.

The request forwarding is used by the owner discovery mechanism, presented in Section 3.4, and during the *UPDATE* request forwarding. Thus, it is enabled if any of the variables has the **replication_range** policy parameter set to a value greater than one or is defined as global and has the **discovery_hops** parameter set to a value greater than zero.

The *UPDATE* request forwarding may require the additional fields (*noACKS* and *noNACKS*), if the *VERIFY* phase is enabled in the **update_pattern** policy parameter for any of the variables. These fields store the cumulative numbers of positive and negative *UACK* messages. The *noNACKS* field can be omitted if all the variables with the enabled *VERIFY* phase have a defined **replication_copies** policy parameter, i.e., do not require negative *UACK* messages. The *node_no_t* type is defined as an integer type of the same size as the *node_addr_t*, and thus, able to store a value equal to the maximum number of addressable nodes.

All these application specific types are defined in the *tinyDSMTypeDefs.h* header file.

Measurements were taken in order to estimate the complexity of the functions providing the access to the request buffer and to evaluate the possible frequency of these operations assuming a given clock frequency of the processing unit. Table 4.1 provides these measurements performed on the IHPNode hardware platform (see Section 2.1.1) with the IHPOS operating system (see Section 2.1.2). The source code was compiled with the default optimization settings in the Code Composer IDE [118]. The measurements were taken in clock cycles to make them independent from the actual clock frequency. Additionally, these measurements can be used to estimate the required clock frequency to achieve the requested functionality.

Two setups were tested; one with the support for FIFO queue and one without. In both cases the sizes of the buffer parts for local and external requests were 50 elements each, with 20 elements shared between both parts of the buffer. This resulted in the total buffer size of 80 elements.

The measurements in Table 4.1 provide the values of the minimum and the maximum clock cycles required for executing the given function. They show that there is still room for optimizations. The best case values cover cases, where the request buffer is empty. In this case, there is no need to check many elements while allocating and also no actual action is necessary while accessing the request buffer with the other functions. The worst case values include situations, where the buffer is full and it is necessary to go through all the elements in the buffer. Additionally, in case of the *reqBuf_timeoutFired()*, all the elements are marked as out-dated, as well.

The initialization of the request buffer with the *reqBuf_init()* function and releasing

Table 4.1: Complexity of the request buffer access functions

Function	FIFO queue		No FIFO queue	
	Min [cycles]	Max [cycles]	Min [cycles]	Max [cycles]
reqBuf_allocateElement()	258	2790	153	2655
reqBuf_getNextElement()	35	109	35	96
reqBuf_isRequestInBuffer()	44	6849	44	6849
reqBuf_timeoutFired()	50	14085	50	10541
reqBuf_init()		14590		13470
reqBuf_releaseElement()		264		228

the buffer element are based on the system standard function *memset()*. Calling the *reqBuf_releaseElement()* function for FIFO enabled request buffer, clears and removes the element from the queue. Thus, requires more clock cycles to complete.

The local variables and metadata

The *local variables and metadata* structure contains the local copies of the variables and the configuration data that describe all the shared variables defined in the current tinyDSM setup. This set of local copies contains exactly one instance of each defined variable, i.e., one instance of each array variable (own entity) and one instance of the single entity of each global variable. All these instances are the most recent ones available at the local node.

A simplified SQL like description of the *local variables and metadata* structure is presented in Listing 4.14. It contains exactly one record for each defined variable and each of these records initially contains at least the identity of the variable in the *var_id* field, which is the primary key in the table and the configuration data in the *config* field that describes the given variable and its type. The other fields in the record can be initially empty and their values change, as the knowledge of the node on the variables changes. These other fields in all the records contain the current values and timestamps for the local entities of array variables and for the single entities of the global variables. For the latter, the fields also store the addresses of their owners. The *timeout* field is a counter that is decremented by an external timer and if it reaches zero the stored value is marked as not valid. The start value for the *timeout* field is defined by the **variable_timeout** policy parameter for each variable and is reset every time a new instance of the variable is put into the storage.

In order to make the core of the tinyDSM middleware independent from the internal realization of this storage module a functional interface was established to access the content of the storage (see Listing 4.15).

```
CREATE TABLE local_variables_and_metadata(
    var_id      INTEGER NOT NULL UNIQUE,
    value       INTEGER,
    timestamp   INTEGER,
    owner       INTEGER,
    timeout     INTEGER,
    config      INTEGER NOT NULL,

    PRIMARY KEY ( var_id )
);
```

Listing 4.14: A SQL like description of the local variables and metadata structure

```
error_t var_init(void);

uint8_t var_getSize( var_id_t var_id );
bool var_isGlobal( var_id_t var_id );
bool var_isEvent( var_id_t var_id );
bool var_isSigned( var_id_t var_id );

bool var_isSet( var_id_t var_id );
bool var_isOwnerSet( var_id_t var_id );
node_addr_t var_getOwner( var_id_t var_id );

error_t var_getValueTS( var_id_t var_id, value_t *value,
        ts_t *timestamp );
error_t var_setValueTsOwner( var_id_t var_id, value_t value,
        ts_t timestamp, node_addr_t owner );

void var_timeouterFired(void);
```

Listing 4.15: The functional interface to the local variables and metadata storage module

All the nodes that constitute one system share the configuration of the defined variables. Thus, the read only configuration data is global for all nodes in the network. The configuration parameters describing a chosen variable can be read using the *var_isGlobal()* and the *var_isEvent()* functions. The first function states, if the variable is defined as a global one and the second, if the variable is associated to an event. The parameters of the data type, defined for the variable, can be read using *var_getSize()* and *var_isSigned()*. The first one returns the size of the data type chosen for the variable. The information, if the type of the variable is signed or not, can be read using the second function.

The state of the variable in the storage on the local node changes as the variable data is changing. For each variable in the storage there are two state parameters and they can be read, using the *var_isSet()* and the *var_isOwnerSet()* functions. The first states if the value and timestamp are set and valid, the second if the address of the owner is set.

The address of the node that owns the instance of a given variable, available in the storage, can be read using the *var_getOwner()* function. But, as already mentioned, this information is only important for global variables, because for array variables it will always return the local address, since the storage contains only own instances of these variables.

Since the value and the timestamp belong together, they can be read from the storage using a single function. The *var_getValueTS()* returns both, the value and the timestamp available in the stored instance of the chosen variable.

Writing the instance into the storage is done using the *var_setValueTsOwner()* function that specifies all the three fields; the value, the timestamp and the owner of the instance of the given variable to be stored. This function also changes the state, if necessary, i.e., the *value* and the *owner* fields are marked as set and valid.

The *var_timeouterFired()* function is triggered by an external timer. It decrements the *timeout* fields and invalidates the out-dated instances.

The *var_init()* function shall be used during the initialization of the middleware. It contains the necessary operations to put the content of the structure in the operational state.

The implementation of these above mentioned functions shall also protect the stored data from concurrent modifications resulting in an unpredictable state. Also reading an instance, which is currently modified in some other place in code, can result in erroneous data and shall be prohibited.

The actual internal data structures are generated by the tinyDSM pre-compiler. There are many different ways how the data can be represented and optimized depending on the requirements of the application. However, for the tinyDSM pre-compiler three options were chosen and one of them can be chosen by a command line parameter. They are the *array* representation, the *individual* representation and a mixture of these both, the *individual-array* representation. These representations were chosen since the first two are the two extremes regarding the memory overhead and data access overhead, i.e., they provide either optimal code size for the accessing functions or a memory usage optimized representation of the data. The third representation is a kind of golden mean, trying to combine both, the optimum memory usage and the compact access functions. But the possible internal representations of the storage have also other features. These will be explained later with the description of each representation.

The array representation is the most memory consuming, but provides simpler access to the stored data. It is a straight forward implementation of a data storage to store the data described in Listing 4.14. It restricts the identities of the variables, i.e., the values in each *var_id* field in the SQL representation, to be a continuous set of integer values starting with 0 and smaller than the constant *NUMBER_OF_VARIABLES*, defined by the tinyDSM pre-compiler, based on the number of defined variables. This allows using these identities of variables directly as indices in the array of structures of the *variable_t* type (see Listing 4.16) to represent the *local variables and metadata* storage. The fields of each *variable_t* structure are initially set according to the definition of its corresponding variable.

```
typedef struct variable_t{
  value_t value;
  ts_t timestamp;
  node_addr_t owner;
  timeout_t timeout;
  uint8_t config:5;
  uint8_t state:3;
} variable_t;

variable_t var_variables [NUMBER_OF_VARIABLES];
```

Listing 4.16: The *variable_t* structure and definition of the *local variables and metadata* storage in the array representation

The *value*, *timestamp* and *owner* fields in the *variable_t* structure, together with the index of the structure in the *var_variables* array, so the *var_id*, represent the stored instance of the variable. The timeout field is used to detect out-dated instances of variables, for which the *timeout* periods were defined. For variables without a defined **variable_timeout** policy parameter, this field is always zero.

The four above mentioned fields use types already mentioned in the description of the *request_t* structure. As already mentioned, all these types are defined by the tinyDSM pre-compiler to be capable to store data of every variable.

The configuration of a variable is stored in the *config* field. As already mentioned, it includes the information if the variable was defined as a global one and if it is associated with an event. It also includes the information about the type of the variable. The tinyDSM middleware was originally designed to provide support for sharing unsigned integer types available in the C programming language, so with sizes ranging from one to eight bytes. Thus, three bits can be used to represent the size of the type decreased by one. Having the size of the type, it is possible to optimize the size of storage and transmitted packets to the exact needs. However, having only the size information is not enough to interpret the value of a variable correctly, if the type is a signed one. The correct interpretation is important, e.g., by casting the value to a larger type or if it shall be allowed to freely compare variables with signed and unsigned types, while evaluating event equations. In that case, it is necessary to store the additional information if the type is signed. And since the sizes of integer types are always powers of two, it is sufficient to store the exponent to have the size information available. This allows storing both, the size of the type and the information if it is signed or not on three bytes. This solution requires taking a logarithm of base two from the value returned by *sizeof(type)*, for each defined variable, during the initialization of the structures. It is an operation on constants and there are only four allowed values, so it can be done using a macro. Another macro detects if the type of a variable is signed. It tests if casting a negative value to the type of the variable results in a value that is recognized as smaller than zero. Both these tasks can be done by the C compiler for the target platform during the initialization. This solution allows the tinyDSM compiler to generate the configuration without knowing the details on the types for a specific platform. Anyway, in order to make the configuration of a tinyDSM-based application transferable between platforms, it is advantageous to use platform independent types with specified size, e.g., *uint16_t* instead of *int* or *short*.

In general, the tinyDSM core does not provide any type checking, e.g., while writing a value to a variable. It is left to the application engineer. But, with the information if the type is signed, the stored values can be at least protected from being demolished during the processing and storage. Thus, it is a tool for the application engineer, to help her.

It is also possible to define variables of floating point types. But, in such a case, the integer type *value_t* is simply used as a storage place for the floating point content. It may also generate erroneous configuration if, for the specific platform, the size of *float, double* or *long double* type is not a power of two or is larger than the largest integer type. Using these variables in event equations can also result in an unpredicted behaviour.

The code generated by the tinyDSM pre-compiler can either take into account that the variables can have signed types or handle all variables as if they were of unsigned types. This is a command line parameter used at the compile time by the application engineer. It influences the internals of the generated functions, due to different initialization data and its interpretation. Example sets of constants used to represent and extract the configuration data from the *config* field are shown in Listing 4.17, for the setting, where all the variables are handled as unsigned, and in Listing 4.18, for the sign-respective handling of variables.

The current state of the stored instance is available in the *state* field. It indicates if the data fields contain valid values. Additionally, to support internal protection of the data the field includes a lock flag, which indicates that the data is currently being changed. Example constants, used for flags in the *state* field, are shown in Listing 4.19. The *value, timestamp* and *owner* fields are set with one call of the *var_setValueTsOwner()* function, thus, their validity flags are set simultaneously. But,

```
enum varconfig{
  ISEVENT    = 0x10,
  ISGLOBAL   = 0x08,
  SIZEMASK   = 0x07
};
```

Listing 4.17: Example constants for the configuration of a variable - ignoring the sign

```
enum varconfig{
  ISEVENT    = 0x10,
  ISGLOBAL   = 0x08,
  ISSIGNED   = 0x04,
  SIZEMASK   = 0x03
};
```

Listing 4.18: Example constants for the configuration of a variable - respecting the sign

there is one exception, which is the initialization of a global variable. In this case all the nodes in the network have a valid content in the *value* field set at the zero timestamp, but the *owner* is not specified, so the content of *owner* field is not valid. An opposite situation occurs in the case of a global variable, for which a timeout period was defined. After it is set by its owner, both *value* and *owner* fields have valid values. But, as soon as the timeout period elapses, the *value* field is invalidated. The *owner* field is still valid, but there is no valid value for that variable available anymore.

```
enum varstate{
  ISLOCKED    = 0x01,
  ISSET       = 0x02,
  ISOWNERSET  = 0x04
};
```

Listing 4.19: Example constants for the state of a local instance

In the array representation of the *local variables and metadata* storage the functions defined in Listing 4.15 simply access the appropriate fields in the *variable_t* structure for the corresponding *var_id*. Thus, these functions are compact. On the other hand, the data types in the structures are defined to be able to store the data of all the defined variables. In a pessimistic case, this can lead to huge memory waste. Even if only one of the variables is defined with the *uint64_t* or *int64_t* type, all the structures for all other variables foresee this maximum amount of memory to store their values, even if the other variables were defined as the *uint8_t* or *int8_t* type variables. And, if only one variable has a defined **variable_timeout** parameter, then all the others also have the *timeout* field in their corresponding *variable_t* structures. Another huge disadvantage of the array representation is the need to initialize all the fields in the structures, what requires additional code memory.

In order to optimize the memory requirements of the *local variables and metadata* storage the individual representation can be chosen. In this representation the required fields of the database table record as defined in Listing 4.14 are represented by individual data of the exactly required type. And this applies for each record representing each variable in the storage.

Assuming an example definition of a shared variable:

distributed **global timestamp_size**:1 **variable_timeout**:200 *int8_t* **temperature**;

The individual representation of a record for the example shared variable called *temperature* is shown in Listing 4.20. The *int8_t* type is the type of the *temperature* variable, exactly as it is specified in the definition. The *uint8_t* is the type used by the version number according to the value defined for the **timestamp_size** policy parameter. The **variable_timeout** policy parameter defines a timeout period for the variable. The *uint8_t* type is defined based on the defined timeout period and the common timeout period calculated for all the variables. The *temperature* variable has a defined **global** parameter, thus, it is a global variable and it is necessary to store the address of the owner of the standard address *node_addr_t* type. The configuration of the *temperature* variable and state of the available instance is stored in the *temperature_varinfo* variable. The *varinfo_t* type is defined as shown in Listing 4.21. It contains two fields, *config* and *state*. They contain the same information, as the *config* and *state* fields in the *variable_t* structure and the same methodology is used to initialize and interpret their content.

```
int8_t            temperature_value;
uint8_t           temperature_timestamp;
uint8_t           temperature_timeout;
node_addr_t       temperature_owner;
varinfo_t         temperature_varinfo;
```

Listing 4.20: The individual representation of an example shared variable

```
typedef struct varinfo_t{
  uint8_t config:5;
  uint8_t state:3;
} varinfo_t;
```

Listing 4.21: The definition of the *varinfo_t* structure type

This individual representation results in a large number of individual variables in the source code of the storage. For each defined shared variable, the tinyDSM precompiler individually generates a set of data items representing its record in the *local variables and metadata* storage. These local variables are defined exactly as needed, regarding their type and existence. Thus, from the RAM memory usage perspective this solution is the most optimal. However, to manage these local variables and to access their content using the identities of the shared variables, so according to the primary key defined for the storage, it is necessary to use, e.g., large *switch* constructs resulting in a larger code size of the functions accessing the data.

Thus, the individual representation may require less RAM memory for the storage, compared to the array representation. It may also require less initialization data, since every field can be initialized individually and only if necessary. However, its code overhead for accessing the data may exceed the additional data that needs to be programmed on the nodes as initialization data.

In order to keep the compact access functions while reducing the size of the initialization data the individual-array representation can be used, as a solution between these two mentioned above. It allocates the same amount of memory for the storage as the array representation, but reduces the size of the initialization data by storing the fields in separated arrays indexed by the identifiers of the variables. The definition of the storage in the individual-array representation is shown in Listing 4.22. It uses the same *varinfo_t* type as used in the individual representation to store the configuration and the same types as the array representation to store the instances.

ts_t	var_timestamps [NUMBER_OF_VARIABLES] ;
node_addr_t	var_owners [NUMBER_OF_VARIABLES] ;
timeout_t	var_timeouts [NUMBER_OF_VARIABLES] ;
value_t	var_values [NUMBER_OF_VARIABLES]
varinfo_t	var_infos [NUMBER_OF_VARIABLES]

Listing 4.22: Definition of the *local variables and metadata* storage in the individual-array representation

The fields that need to be initialized with arbitrary values, so the values and configurations, can be initialized during the definitions of their arrays. In contrast, the arrays that contain fields that need only to be cleared, can be initialized in the *var_init()* function, e.g., using the *memset()* standard function. This solution significantly reduces the size of data needed to be programmed on each node as initialization data, while keeping the simple access functions. However, this representation does not optimize the RAM memory consumption for storage.

The tinyDSM pre-compiler generates the representation chosen by the application engineer, but it is a straight forward extension to support this decision for the specific configuration, by calculating the costs of each representation and choosing the one that shows the best characteristics of the chosen parameters.

The three proposed representations and their features show how complex it actually is to program small resource constrained devices in an optimal way and to which extent an implementation decision can influence the performance of the system. In order to investigate the properties of each representation for an example configuration three versions of the *local variables and metadata* storage were generated. These were tested in a test application, without the other parts of the middleware, just to evaluate the required program memory, the size of the initialization data and the time needed for accessing the data.

To define a kind of start point for the comparison, a fourth test storage was compiled. This fourth storage is called the *empty* representation, because none of the data is initialized and the access functions only test if the *var_id* is correct to allow their integration in the test application. The empty storage is a skeleton storage and provides the information on the minimal costs, in the senseless case, where no variables are defined.

The test configuration is as follows. One hundred shared global variables of the *uint32_t* type are defined and each of these variables has a defined timeout period and an initial value. The *timeout_t* type is actually the *uint16_t* type and the *ts_t* is the *uint32_t*. The *varinfo_t* is actually equal to the *uint8_t* and the *node_addr_t* is equal to *uint16_t*. This configuration requires initializing all the fields except the *owner* field. The large amount of defined shared variables was chosen to make the differences between representations more significant and thus, more visible.

The aim of the test was to check the costs of each representation for the same settings. Thus, the configuration was chosen in a way that it cannot be optimized, resulting in worst case scenarios without using the optimization advantages of each representation.

The test application initializes the storage using the *var_init()* function, then writes an instance for each variable, stored in it, using the *var_setValueTsOwner()* function, then reads each instance, using the *var_getValueTS()* function and finally calls the *var_timeouterFired()* function several times, to invalidate the instances. The amount of clock cycles required by each of these operations is measured by the timer. The measurements are provided in Table 4.2. The measurements are given in clock cycles, making them independent from the frequency of the microcontroller. The number of clock cycles is also the straight forward concept to measure and indicate complexity.

Again, the measurements were performed on the IHPNode hardware platform with the minimal support of the IHPOS operating system, to reduce the code size overhead. The only used modules from the IHPOS was the timer, to count the amount of clock cycles and the USB output, to print the debug messages on a PC connected to the examined node. The source code was compiled with the default optimization settings in the Code Composer IDE [118]. The size of the code required by each representation and the size of the initialization data that also needs to be programmed onto the device

Table 4.2: Clock cycles required by the access operations of the *local variables and metadata* storage

Storage Representation	Write [cycles]		Read [cycles]			Init [cycles]
	Success	Failure	Success	Wrong var_id	Not set	
empty	63	66	42	45	45	11
array	271	66	180	45	87	11
individual array	137	66	100	45	59	2022
Individual	117	69	125	48	70	11

are provided in Table 4.3.

The timing measurements for the four representations are shown in Table 4.2. An interesting observation can be made for the empty storage. The measurements show the influence of the amount and types of parameters used by a function on the number of cycles required to call the function. The functions for the read and write operations differ only in the number of parameters and their bodies and return types are the same. However, they require a significantly different number of clock cycles to be called and to return.

The following paragraphs explain the measurements presented in Table 4.2, by describing the test application in more details. The test application distinguishes between two cases for writing and reading of the instances. The operation can be successful or a failure. Additionally, in case of reading, the failing can have two reasons; either the provided *var_id* is incorrect or, for the chosen variable, there is no valid instance in the storage, i.e., it is not set.

The similar values for the measured timings for the empty storage and the array-based representations can be explained by the fact that they check the correctness of the provided identity of the variable in the same way, i.e., it has to be within the array index range. If it is not the case, the access functions return with an error. In case of the individual representation, the identity is incorrect, if it is not assigned for any variable and was not found in the switch statement.

If the *var_id* is correct, the read operations need to check if the instance, available in the storage, is valid. This test requires accessing the state of the instance. Comparing the measurements for both cases where the read operation failed, indicates the cost of this check for a representation. These values give already some idea on the differences between the representations.

The actual data access occurs only if the read or write operation is successful. And the measurements for these successful accesses show the differences in the complexity between the representations. An interesting observation can be made comparing the timings of both array based representations. In the array representation the read and write operations are about twice that expensive, as their respective operations in the individual-array representation. This can be caused by the fact that in the array representation the access requires both, traversing through the array and through the structure. This significant difference makes the individual-array a very attractive alternative to the array representation.

The individual-array representation is the only one where the *var_init()* function is used to initialize the storage. This effort is actually an optimization, because it allows reducing the size of the initialization data–the values in the array of timestamps are cleared in the *var_init()* function. The body of the *var_init()* is in this case only a single *memset()* function, so the additional increase of code size is marginal and the *var_init()* function is called only once, at the application start.

In case of the individual representation, the cost of the write operation is about 17 per cent lower than for the individual-array representation. In contrast, the read operation is 25 per cent more expensive, comparing the same two representations. There is a slight difference in the complexity of the read and the write operations for the individual representation and the ratio between these is different, compared to the array based representations. This is caused by the fact that reading requires accessing the state field and returns with an error, if the stored value for the instance is not valid. This significantly increases the complexity of the read operation, making it more expensive than the write operation, even though the latter accesses more fields.

Since the number of defined variables is quite large, the size of the code needed for such large switch statements, used by the individual representation, results in very large program size. Table 4.3 shows the sizes of the code and initialization data for the examined representations. Taking the empty storage as the reference level, the array based representations require between 300 bytes and 350 bytes of code for the accessing functions. In contrast, the individual representation generates over 15 Kbytes of code.

In the worst case, where all the defined shared variables have to be initialized, the individual representation generates also enormous amount of initialization data. For the chosen test configuration the individual-array representation needs the least initialization data, the array representation requires about the double of it. And the individual representation needs almost four times more initialization data, than the individual-array representation. This is caused by the way the data is initialized and by the granularity of the storage. The granularity is defined by the number of independent data units, i.e., variables or structures that have to be initialized. The initialization data for a data unit consists of a pointer to the unit and the complete content of the unit. The test was performed on the IHPNode hardware platform, where a pointer is represented by four bytes and the processor word has the size of two bytes. The data is aligned on the boundary of the processor word, making the processor word the smallest piece of data that can be used for initialization, even if the initialized data

Table 4.3: Code size and initialization data size requirements of the *local variables and metadata* storage representations

Storage representation	Code size [bytes]	Initialization data size [bytes]
empty	1402	46
array	1748	1450
individual array	1690	758
individual	16992	2846

unit is smaller. This influences the actual size of the initialization data as well as the actual size of the RAM memory allocated for the storage.

The fields that need to be initialized are the *value*, *config*, *timeout* and *timestamps* fields. These need in total 1100 bytes of pure initialization data. The individual representation represents the fields for each instance as individual variables in the source code. This causes the most initialization overhead, because for the total of 400 data units, which need to be initialized, a total of 1600 bytes is used by the pointers to these units. Additionally, the initialization data for the *config* fields are extended to the size of processor word, causing additional 100 bytes of wasted memory. In total, 2800 bytes initialization data is required for the individual representation.

In case of array based representations, the overhead caused by the pointers is much smaller. In case of the array representation, there is only one data unit to be initialized– the main array of *variable_t* structures. And thus, only one pointer is necessary. However, a data unit has to be initialized as a whole, so even the *owner* fields have to be initialized, causing additional 200 bytes of initialization data. Additionally, the size of a single *variable_t* structure is 13 bytes and due to the alignment needs to be extended to 14 bytes, what causes 100 bytes overhead. Thus, a total of 1404 bytes of initialization data is required for the array representation.

The individual-array representation allows initializing each array separately. Additionally, for the shared variables with defined initial values the timestamps have to be set to zero, what allows setting them in the *var_init()* function. This reduces the size of the initialization data by 400 bytes. Further, the one-byte *config* fields are contained in one array, whose size is a multiply of the processor word. Thus, the size of the initialization data for the three arrays is 712 bytes, what makes the individual-array representation the least demanding.

Another parameter is the amount of RAM memory required for the storage. The individual-array representation requires 1300 bytes. If the declaration order of variables in the source code, generated by the tinyDSM pre-compiler, is optimal, the individual representation requires also 1300 bytes. The array representation requires 1400 bytes,

Table 4.4: The complexity of the validation check for the *local variables and metadata* storage

Storage representation	Timeout fired [cycles]		
	case 1	case 2	case 3
empty	9	9	9
array	8521	14121	4521
individual array	2821	5721	1821
individual	1210	3810	510

and thus, causes a waste of 100 bytes of RAM memory, due to alignment of each *variable_t* structure on the boundary of the processor word.

Another important parameter of a representation is the time it requires for checking if the stored values are still valid. Table 4.4 presents the measurements for the complexity of the validation check done by the *var_timeouterFired()* function for each representation. This parameter is very important, since this validation check routine is called periodically and its complexity influences the performance of the complete system. The presented measurements show the timings for three cases. The first case is the case, where all timeout counters of all instances are decremented and tested, but none instance has to be invalidated. The second case is similar to the first one, but all the instances are invalidated, thus, this is the worst case. The third case is the best case, all counters are already clear and none of them is decremented or tested. It represents the situation, where all instances are already invalid. These measurements specify the spectrum of the costs of executing the *var_timeouterFired()* function, depending on the dynamic state of the storage in each representation. The values for case 3 are the best case, where those for case 2 represent the worst case. The average cost is influenced by multiple factors and is hard to predict due to high spread of the potential dynamics of the system.

In a situation, where none of the variables has a defined timeout period, the tinyDSM pre-compiler generates an empty *var_timeouterFired()* function. The costs of calling an empty function are given by the measurements taken for the empty storage. Calling a function without parameters and return value requires nine clock cycles on the examined hardware platform. Such senseless behaviour can be optimized by the compiler, but in order to reduce the influence of such optimizations on the measurements, the compiler is not working in an aggressive optimization mode.

These measurements show that the spectrum of performance and complexity can be very broad, depending on the chosen internal representation of the *local variables and metadata* storage. They also show that the individual-array is the most preferred representation for this storage. It combines small memory footprint with efficiency. The array representation is actually out-performed by the individual-array representation in every of the measured parameters.

But, if the RAM memory usage is the predominant objective, it may be reasonable to go for the individual representation. This applies especially for specific configurations with few variables with large types and many with small types. If the RAM memory overhead, generated by using the common *value_t* for storing the values for all variables, is not acceptable, but additional code size is not a problem, the individual representation is the best choice. The access functions of individual and individual-array representations are comparable, but the validation check for the former requires in average only half of the time needed for the latter.

Another important advantage of the individual representation is that it allows defining arbitrary identities of the variables. This feature can be used to increase the flexibility of the tinyDSM middleware, e.g., by defining shared variables shared between different configurations for different systems. In order to provide the arbitrary identities of the variables in the array based representations a function that maps these identities to the indices is necessary.

The external variables and history

The *external variables and history* storage contains the instances of all foreign entities the node decided to replicate or was forced by the policy to do so. It also contains the history of these entities, as well as the history of all own entities. The size of the history for the entities of each variable is defined by the **replication_history** policy parameter. Since multiple instances of the same entity may coexist in this storage, these are ordered and distinguished by the *timestamp* field. Thus, the informational function of the *timestamp* field, as it was in the *local variables and metadata* storage, is in case of the *external variables and history* storage enhanced with the ordinal meaning.

Listing 4.23 provides a SQL like description of the storage. Three fields have the data addressing function, i.e., the actual data, stored in the *value* field, is located using the identity of the variable, the address of the owner and the timestamp. The optional counter in the *timeout* field allows checking the validity of the stored value.

Due to its potential high storage demand, the *external variables and history* structure is closely coupled with the permanent data storage. It is actually a management layer on top of the flash memory functionality provided by the operating system and indirectly by the OS adaptation layer.

The internal structure of the storage can be realized in many ways and again, to make the core of the tinyDSM middleware independent from the actual realization, the *external variables and history* storage has a defined functional interface (see Listing 4.24). The interface consists of two immediate return functions that provide the information on the state of storage (*ext_isBusy()*) and on the content of the stor-

```
CREATE TABLE external_variables_and_history(
    var_id      INTEGER NOT NULL,
    owner       INTEGER NOT NULL,
    timestamp   INTEGER NOT NULL,
    value       INTEGER NOT NULL,
    timeout     INTEGER,

    PRIMARY KEY (var_id, owner, timestamp)
);
```

Listing 4.23: A SQL like description of the external variables and history structure

```
bool ext_isInStorage(request_t* data);
bool ext_isBusy(void);

error_t ext_set(request_t* data);
error_t ext_get(request_t* data);

void ext_setDone(request_t *data, error_t result);
void ext_getDone(request_t *data, error_t result);
```

Listing 4.24: The functional interface of the external variables and history storage

age (*ext_isInStorage()*) and two pairs of split-phase functions to read (*ext_get()* and *ext_getDone()*) and write (*ext_set()* and *ext_setDone()*) the data. These functions operate on the elements of the request buffer and store or read the instances contained or described in these.

As already mentioned, the storage is coupled with the underlying flash memory layer. This was the reason for the access to the stored data to be realized in the split phase manner. The flash memory devices may require more time for accessing their content, what, together with additional management time and accesses, could result in enormous blocking of the system. The *ext_isBusy()* function is used to control the parallelization of the accesses, depending on the capabilities of the underlying hardware and software layer.

The *ext_isInStorage()* function provides the information if any instances of a chosen entity are available in the storage. It only informs that the combination of identity of a variable *(var_id)* and the address of the owner of the entity *(addr)* exist in the storage, without providing any information about the values or their corresponding timestamps or versions.

One of the most important features of the flash storage is the data persistence. It helps to keep the data, even if the node encountered some temporal energy problems that led it to a reset and the content of the RAM memory is lost. But, in order to be able to interpret the data in the flash memory in the correct way, it is necessary to create a recovery strategy that allows the node to restore its knowledge, after a reset. The common part of all the recovery strategies is specifying a fixed place in the flash storage that stores the information about the last known state of the data. As already mentioned, the flash memory is in general slower than the RAM memory. The greater access time is caused by the fact that the data is not available at place, but needs to be accessed, e.g., via a serial interface. Additionally, it requires additional management layer to cope with the erasing of the blocks, before the memory can be written. Actually, this nature of the flash memory causes the most of the problems and management overhead. But, since there is no cheap alternative for flash to date, it is necessary to cope with that, using more elaborated management layers.

In general, there are two approaches, either avoiding the use of the RAM memory for storing the temporal extract of the state, or creating an additional structure in flash to store the state of the data each time it changes. Both these approaches have advantages and disadvantages. Storing some of the management data in RAM results in faster operation, but induces storing more data as the state changes and causes the system to be more vulnerable to failures caused by the state loss. There is a trade-off between dependability and performance. Storing the data in a structure entirely in flash may cause huge delays caused by the traversing through the flash storage to find the requested data.

An ideal solution is to combine the two approaches, i.e., having a standalone and self-contained flash storage with a defined recovery point and integrated management data combined with a helper management structure in RAM memory to speed-up the access to the data. The huge advantage of such a solution is that the size of the helper data can be adapted to the needs of the application and to the available resources, i.e., according to the application requirements and definition, as well as to the dynamic environment, the helper data can be constructed to provide the best performance with the available amount of RAM memory, but it can be also completely left out. Additionally, if the data in RAM is lost it can also be recovered from the structure of the data in flash, if necessary.

The instances stored in the *external variables and history* storage can be represented as a three-dimensional matrix of values, where the coordinates are represented by the other fields of the instance; the identities of the variables *(var_id)*, the address of the owner *(addr)* and the timestamp or version of the instance *(timestamp)*. The complete matrix represents the total knowledge of the network. The size of the *var_id* dimension of the matrix is fixed and specified by the configuration, i.e., by the definitions of the shared variables. For dynamic networks the *addr* dimension may change with time, some nodes may disappear, some new may appear. The *timestamp* dimension grows with time. The data available on a single node represents only a part of the total knowledge. Figure 4.13 visualizes a storage with historical data of five entities of two

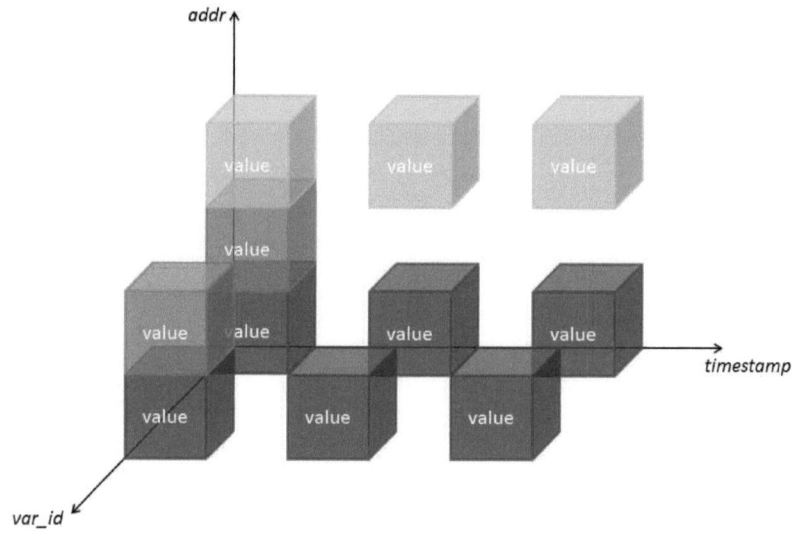

Figure 4.13: The 3D visualization of the external variables and history storage

variables belonging to three nodes. It shows that it is not necessary for the matrix to be full.

In order to store the matrix in the one-dimensional flash memory, it is necessary to find the optimum serialization of the matrix, which does not require traversing through the complete memory to find the requested data. There are many solutions that provide different flexibility and performance figures. One of them is creating a three dimensional data structure based on linked lists (see Figure 4.14). Due to the erasing of the flash memory, which is possible only in blocks, the most natural way to store the data in the flash memory is a circular buffer consisting of multiple erase blocks. The instances are stored in structures of the *flashdata_t* type (see Listing 4.25). Thus, each requires the same and a priori known amount of memory. In the *flashdata_t* structure the instance of the variable is extended by the flags field and three flash pointers, i.e., three addresses in the flash memory address space. These pointers are used to create the links between the data in the matrix. The constants presented in Listing 4.26 are used by the *flags* field to indicate that the structure is not the last in a given dimension, i.e., to indicate that its pointers are pointing at other structures. During the erasing process, the values of all flash memory cells in the erased block are set to ones. For every single cell this value can be changed to zero during writing.

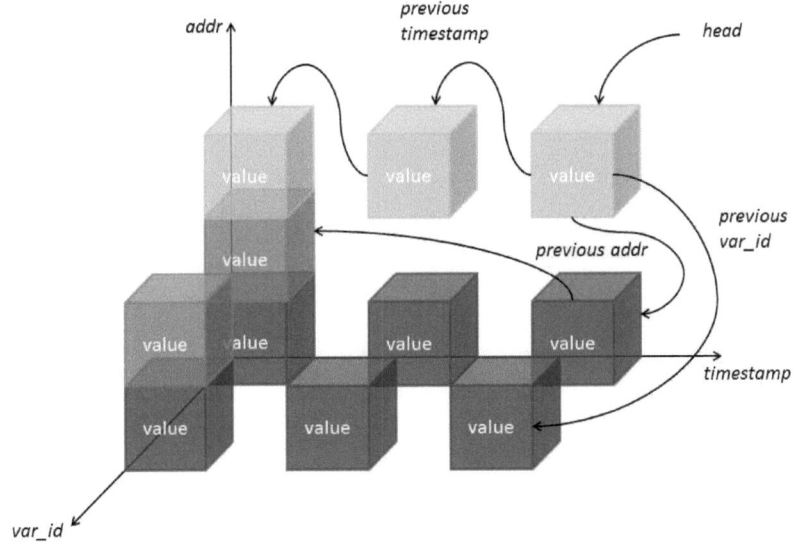

Figure 4.14: Serialization of the three dimensional matrix–a sketch

Using this feature, it is possible to update the value that is written in the *flags* field, to remove the connection to the previous structure in the chosen dimensions.

These *flashdata_t* structures are stored in the circular buffer starting from its first address. The first stored structure cannot point at anything. Thus, its pointers are deactivated in the *flags* field. As new instances are stored in the storage, their pointers in the *flashdata_t* are set to point at the right structures already stored or are deactivated, if there is no structure to point at, in the particular dimension.

On a read or write access, it is necessary to find the preceding instances in the three dimensions. Finding the right structure requires traversing through the already stored ones. To optimize this process a helper structure in RAM memory can be used. The minimum set of management data in RAM consists of the pointer to the most recently stored structure *(head)* and the address of the oldest structure *(last)*. Based on these two addresses, it is possible to calculate the remaining memory size.

A clean-up strategy specifies the behaviour in case the amount of remaining memory is smaller than a defined threshold. The simplest strategy in this case is just cleaning the erase block with the oldest instances and removing the connections to these from the remaining structures. Other strategies include conservation of some data from the erase block to be cleared.

```
typedef struct flashdata_t{
  var_id_t var_id;
  node_addr_t addr;
  ts_t timestamp;
  value_t value;
  uint32_t prev_var_id;
  uint32_t prev_addr;
  uint32_t prev_timestamp;
  uint8_t flags;
} flashdata_t;
```

Listing 4.25: Definition of the *flashdata_t* structure type

```
enum flashdata_flags{
  HAS_PREV_VAR_ID      = 0x01,
  HAS_PREV_ADDR        = 0x02,
  HAS_PREV_TIMESTAMP   = 0x04,
  IS_VALID             = 0x08
};
```

Listing 4.26: Constants used for the *flags* field in the *flashdata_t* structure type

Since the instances of entities are stored in series, it is reasonable to specify the requested size of the history for each entity, i.e., the required and allowed amount of instances. This helps to protect the flash from being filled by unnecessary data. If the amount of data stored in the flash memory reaches a threshold, during the clean-up the requested size of the history helps to decide how many instances of each entity shall be kept. The array of values chosen for the **replication_history** policy parameter specifies the history size for every hop distance from the source node. The policy may additionally specify the way the specific instances from the stored ones are chosen to be kept. For instance, instead of keeping only the last values of some entity, it may be reasonable to keep the history of the changes over the entire time, e.g., by computing average values for interpolated timestamps over the available data. This decision is specified by the data retention strategies. Currently, tinyDSM only supports keeping the most recent instances, as defined by the **replication_history** policy parameter.

If a variable has a defined timeout period, the instances of its entities have to be monitored if they are still valid. However, in case of the *external variables and history* storage, a periodic check of all the stored instances is not reasonable. Instead, the stored instances are checked during the read and clean-up operations, based on the value in the *timestamp* field and the current time. The invalid instances are simply marked as not valid, using the *flags* field (see Listing 4.26).

4.5.3 The communication interfaces

The tinyDSM middleware uses radio and serial communication. These are used for different purposes. The radio is the primary communication means and is used for the inter node communication. In contrast, the serial interface is used to connect to and communicate with devices not capable to use the primary channel, like a PC or PDA, allowing these to access the data stored in the network.

The tinyDSM middleware uses the radio interface to exchange its messages between nodes. These messages are extracts of the requests represented by the *request_t* structure and contain only the data required to be transmitted. Actually, the content of the message depends on the operation the request represents, but currently, the same format of the packet is defined for all operations. It is defined by the *radiodata_t* structure type presented in Listing 4.27. The structure contains all the data required to transfer all the requests possible in the tinyDSM middleware. The fields in the structure contain the same data, as their corresponding fields in the *request_t* structure.

```
typedef struct radiodata_t {
  uint8_t operation:3;
  uint8_t opflags:3;
  var_id_t var_id;
  node_addr_t addr;
  ts_t timestamp;
  value_t value;
  error_t result;
  reqno_t reqno;
  node_addr_t reqSrcAddr;
  hops_t hops;
  node_no_t noACKS;
  node_no_t noNACKS;
} radiodata_t;
```

Listing 4.27: Definition of the *radiodata_t* structure type

Having one structure that holds all message types simplifies the handling of the radio packets and unifies the transmission costs for all requests, but is not optimal regarding the amount of data that is transmitted over the medium. In order to limit the size of the data packets to the absolute minimum, an alternative *radiodata_t* structure like, the one presented in Listing 4.28 can be used. It consists of three parts. The first is the fixed data part consisting of the *operation, opflags, reqno* and *reqSrcAddr* fields. These fields are used in all the requests. The second part is the *contentflags* field that contains flags that indicate the actual content (and the size) of the third part–the byte array containing the data of the required set of fields for the given request. And since the data is put into the byte array one after another and only the required data fields from the original *radiodata_t* type are used, it is possible to send packets with

```
typedef struct radiodata_t {
  uint8_t operation:3;
  uint8_t opflags:3;
  reqno_t reqno;
  node_addr_t reqSrcAddr;
  uint8_t contentflags;
  uint8_t data[sizeof(var_id_t) +
               sizeof(node_addr_t) +
               sizeof(ts_t) +
               sizeof(value_t) +
               sizeof(error_t) +
               sizeof(hops_t) +
               sizeof(node_no_t) +
               sizeof(node_no_t)];
} radiodata_t;
```

Listing 4.28: Example definition of an alternative *radiodata_t* structure type

the most optimum size. Before a packet is sent, the request needs to be analysed, the required fields are inserted into the data field and their corresponding flags are set in the *contentflags* field. This solution allows reducing the amount of sent data, but requires parsing the content of the data array to access the fields of the request stored in it. And, since the data is decomposed into a standard *request_t* structure on reception, it is further possible to avoid sending fields with value equal to zero.

Measurements were taken, in order to evaluate the advantages and costs of the alternative *radiodata_t* structure, compared to the fixed size version. The different request types require different fields to be transmitted (see Table 4.5). And since none of the requests require the complete set of fields, the size of the transmitted messages can be optimized. The *ALT* request column represents the fixed and optional fields that can be used in the alternative *radiodata_t* structure. The *FIXED* request column represents the *radiodata_t* with the fixed size, where all the fields are transmitted by default.

As already mentioned, the alternative version of the *request_t* structure was constructed this way that the data required by all the requests is send in individual fields of the structure and the optional data is stored in the *data* field with a variable length. This approach requires encoding of the request into a *radiodata_t* structure to be transmitted and decoding in a request from a received *radiodata_t* structure. In case of the fixed size *radiodata_t* structure the encoding and decoding corresponds to the copying of *request_t* fields into the *radiodata_t* structure and vice versa. The final size of the message to be sent and the actual complexity of the encoding and decoding depend on the sizes of the types specified by the current tinyDSM configuration. In order to take the measurements the types were specified as provided in Listing 4.29.

Table 4.5: Message fields required by the tinyDSM requests

Required fields	Request message							
	GET	SET	UPD	ANS	SACK	UACK	ALT	FIXED
operation	+	+	+	+	+	+	+	+
opflags	-	-	O	-	-	-	+	+
Reqno	+	+	+	+	+	+	+	+
reqSrcAddr	+	+	+	+	+	+	+	+
var_id	+	+	+	-	-	-	O	+
Addr	O	O	+	O	O	-	O	+
timestamp	O	-	+	+	+	-	O	+
Value	-	+	+	+	-	-	O	+
Result	-	-	-	+	+	+	O	+
Hops	O	O	O	O	O	O	O	+
noACKS	-	-	-	-	-	O	O	+
noNACKS	-	-	-	-	-	O	O	+
Required: + Not required: - Optional: O								

The minimum and maximum size of the message for these defined types on the IHPNode hardware platform, are provided in Table 4.6, for each kind of request. This range is caused by the fact, that some of the fields are optional in the request, e.g., while issuing a read request, it is possible to specify the desired timestamp of the instance to be read, but it is optional. Additionally, if a field is required but its value is zero then it is not transmitted and is decoded as zero.

The absolute minimum and maximum size of the alternative *radiodata_t* is given in the *ALT* column. None of the requests can go below this minimum and it can also be seen that none of them requires the maximum. The fixed size *radiodata_t* structure requires always the same amount of data to be sent. Due to the combination of the type sizes the maximum alternative *radiodata_t* is equal to the size of the fixed version, even that it has an additional field–the *contentflags*.

The measurements show that the size of the fixed size message can be reduced to less than one third, i.e., only 7 bytes compared to 24 bytes. However, this reduction causes higher processing costs. Table 4.6 provides also the minimum and maximum number of clock cycles needed for encoding and decoding. Copying the fields from *request_t* structure to the fixed size *radiodata_t* (encoding) requires 178 clock cycles; decoding requires 183 clock cycles. For the alternative *radiodata_t* structure the maximum encoding cost is equal to 474 cycles, which is less than three times of the cost for the fixed size structure. In case of the maximum decoding cost, for the alternative structure, this ratio is even smaller–it is slightly above two. For the UACK requests, the minimum

```
typedef uint16_t node_addr_t;
typedef uint16_t node_no_t;
typedef uint32_t ts_t;
typedef uint32_t value_t;
typedef uint8_t  var_id_t;
typedef uint16_t reqno_t;
typedef uint16_t timeout_t;
typedef uint8_t  hops_t;
typedef uint8_t  bufsize_t;
typedef uint8_t  error_t;
```

Listing 4.29: Example type definitions for the message size related measurements

Table 4.6: Measured size of request messages and the complexity of request encoding and decoding

Measured parameter	Request message							
	GET	SET	UPD	ANS	SACK	UACK	ALT	FIXED
Size [Bytes]								
minimum	8	12	18	15	11	7	7	24
maximum	15	15	19	19	15	13	24	24
Encoding ($request\_t -> radiodata\_t$) [clock cycles]								
minimum	218	299	426	321	240	167	167	178
maximum	393	401	474	471	390	374	633	178
Decoding ($radiodata\_t -> request\_t$) [clock cycles]								
minimum	198	261	371	285	222	159	159	183
maximum	348	348	411	412	349	334	546	183

encoding and decoding costs are even below these for the fixed size structure.

These measurements, combined with the computation and data transmission costs for the IHPNode hardware platform, show that for a real world application the alternative *radiodata_t* structure is the only choice. The additional costs for the encoding and decoding are fully covered by the savings due to the reduction of the message sizes.

The serial interface is used to allow devices, not able to communicate with the nodes in the radio communication channel, to access the data stored in the network. This interface is a kind of extension to the functional interface provided to the application layer on the node, i.e., it allows issuing requests and receiving replies to these. The device connected to the node constructs the requests using the fields in the *serialdata_t* structure presented in Listing 4.30. This structure type is also used to store the replies. The complete handling of the request happens on the node that plays the role of a gateway. All the requests are sent to the network on behalf of the gateway node. After the request is handled and a reply is available, the reply is provided back to the requester device, using the serial interface.

```
typedef struct serialdata_t{
  uint8_t operation;
  var_id_t var_id;
  node_addr_t addr;
  ts_t timestamp;
  value_t value;
  error_t result;
} serialdata_t;
```

Listing 4.30: The definition of the *serialdata_t* structure type

The serial interface allows partial moving of the application logic to the device connected to the gateway node. However, the interface does not provide all the features of the functional interface of the tinyDSM middleware.

Currently, it is only possible to process the requests issued via the serial interface one after another. It is not possible to handle a new request, until the current request is processed and a reply is issued. In order to support parallel processing of requests, the request number should be transmitted back to the device and the number should be included in the reply.

The serial interface is currently a pure pull interface, i.e., it is not possible to receive notifications on event detection via the serial interface. The states of the event variables can be queried. A push service in the middleware on the gateway node also requires identification of requests to avoid misinterpreting the pushed data on the external device. It also requires a mechanism to enable and disable the pushing of the data. All these mechanisms are possible extensions to the current tinyDSM implementation.

4.5.4 The Replication Logic module

The *replication logic* module consists of functions that control the behaviour of the middleware, while handling of the instances of the variables. These functions are generated by the tinyDSM pre-compiler according to the values chosen for each defined variable for the policy parameters introduced in Section 4.4. These functions are listed in Listing 4.31. The functionality they provide requires diverse input parameters, but in general, these functions are based on the information about the kind of the request and the variable in question. Thus, it is reasonable to use the elements from the request buffer as parameters for most of these functions. They are to be used in the core of the tinyDSM middleware and they are, de facto, the interface to the virtual policy module. Their dependencies on policy parameters are given in Section 4.4.

The replication logic functions can be split into two groups. They are either logic or parametric, i.e., they support some logical decisions on handling of the given request or they provide some parameters for the given request according to the policy of the given variable.

The Boolean values returned by the logic functions influence the flow of the processing of the requests. The *repLogic_isAllowedToWrite()* and *repLogic_isAllowedToRead()* functions inform, if the source of the request is allowed to perform the corresponding operation on the given entity of the variable. The *repLogic_shallBeSent()* states, if the given request shall be transmitted using the radio and the *repLogic_shallBeAcked()*, if it requires sending an acknowledgment message. The *repLogic_shallBeStored()* defines, if the data in the request shall be locally stored in the *external variables and history* storage. This decision is taken for the *UPDATE* requests for both own and foreign instances of variables. The *repLogic_isTsInRange()* function is used by *GET* requests with a specified desired timestamp. Based on the tolerance of timestamp comparison, according to the policy for a given variable, this function checks if the timestamp to be checked, is acceptable for the request. The *repLogic_answerNotLocalGets()* specifies, if a *GET* about a foreign entity of a variable shall be answered and the *repLogic_shallForward()*, if the request in question shall be forwarded to other nodes, if the data it is about, is not available locally.

```
bool  repLogic_isAllowedToWrite(request_t *data);
bool  repLogic_isAllowedToRead(request_t *data);
bool  repLogic_shallBeSent(request_t *data);
bool  repLogic_shallBeAcked(request_t *data);
bool  repLogic_shallBeStored(request_t *data);
bool  repLogic_isTsInRange(request_t *data, ts_t tsToCheck);
bool  repLogic_answerNotLocalGets(request_t *data);
bool  repLogic_shallForward(request_t *data);

void  repLogic_setTimestamp(request_t *data)
void  repLogic_setBufferTimeout(request_t *data);
void  repLogic_setRetriesCount(request_t *data);

uint8_t  repLogic_historySize(request_t *data);
bool  repLogic_requestedUpdateCount(request_t *data);
```

Listing 4.31: The functions of the Replication Logic module

The parametric functions can be further divided into two groups. The first group consists of the *repLogic_setTimestamp()*, the *repLogic_setBufferTimeout()* and the *repLogic_setRetriesCount()*. These functions set their corresponding fields of the *request_t* structure, according to the policy chosen for the variable the request in question is about. The *repLogic_historySize()* that belongs to the other group directly returns the defined amount of instances in the history for a given entity of a variable. This amount may vary depending on the distance from the owner of the data, determined by the hops field in the *request_t* structure.

The *repLogic_requestedUpdateCount()* function is both, logic and parametric. It counts the number of acknowledgement messages for a given local *UPDATE* request and returns true, if the amount of them reached the value requested by the policy parameter.

4.5.5 The Event Logic module

The main component of the event logic module is the *eventLogic_evaluate()* function (see Listing 4.32). It is generated by the tinyDSM pre-compiler based on the event equations, as well as on the initialization equations of the non-event variables.

```
void eventLogic_evaluate(request_t *data);
```

Listing 4.32: The functional interface of the Event Logic module

All the logic and arithmetic operations, the equations consist of, are converted by the tinyDSM compiler to their corresponding function constructs. The compiler generates the internal function *evalDD()* (see Listing 4.33) that operates on two parameters of the *eval_t* type (see Listing 4.34) and applies a chosen relation on the value fields of these as long as they are valid. The set of supported operations is produced by the tinyDSM pre-compiler after parsing the equations and includes all arithmetic and logic operations used in these. The *evalDD()* function is used by two helper functions, *evalVD()* and *evalVV()* (see Listing 4.33) that operate either on one shared variable and one immediate value or two shared variables, respectively. These are used in the functional constructs that represent the equations in the *eventLogic_evaluate()*.

```
eval_t evalDD(eval_t va, eval_t vb, uint8_t relation);
eval_t evalVD(request_t *data, var_id_t avid, eval_t vb,
        uint8_t relation);
eval_t evalVV(request_t *data, var_id_t avid,
        var_id_t bvid, uint8_t relation);
```

Listing 4.33: Functions used for constructing the evaluated equations in the Event Logic

```
typedef struct eval_t{
  bool valid;
  value_t value;
} eval_t;
```

Listing 4.34: The definition of the *eval_t* structure type

The *eventLogic_evaluate()* function is called each time a new instance is created or received. This function evaluates all the equations, the variable, the instance belongs to, is a term of. If any of the terms of an equation if not available locally, the equation is not further evaluated. As the equations are evaluated, the function changes the values of the event and non-event variables and, if necessary, it triggers the *event()* callback function to notify the application. As already mentioned, the *event()* function is to be registered at the core of the tinyDSM middleware using the *tinyDSM_registerEventHandler()* function from the middleware interface. The parameters of the *event()* function inform the application about the current value of the given event variable and about the instance that caused the notification (see Listing 4.35).

```
void event( var_id_t event_id , bool evalue , var_id_t var_id ,
            value_t value , node_addr_t addr , ts_t timestamp );
```
Listing 4.35: The *event()* function

4.5.6 The operations

All the above mentioned components are involved in the processing of requests. And as already mentioned, there are two types of application requests. The read and write operations, issued from the application logic or from an external device, allow data exchange in the tinyDSM based system. This section shows, how the above mentioned components interact during the request processing and how they are bound into one system.

In order to monitor the state of the tinyDSM middleware, chosen places in the source code are identified by state marks. Since the tinyDSM middleware is a complex and parallel state machine, the places in the code in combination with the data that reached the given point, constitute to the picture of the current state of the system. This information can be used during simulation and debugging on real nodes and provides the details on the execution of the program and the progress of the request processing. There are several groups of states, depending on the functionality they monitor. These are presented in the state diagrams mentioned in this section.

The probably most fundamental are the request buffer state diagrams presented in Figure 4.15 and Figure 4.16. They present the possible state transitions for the complete lifetime of a request in the request buffer. The allocation of an element of the buffer, to store the request, is indicated by the **BUF1** state for local requests and by the **BUF2** state, for external ones. If there is no room left in the part of the buffer responsible for storing the given request, a transition to state **BUF5**, for a local request or to **BUF6**, for an external one, occurs. The states **BUF3** and **BUF4** indicate, that the allocation was successful. From now on, the buffer element stores the content of the request and may be used to show the progress of the request processing. The lifetime of a request in the buffer ends with releasing the buffer element, indicated by the state **BUF9**, as soon as the processing of the request is completed. It may also happen, that

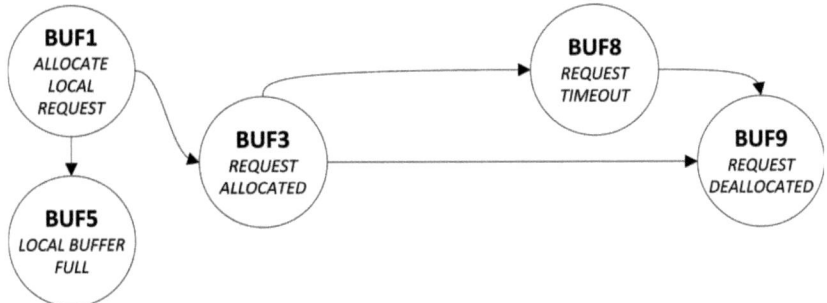

Figure 4.15: State diagram for the request buffer–local request

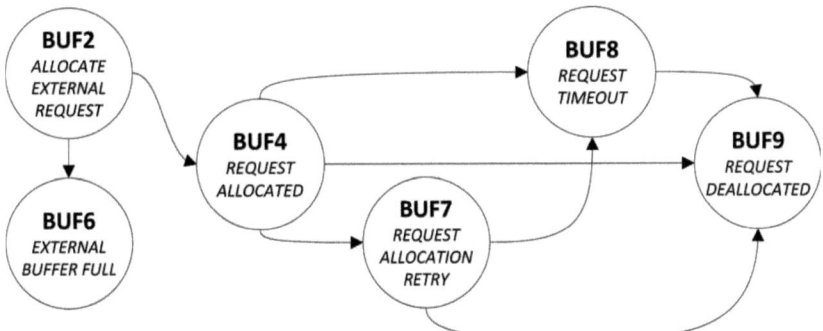

Figure 4.16: State diagram for the request buffer–external request

the defined timeout period elapses, before the request is processed. Such situation is indicated by the **BUF8** state and interrupts the further processing of the request. The *reqstate* field is cleared and the *result* field is set to *ETIMEOUT*.

Before trying to allocate an element in the buffer to store an external request, a check using the *reqBuf_isRequestInBuffer()* function is performed. If the request is detected as already present in the request buffer, then the fact is indicated by the **BUF7** state.

The following two state diagrams, shown in Figure 4.17, are the state diagrams of the accesses to the *external variables and history* storage. The access demand is signaled by setting the *REQBUF_WAIT4STOR* flag in the *reqstate* field of the *request_t* structure that contains the processed request. The **EX1** and **EX4** states indicate the start of a write and a read access, respectively. After the access started, the *REQBUF_WAIT4STORREP* flag is set and the *REQBUF_WAIT4STOR* flag is cleared. The split-phase access to the storage can result either in a success, represented by the states **EX2** and **EX5** or a failure, represented by states **EX3** and **EX6**. As soon as

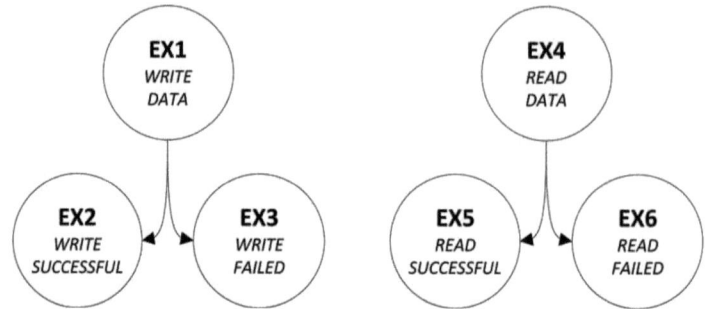

Figure 4.17: The *external variables and history* storage access state diagrams

the result of the access is available, the *REQBUF_WAIT4STORREP* flag is cleared.

The notification state diagram is shown in Figure 4.18. As soon as the request, processed on the local node, is handled locally, there may be a need, to provide the result, of the request processing, to the request source. As it is shown, there are three possible notification channels that correspond to the source of the request; the serial interface, the functional interface and the radio interface. In case of the first two, the notification is mandatory. For the radio interface, it is possible to skip the notifications for specific requests, to reduce communication costs. The state **NOT1** indicates the start of the notification process. Transition to one of the states; **NOT2**, **NOT3** or **NOT4**, reveals the interface, used for the notification. For the serial port and radio communication, it is also possible, that the delivery of the notification fails, after a number of retransmission approaches. This situation is expressed by the transition to state **NOT5** and results in aborting the notification. This maximum retransmission number is specified by the *retries* field in the *request_t* structure, according to the **local_request_retries** and **external_request_retries** policy parameters.

The transmission state diagram is presented in Figure 4.19. It describes the inter node communication, i.e., the complete request and reply exchange. In the data transmission, there is always one sender involved, but there may be multiple receivers.

The transmission starts in the **TR1** state with the demand to send a message containing the tinyDSM request. The demand is indicated by the *REQBUF_WAIT4SEND* flag, set in the *reqstate* field of the *request_t* structure containing the request. If the sender expects a reply message, the *REQBUF_WAIT4SENDREP* flag is set as well. If the sending of the message was not possible and failed, in the **TR6** state the sender decides, based on the counter in the *retries* field, if the sending approach shall be repeated. If it is not the case, a transition to state **TR7** occurs, the sending of the message is aborted and the *result* field of the *request_t* is set to *ESENDFAIL*. If the sending was successful, the sender switches to the **TR5** state. On the reception of a

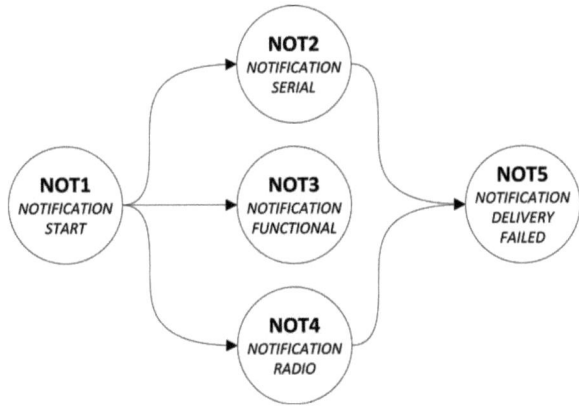

Figure 4.18: The notification state diagram

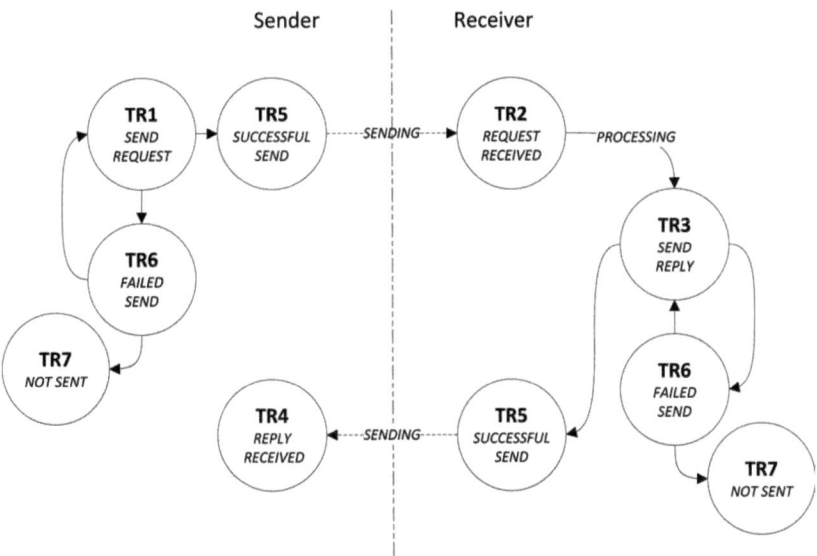

Figure 4.19: The transmission state diagram

request message, the receiver is in the **TR2** state. At that point, the request is available for processing on the receiver node. Depending on the type of the request, there may be a need to send a reply message back to the sender. The start of the sending of the reply message is identified by the state **TR3**. The states **TR5**, **TR6** and **TR7**, indicate the progress and the result of the sending approach, similar as it was for the sending of the request message. The reception of the reply message is identified by the state **TR4**–the request was successfully sent and acknowledged.

The above mentioned state diagrams describe the processing steps that are operation independent, i.e., they are applied in different operations, as necessary. But, in order to create the processing plan for an individual request, it is necessary to analyse each request regarding its specific requirements, the policy settings for the variable in question and the data available in the *local variables and metadata* storage. The flags in the *reqstate* field are set according to the results of this analysis. This step is realized in the initial processing phase. The initial processing phase is initiated by setting the *REQBUF_WAIT4INIT* flag in the *reqstate* field of the *request_t* structure.

Figure 4.20 presents the state diagram for the initial processing of a *GET* request. The **GET1** state indicates the start of the initial processing. At that initial point, the request is set to the default processing plan that includes both, access to the *external variables and history* storage and to the data on other nodes, over the radio communication. Thus, per default, all the flags in the *reqstate* field that indicate these processing steps, are set. Thus, the following transitions represent the restrictions that induce the changes in the further processing plan, until the final analysis result is available in state **GET7**. If none of the restriction applies, the default processing plan is realized.

State **GET2** indicates, that the read operation is not permitted. This decision is provided by the *repLogic_isAllowedToRead()* function, based on the policy for the variable. In the **GET2** state, the result field is set to *ENOTALLOWED* and the *reqstate* field is cleared.

If the request asks about data that is available in the *local variables and metadata* storage, then the request can be fulfilled immediately, what is indicated by the transition to the **GET3** state. Since this situation can happen for an entity of an array variable that is owned by the local node or a global variable, these checks require the knowledge from the metadata and may involve the *repLogic_isTsInRange()* function, as well. The occurrence of the **GET3** state indicates, that the request is actually already fulfilled, and any further accesses are unnecessary. Thus, after the data fields (*value*, *timestamp* and *addr*) are set, the result field is set to *SUCCESS* and the *reqstate* field is cleared.

The **GET4** state indicates, that the radio access was removed from the processing plan, i.e., the *REQBUF_WAIT4SEND* and *REQBUF_WAIT4SENDREP* flags were explicitly cleared. This means that the transmission of the request to other nodes is disabled. This situation occurs for requests from foreign nodes, where the policy, for the variable in question, disallows middleware layer forwarding of *GET* requests. This decision is provided by the *repLogic_shallForward()* function.

If a foreign node asks about an entity of a variable that is not owned by the local node, then the local node may check, if it has the data available in its *external vari-*

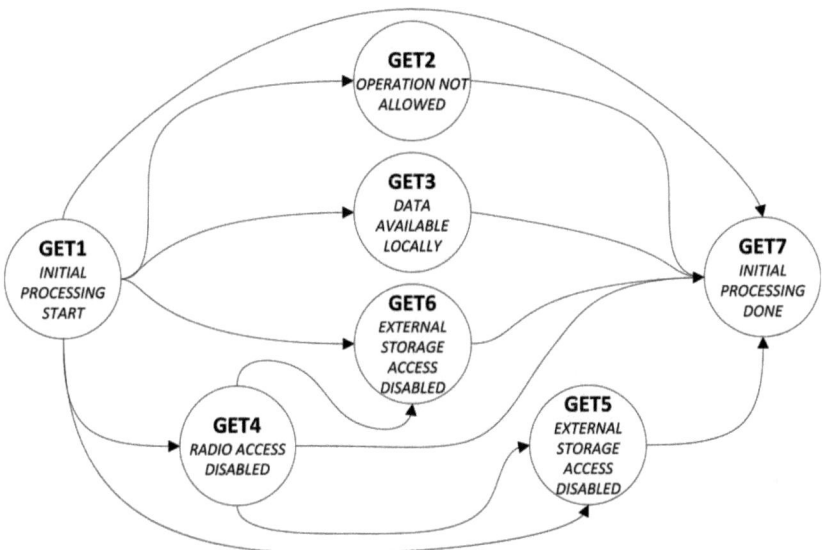

Figure 4.20: The state diagram for the initial processing of a GET request

ables and history storage. However, it is only allowed, if the policy, for the variable in question, allows that, i.e., the *repLogic_answerNotLocalGets()* function returns *true* for the current request. If it is not allowed, a transition to state **GET5** occurs, indicating, that the access to the storage is removed from the processing plan, i.e., the *REQBUF_WAIT4STOR* and *REQBUF_WAIT4STORREP* flags are explicitly cleared. These flags are also cleared, if the storage does not contain the requested data, what is indicated by the *ext_isInStorage()* function, by returning *false*. But, in this case a transition to state **GET6** occurs.

Figure 4.21 shows the state diagram for the initial processing of a *SET* request. For a *SET* request, the creation of the processing plan, is done in the opposite way, compared to the one for a *GET* request. At the starting point, indicated by the **SET1** state, the default processing plan includes no processing steps and it is extended depending on the result of the request analysis, to reach its final version in state **SET5**. The *result* field is set to *FAILED* per default. Thus, if no extension to the default, empty processing plan, happens, the request fails.

If the operation is not allowed, what is decided by the *repLogic_isAllowedToWrite()* function, a transition to **SET2** occurs. Similar to the case for a *GET* request, the *result* field is set to *ENOTALLOWED*, no further analysis is done and the request fails.

State **SET3** indicates, that the request was issued by the local node or the *rep-*

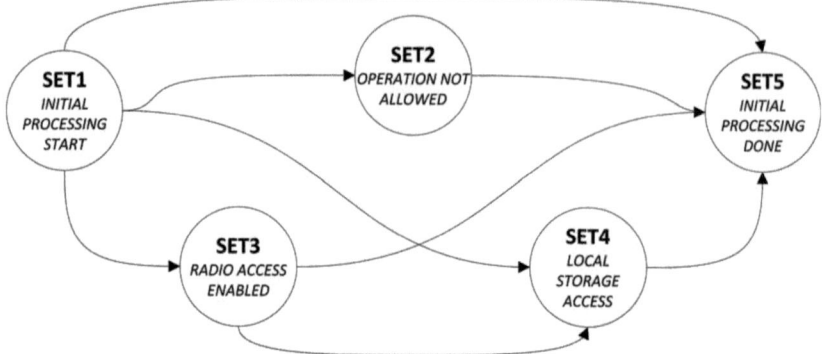

Figure 4.21: The state diagram for the initial processing of a SET request

Logic_shallForward() function allows forwarding of this *SET* request. Thus, the transmitting of the request over the radio is added to the request processing plan, i.e., the *REQBUF_WAIT4SEND* flag, in the *reqstate* field, is set. If, according to the result of the *repLogic_shallBeAcked()* function, the request requires an acknowledgment, then the *REQBUF_WAIT4SENDREP* flag is set as well.

A transition to the state **SET4** indicates, that the entity of the variable to be written, is owned by the local node or the variable is a global one without a defined owner. In this case, the local node marks the value to be written by a timestamp or version number, generated using the *repLogic_setTimestamp()* function, according to the chosen policy, sets itself as the owner of the entity and performs a write operation on the *local variables and metadata* storage. Further, the request operation is changed to *UPDATE* and the *reqstate* field is cleared. The *SET* request is accomplished and now the second phase of the *SET* request, i.e., the *UPDATE* request, is to be realized.

Figure 4.22 presents the state diagram for the initial processing of an *UPDATE* request. The request processing plan is created similar as it was done for a *SET* request. At the initial **UPD1** state, the default processing plan includes no processing steps and is extended, according to the result of the analysis of the request. The default value in the *result* field is *ENOTREPLICATED*. Again, if no extension to the default processing plan occurs, until the final **UPD5** state, the request fails and the data, it provides, is not replicated in the *external variables and history* storage on the local node and the request is also not send to other nodes.

As already mentioned, the *UPDATE* request is an internal request type generated by the middleware as a result of a *SET* request. Thus, since it is a part of a write operation, the *repLogic_isAllowedToWrite()* function decides, according to the policy of the variable, if the operation is permitted. If the operation is not allowed a transition to state **UPD2** occurs and the initial processing of the request is finished, after the

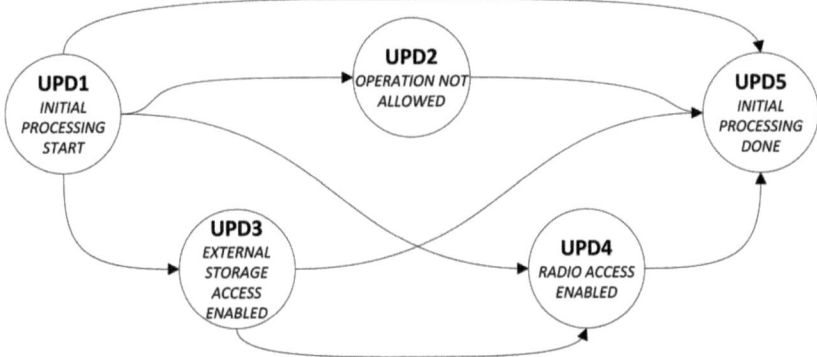

Figure 4.22: The state diagram for the initial processing of an UPDATE request

result field is set to *ENOTALLOWED*.

At that point, the new data is used to check, if it triggers any of the defined events, i.e., the *eventLogic_evaluate()* function is called. If the data caused a change to any of the event variables the *IFLAG_INTERESTING* is set in the *intflags* field for the request.

Based on the *intflags* field and the variable's policy, the *repLogic_shallBeStored()* function decides, if the data in the *UPDATE* request shall be locally stored in the *external variables and history* storage. This function controls the ratio between the setting of an entity and storing these changes in the storage, using the instance filtering mechanism introduced in Section 3.6. A positive decision is indicated by the transition to the **UPD3** state. In this case, the processing plan is extended by the access to the storage, i.e., the *REQBUF_WAIT4STOR* flag, in the *reqstate* field, is set.

For a locally stored instance of an own entity, the node may send an *UPDATE* request to other nodes, so they can update their copies of the entity. This decision is provided by the *repLogic_shallBeSent()* function. This function controls the ratio between the storing of the changes in the *external variables and history* storage of the owner and sending the *UPDATE* request to other nodes to update their storages–the second filter supported by the instance filtering mechanism. The positive decision is indicated by the **UPD4** state and causes setting the *REQBUF_WAIT4SEND* flag in the *reqstate* field of the request. If, according to the function *repLogic_shallBeAcked()*, the request requires an acknowledgment, then the *REQBUF_WAIT4SENDREP* flag is set as well. This function updates also the *opflags* field of the request, according to the policy for the given variable and following the chosen replication strategy.

For *UPDATE* requests issued by foreign nodes, the radio transmission may be also enabled, if the policy of the variable in question allows middleware layer forwarding of *UPDATE* requests. A positive decision, provided by the *repLogic_shallForward()*

function, triggers a transition to the **UPD4** state. The *REQBUF_WAIT4SEND* flag is set in the *reqstate* field and, if required by the *repLogic_shallBeAcked()* function, the *REQBUF_WAIT4SENDREP* flag is set as well.

After the initial processing phase, the request processing plan is created and needs to be applied. The state diagram in Figure 4.23 shows the possible steps in the processing of a request, as they were described in detail above and the possible transitions between these. It has to be noticed here, that the access to the *external variables and history* storage has higher priority than the radio access. Now, the mapping between the integrated request processing state diagram and the detailed individual state diagrams will be explained.

The request buffer state diagrams (see Figure 4.15 and Figure 4.16) span over **PROC1**, **PROC2** and **PROC8**. The states **PROC1** and **PROC2** include the request buffer allocation for local and external requests, respectively. The buffer element release occurs in **PROC8**. In **PROC2**, it is also checked, if an external request is already present in the request buffer. The request buffer element timeout is an event that is asynchronous to the processing–it is triggered by the external timer.

The initial processing state diagrams (see Figure 4.20, Figure 4.21 and Figure 4.22) are entirely included in the **PROC3** state. Similar applies for the *external variables and history* storage access state diagrams (see Figure 4.17); they are included in the **PROC4**. Additionally, in **PROC4**, if the read access to the storage was successful (state **EX5**), the *REQBUF_WAIT4SEND* and *REQBUF_WAIT4SENDREP* flags in the *reqstate* are cleared, because no radio access is required anymore.

The transmission state diagram (see Figure 4.19) is used in **PROC5**, **PROC5**, **PROC8** and **PROC7**, as shown in Figure 4.23. The **PROC8** state includes also the notification states shown in Figure 4.18.

A write operation from the application logic starts with a call to the *tinyDSM_set()* function, available at the interface the middleware provides to the application (see Listing 4.2). This function takes the identifier of the variable (*var_id*), the value to be set and the pointer to the address of the owner of the entity to be written (*addr*) as parameters. In case the variable is a global one or the own entity of an array variable shall be written, the *addr* parameter may be a NULL pointer. The function returns the request number or zero, if the issuing was not successful, e.g., because there was no room left for the request in the request buffer. The request number allows the application to match the reply with the corresponding request it issued. The replies for the write operations are provided by the middleware to the application using the callback function *tinyDSM_setDone()*, registered using the *tinyDSM_registerSetDone()* function from the functional interface.

The read operation starts with a call to the *tinyDSM_get()* function. It takes the identifier of the variable (*var_id*), the pointer to the address of the owner of the entity to

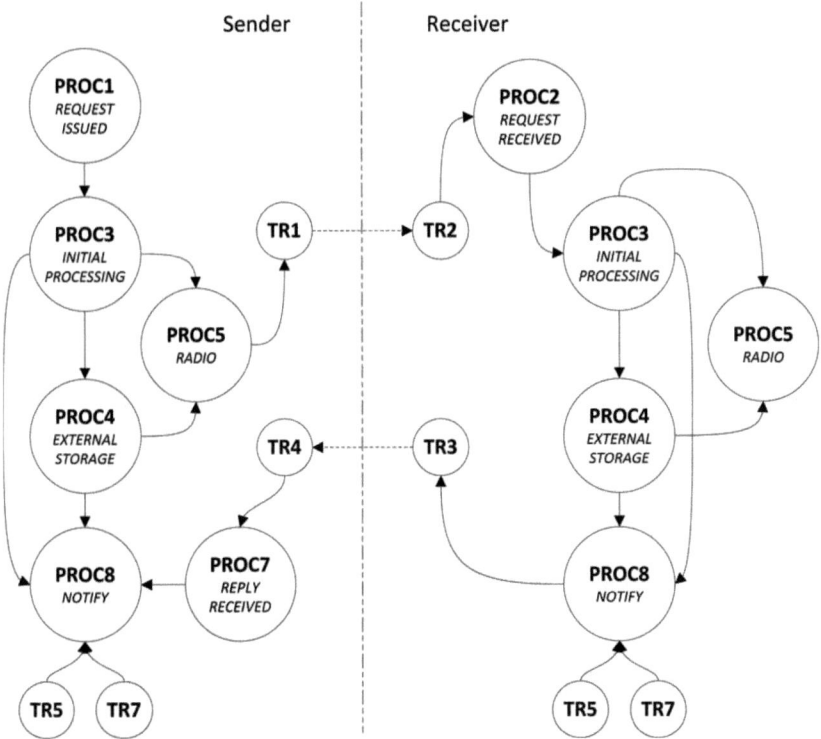

Figure 4.23: The request processing state diagram

be read (*addr*) and the desired *timestamp* of the value to read as parameters. The *addr* parameter may be set to NULL, if the variable is a global one or the own entity of an array variable shall be read. It the *timestamp* parameter is set to NULL, then the most recent value will be read. Again, to make it possible to match replies with the issued requests, the *tinyDSM_get()* function returns the number of the request. The replies for the read operations are provided to the application using the callback function *tinyDSM_getDone()*, registered using the *tinyDSM_registerGetDone()* function.

Similar applies for requests issued by the device connected to the node via the serial interface. The difference is, that the device has to construct the request on its own, i.e., it has to fill the *serialdata_t* structure with the data describing the request and send it to the node. As soon as the request is handled, the external device receives a reply message of the same format.

These descriptions show, that from the perspective of an application, the access to the tinyDSM middleware is easy and similar for both kinds of requests, as well as for both supported interfaces. However, internally, the two operations, read and write, differ significantly and also cause different messages to be exchanged between the nodes.

Chapter 5

Consistency Model Evaluation

This chapter discusses the memory consistency models, introduced in Section 2.2.2, in the WSN context and provides the implementations of the chosen models within the tinyDSM framework. These implementations are realized under the assumption, that the request propagation mechanism proposed in Section 3.1 provides the reliable broadcast functionality. But since this mechanism certainly does not provide all the features required by the reliable and atomic broadcast, the implementations and the mechanism itself, are evaluated in this respect. The implementations are also evaluated regarding their operation costs. As shown in Section 2.1.1, the main cost factor for a WSN is the amount of transmitted data and, maybe even more important, the amount of received data. Other cost factors are the memory required for code and local storage (flash and RAM), as well as the processing costs. Additionally, the data transmission and computations induce the fourth factor, i.e., delay.

5.1 The evaluation setup

For the evaluation a test network of 16 IHPNode nodes was chosen. The microcontrollers run at 1MHz clock speed and the nodes use the CC2500 and CC2520 radio transceivers to exchange the data. The nodes are working under the control of IHPOS operating system. The size of the network already involves multi-hop communication, but it is still feasible to handle the test results collected for the real nodes.

Figure 5.1 shows the topology of the network. The arrows represent the bidirectional links between the nodes and only nodes connected by these arrows can directly communicate. In a laboratory setup with small distances between nodes, even the weakest sending power of the radio transceiver causes all the nodes to overhear the data traffic. Thus, in order to provide the desired communication conditions, it was necessary to specify the network statically and extend the radio driver with a packet

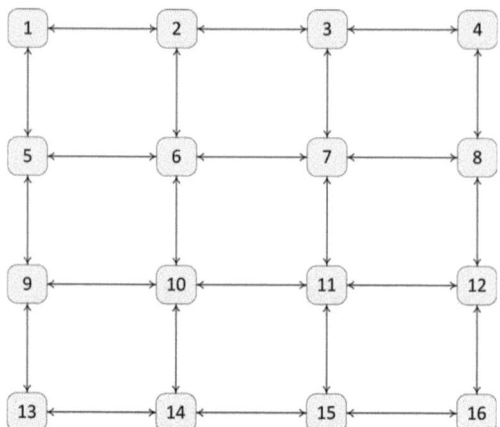

Figure 5.1: The topology of the network used for the evaluation on IHPNode nodes

filter that allows reception of messages only from a given set of nodes. This set is defined according to the topology shown in Figure 5.1.

In fact, the radio transceiver of each node receives messages from all other nodes. Thus, the actual conditions, regarding communication, are much more rigorous than it might be read from the given topology. This complicates the medium access and causes that the actual traffic is higher than the one observed by the layers on top of the radio filter on each node. Additionally, the ALOHA-like medium access (MAC) protocol, used by the CC2500 radio, does not provide any means to protect the data, it simply sends the data without checking the channel and without delivery verification. The CC2520 radio performs a clear channel assessment (CCA) check before sending the data. In this case, the ability to sense the communication between any nodes in the network, protects from the hidden terminal problem.

The choice of such a simple MAC protocol was influenced by the fact that the tinyDSM middleware shall work independent from the underlying protocol stack. It can use any protocol stack, but it shall not make any assumption about the quality of the services provided by the protocol stack. Thus, tests with specific and maybe more sophisticated MAC protocol would bias the results and would not show the results or problems in a full spectrum.

The measured time required by the radio driver, to transmit a single *radiodata_t* structure, is slightly below 5 ms, for the CC2500 and about 8 ms, for the CC2520. This is a quite large value, considering the size of the structure, which is only 20 Bytes and the configured data rate at 400 kbps, for the CC2500 and 250 kbps, for the CC2520. The large delay can be caused by frequent switching between radio states in the current radio drivers, as well as the CCA check.

Table 5.1: The content of the state notification data

Field	Description
timestamp	The local timestamp at the processing node.
state_id	The identifier of the state mark.
node_id	The address of the processing node.
operation	The operation of the processed request.
address	Address of the owner of the data item, the request is about.
result	The current result of the request processing.
req_no	The sequence number of the request at the issuing node.
req_src	The address of the issuing node.
hops	The number of hops the request should be forwarded.
noACKS	The cumulative number of positive acknowledgments. Applicable only for the replies to update requests.
msg_src	Address of the node that was the immediate sender of the request message.

The state marks, introduced in Section 4.5.6, are used to monitor the current state of the processing of each request on the nodes. When the processing of a request on a node reaches one of the defined states, the description of the state and the extract of the information on the request is collected together. This state data is then transferred using the serial interface, e.g., to a PC and can be further analysed in detail. In the test setup, all the nodes were connected via USB to a single PC, where a listener application was collecting the incoming state data and storing it in a text file. Section 4.5.6 explains the meaning of each state and presents the state diagrams to show the interdependencies of these states.

The chosen data set to represent a request state is shown in Table 5.1. The size of the data is 20 Bytes, but since the data is transmitted as text string, the actual data is 59 Bytes or 472 bits. Each byte of the state data is represented by the two characters of its hexadecimal textual representation. The bytes in the text string are additionally separated by colons, to simplify their interpreting.

The current driver for the serial port in the IHPOS blocks the processing during data transfer. Thus, to reduce overhead and to avoid the serial transmission to become a bottleneck, the serial interfaces of the nodes were configured to transmit the data at 1Mbps.

An example state chart for a read request is given in Figure 5.2. It shows the states during the processing of a read request issued by *node2* to *node1*, in the test network using the settings presented in Table 5.2. The processing of this particular request uses

Table 5.2: The initial settings chosen for the evaluation and the resulting parameters

Setting	Value
Radio	CC2500
Radio datarate	400 kbps
Serial datarate	1 Mbps
Defined variables	global variable A, $uint32\_t$
Replication Range	6 hops
Replication Density	100 %
Common timeout unit	250 ms
Request timeout	750 ms
Forwarding delay	10 ms * (node_id-1)% 4
Radio message transmission	5 ms
Serial state transmission	0.5 ms

the CC2500 radio and a single hop communication, so the request forwarding is not involved. The complete operation, starting with request buffer element allocation at the issuing node and ending with its releasing takes less than 200 ms. It is noticeable that the order of causally related states, like sending and receiving of the same message by the two nodes, is sometimes wrong. This is caused by the serialization of the state notifications generated in parallel on different nodes, necessary on the PC at the message reception time. Knowing that, e.g., for the reply message, the state **TR5** on *node1* shall precede the **TR4** on *node2*, allows correcting the chart and allows to verify the flow logically. However, this inaccuracy puts the timing results in question. Due to the lack of more accurate monitoring means, these timing results are used in the further discussion, but only for estimation purposes. Fortunately, the order of states observed on a single node reflects the actual order of their occurrence. Additionally, the inclusion of the local timestamps in the state data helps to estimate the correct order of the states on multiple nodes, to some extent. The clocks on different nodes are not synchronized, but run at about the same frequency, taking the allowed oscillator inaccuracy into account. Thus, comparing the time differences of states observed on a single node and having some states as anchors on different nodes, the order can be corrected.

Example state charts for write requests in a system with replicas are presented in Figure 5.3 and in Figure 5.4. Both these charts show the states monitored on two nodes, i.e., they show a write request performed locally by *node1* and issuing of the resulting update request received by *node2*, in the test network using the settings shown in Table 5.2. Figure 5.3 shows the case, where the update requests are only forwarded, without waiting for acknowledgments. This represents the plain update requests as mentioned in Section 3.2. In this case, the source of the request (*node1*) and the

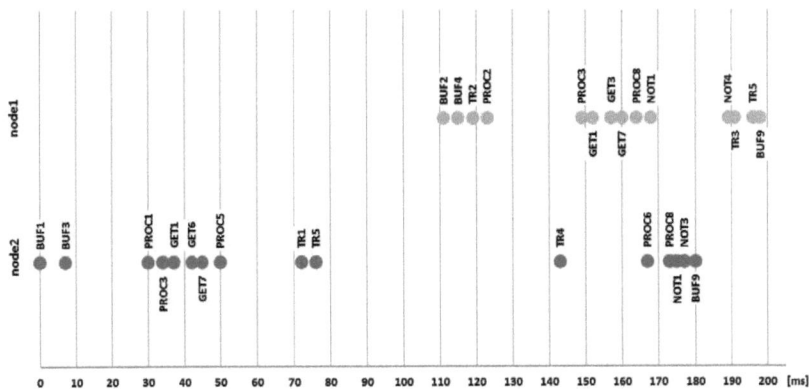

Figure 5.2: The states during the processing of a read request

forwarding nodes (in this example, only *node2*), keep the forwarding request in the request buffer for a single request timeout period to avoid loops in the forwarding tree. The *node2* receives the update request (in state **TR2**), updates its local replica of the variable (state **UPD5**) and sends the request to other nodes (state **TR5**). Then, these two nodes wait for the request to timeout. This is, of course an abstraction of the whole process, that happens on these two nodes. Again, incorrect order of some states of these two monitored nodes can be observed. Additionally, it can be noticed, that the actual timeout period is not equal to the defined 750 ms, but is about 650 ms, for both nodes. This is caused by the fact, that the defined timeout period is internally defined as an amount of common timeout units (CTUs) as defined in Section 4.5.2. The external timer triggers the request timeout routine every time a CTU elapses, i.e., the length of the CTU defines the resolution of the timeout definition. Thus, it may happen that a request is issued exactly at the moment the external timer triggered the timeout routine and the timeout period is exactly as defined. On the other hand, it may also happen, that the request is issued just before the timer triggers, causing the timeout to be effectively one CTU shorter than defined. Thus, since the timeout routine requires processing time, there is a trade-off between the accuracy of the timeout period definition and the processing overhead. The chosen settings result in an effective request timeout period in a range between 500 ms and 750 ms. From the chart, it can be noticed, that for *node1*, it could be enough to keep the request in the request buffer for about 250 ms to protect from loops in the forwarding tree. This can lead to an idea, to introduce the possibility to define a separate timeout period for forwarded requests. This solution could help to reduce the use of the request buffer elements and, as a result, would allow handling more requests or reducing the size of

Table 5.3: The state marks chosen to be monitored in the test network

State	Description
PROC1	The initialization of the request.
TR2	Reception of a request.
TR4	Reception of a reply to a request.
TR5	Successful sending of a message.
TR6	Failure in sending of a message.
NOT3	Notification of the application about the result of the request processing.
UPD5	The completion of the initial processing of an update request.

the request buffer.

Figure 5.4 presents the case, where the forwarding nodes also wait for the replies. Thus, the nodes keep the request in the request buffer for the maximum time, necessary for the processing of the request. This time is defined by the hop distance defined by the request source. In the example, the **replication_range** policy parameter defines the forwarding distance to be 6 hops. Thus, the two involved nodes set the timeout period of the request accordingly to the value of the *hops* field in the request. It is six and five, for *node1* and *node2*, respectively.

The above mentioned procedure, applied for a larger number of monitored nodes, can generate enormous amount of data, complicate its handling and presentation. Thus, it is necessary to restrict the set of monitored states to the absolute minimum. The chosen states to be monitored are given in Table 5.3. They allow the identification of the request initialization, in state **PROC1** and notification about the processing result, in state **NOT3**. Additionally, exchanging the request messages between the nodes (states **TR2**, **TR4**, **TR5** and **TR6**) and updating the local replica, identified by the state **UPD5**, are monitored as well. Based on the fact, that only write operations are actually visible to all the nodes, this set is enough for the evaluation of the memory consistency models. It is also assumed, that only write operations change the current state of the system and, that as soon as the value of a data item is updated, a potential read operation can follow. This holds for both, replicated and not replicated data items.

The charts in Figure 5.5 and in Figure 5.6 present the states monitored on all 16 nodes during a write operation issued from *node1* without and with update acknowledgments, respectively. Thus, they correspond to the charts for write operations shown in Figure 5.3 and in Figure 5.4, i.e., they show the propagation of the update requests triggered by a write request, but consider only the states mentioned in Table 5.3.

In order to reduce the chance for collisions during the request forwarding, a delay

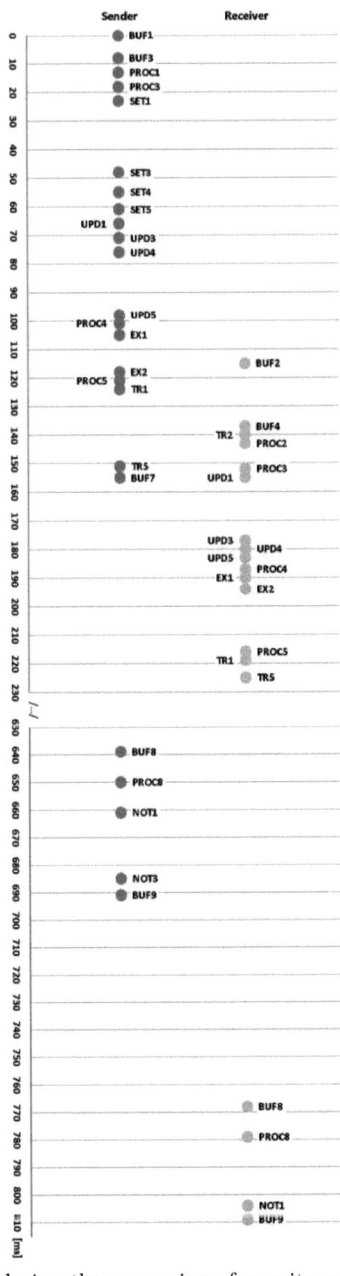

Figure 5.3: The states during the processing of a write request without update acknowledgments

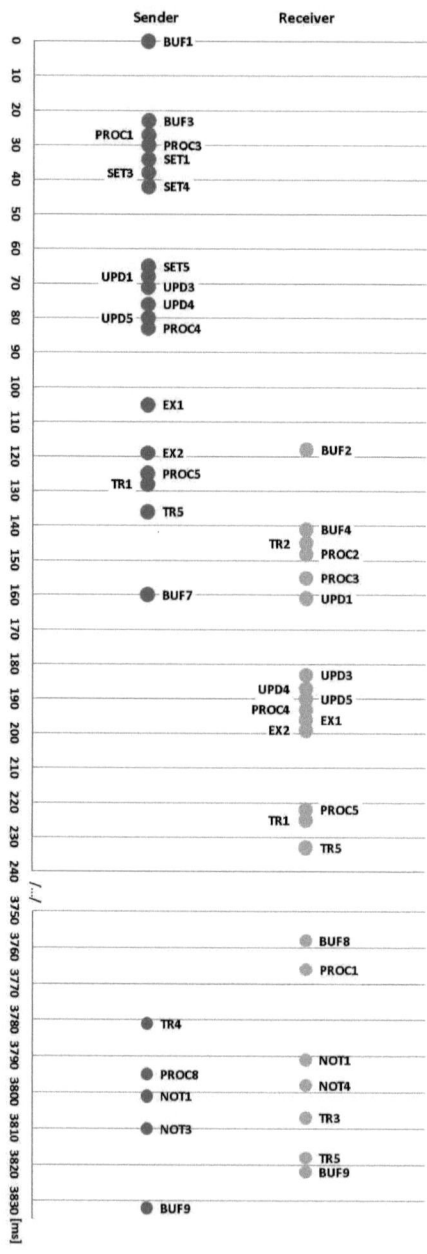

Figure 5.4: The states during the processing of a write request with update acknowledgments

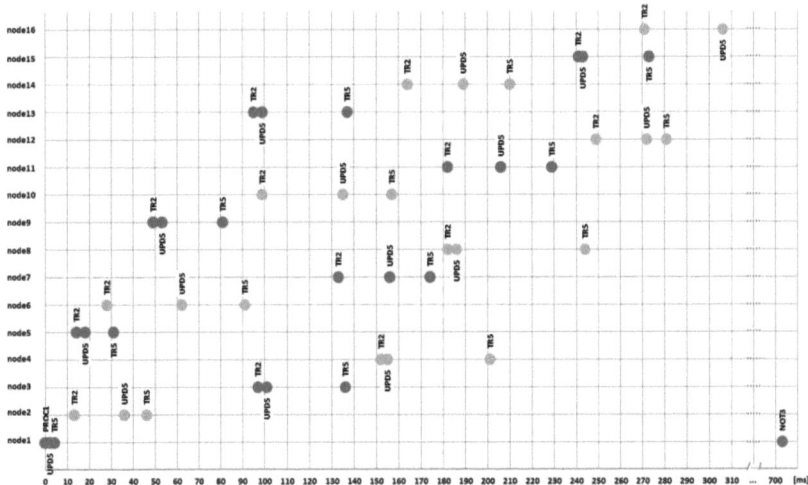

Figure 5.5: The monitored states of a write request without update acknowledgments

was added before sending a message, to provide a temporal dispersion of messages. The value for the delay is determined by the address of the node ($node\_id$) as specified in Table 5.2. The delay period is computed by each node individually, and is a multiply of a constant delay (10 ms), chosen based on the time needed to send one message. This may slow down the operation, but increases the chance for it to complete, by increasing the robustness of the forwarding mechanism. In an real application, this task is done by the MAC protocol, here it is assumed, that some mechanism for medium access is available.

The update forwarding tree for the chart in Figure 5.6 is presented in Figure 5.7. As already mentioned, the forwarding tree is also used for the convergecast of update acknowledgments. Additionally, the information in these acknowledgment messages is aggregated, i.e., the number of positive and negative is accumulated. In the example in Figure 5.7, the arrows represent messages forwarded up the tree and the number next to each arrow represents the number of positive acknowledgments included in the corresponding message.

For the further tests, in order to optimize the system according to the results of the measurements gathered by the above mentioned test runs, a second set of settings was applied. These settings are presented in Table 5.4. In order to reduce the number of message collisions, the CC2520 radio was used, because its driver provides the CCA check functionality. Even though the CC2520 radio provides the CCA check before sending a message, removing the delay from the forwarding mechanism causes an enormous increase in collisions. Additionally, it was observed, that the value for the delay

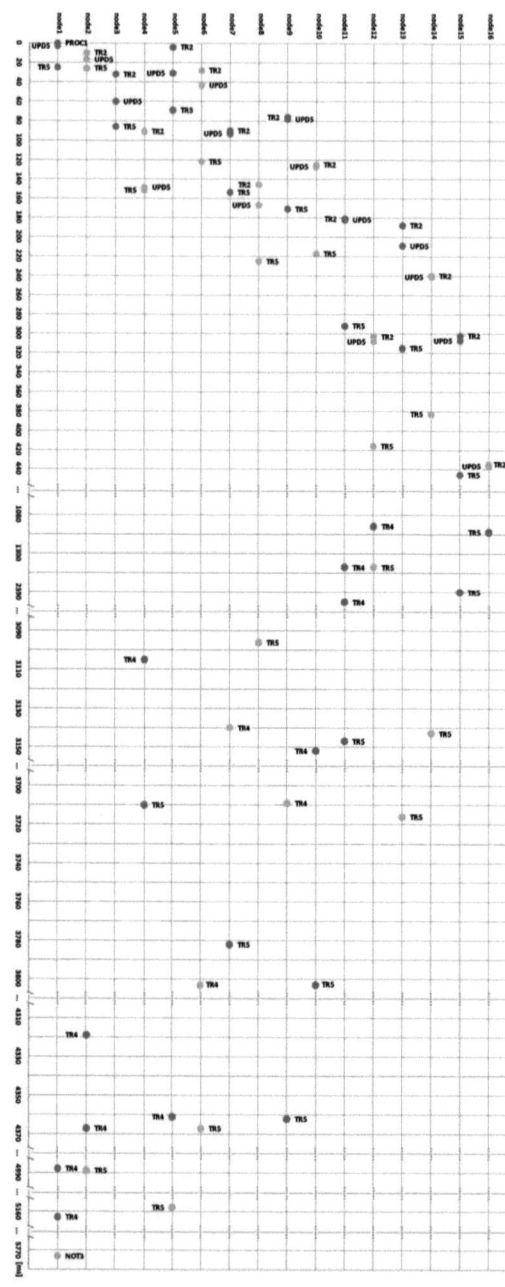

Figure 5.6: The monitored states of a write request with update acknowledgments

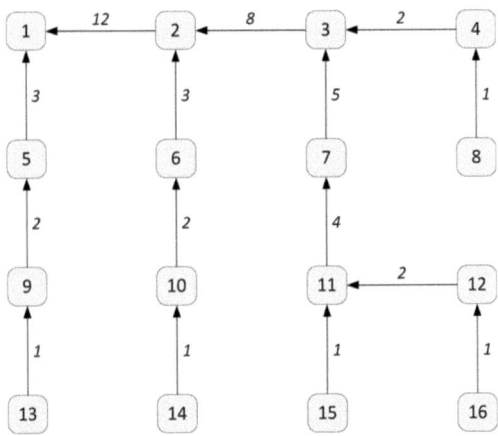

Figure 5.7: The update forwarding tree used for accumulative convergecast of acknowledgments

Table 5.4: The optimized settings chosen for the evaluation and the resulting parameters

Setting	Value
Radio	CC2520
Radio datarate	250 kbps
Serial datarate	1 Mbps
Defined variables	global variable A, $uint32\_t$
Replication Range	6 hops
Replication Density	100 %
Common timeout unit	125 ms
Request timeout	500 ms
Forwarding delay	10 ms * node_id
Radio message transmission	8 ms
Serial state transmission	0.5 ms

based on the modulo operation (see Table 5.2 performs well for requests issued from *node1*, but fails, if the forwarding direction is changed, e.g., the request to be forwarded is issued by *node16*. Thus, in the new settings, each node computes the delay, by multiplying its address (*node_id*) by the constant value of 10 ms. Additionally, the CTU was shortened to 125 ms and the request timeout period to 500 ms (4 CTUs).

Figure 5.8 shows the monitored states for a write request issued by *node16* followed by the propagation of update requests and convergecast of update acknowledgments. This operation was performed with the new settings. It can be noticed, that the time required for the update propagation doubled, i.e., the last update operation (state

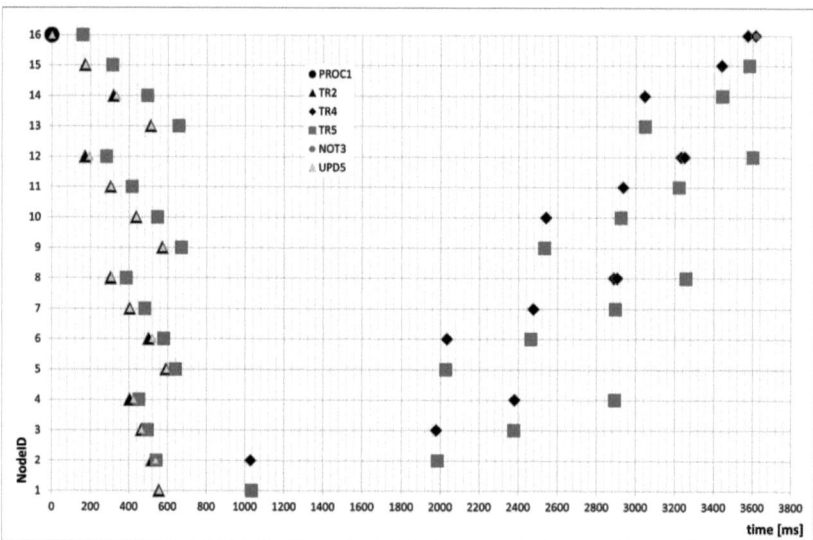

Figure 5.8: The monitored states of a write request with update acknowledgments for the optimized settings

UPD5) was performed after about 600 ms, compared to the 310 ms, for the previous settings. But, the total time required for obtaining the update acknowledgments was reduced by about 36 per cent, the **NOT3** was received after about 3650 ms, compared to about 5770 ms. These two timing changes were caused by the different values used for the forwarding delay (increased update forwarding time) and for the request timeout (reduced acknowledgment convergecast time). These two delay settings are platform (hardware and software) dependent and are subject of fine tuning and optimizations.

The costs for the above mentioned operations can be regarded as fixed, for a given settings. This is due to the fact, that these operations are performed every time in the same way. The delays are almost always the same, since they are determined by the timings defined by the settings, i.e., the processing time is negligible, compared to the request forwarding delay, to the request timeout, or even to the time needed for transmitting a message over the radio. Here both delays are regarded, the delay until the replicas are updated (in the best case all of them) and the delay until the request issuer receives the acknowledgment with the result of the operation.

Similar, the number of sent and received messages is constant for the message forwarding mechanism, considering the network as static. And thus, since the message forwarding is the main building block for the communication in the tinyDSM based system without additional protocol stack, the cost for a single forwarding operation can be regarded as a communication cost unit. The cost of the request propagation is

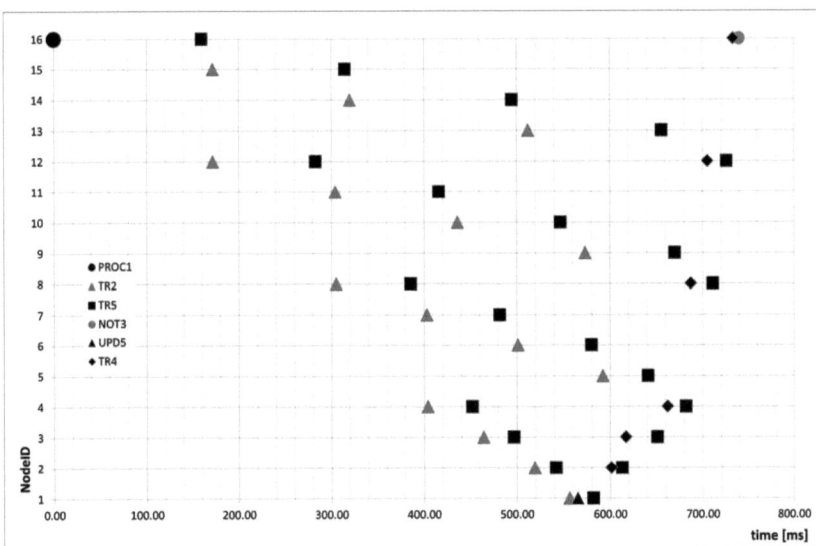

Figure 5.9: An example of a propagated write request followed by a forwarded write acknowledgment

almost equal to the cost of the convergecast performed on the same forwarding tree. In case of forwarding a single message up the tree created for the propagation of a read or write request, the costs are smaller than those for a full convergecast. Figure 5.9 shows an example of such operation. In this example, the write request is issued by *node16*, forwarded (or flooded) using the request forwarding to the *node1*, who performs the write operation on its copy. The acknowledgment for the operation is forwarded using the path, the original request was delivered, back to the request issuer. Thus, in this case the request forwarding mechanism works like a routing protocol, which performs the target discovery during the request forwarding and then directly delivers the acknowledgment, using the created path.

Table 5.5 gives the costs for the operations that can be performed by the request forwarding mechanism, for the possible hop counts in the test network. These costs figures are provided using the number of sent and received messages, for both, flooding and path propagation. The largest hop distance in the test network is equal to six hops. It corresponds to the distance between two node located in opposite corners of the network, e.g., *node1* and *node16*, or *node4* and *node13*. It can be observed, that starting the request propagation by one of the central nodes in the network requires only four hops to reach every node. The numbers for sent messages are given assuming that the nodes that already forwarded a request, do not do this twice. This requirement is satisfied as long as the settings for the request timeout and the actual time needed

Table 5.5: The number of messages sent and received during the request forwarding

Hop count	Messages sent			Messages received			
	flood		path	flood		path	
	min	max		min	max	min	max
1	1	1	1	2	4	2	4
2	3	5	2	8	18	5	8
3	6	13	3	18	40	8	12
4	10	15	4	30	46	10	15
5	13	16	5	40	48	13	18
6	15	16	6	46	48	16	20

for processing and transmitting the requests, correspond. And since the number of received messages is influenced by the number of sent ones, if the above mentioned timing relation is not satisfied, the number of received messages grows exponentially.

For each memory consistency model discussed in the tinyDSM context, three variables (A, B and C) are defined, to show their interdependencies. These interdependencies are often neglected in the discussions on memory consistency models. If necessary, these three main variables are accompanied by other variables, e.g., helper or synchronization variables. If not stated otherwise, all the shared data items mentioned in this discussion are configured to be global shared variables, as specified for the tinyDSM middleware. Here all shared data items are defined using the same settings, if not stated otherwise. The models are evaluated regarding the amount of sent and received messages, as well as the temporal dispersion of the replication process.

For each implemented memory consistency model the evaluation procedure involves the same application accessing the items in the shared memory using the same, defined pattern.

5.2 Consistency models without synchronization

This section discusses the implementation issues for the memory consistency models without synchronization and the feasibility of their realization in the WSN environment within the tinyDSM framework. These memory consistency models are the basic ones, i.e., in the most cases they are used as building blocks for the synchronized and client centric memory consistency models.

5.2.1 Atomic or Strict Consistency

The atomic or strict consistency requires global and total ordering of operations, i.e., the execution moment of an operation determines its location in the global sequence.

In general, the strict consistency is feasible only for not replicated data items. In a distributed system, like a wireless sensor network, this limitation already reduces the parallelism and the overall reliability of the system.

Additionally, the span of the operation cannot be defined as stated in Section 3.9 and the start of an operation has to be identified by the time of its initiation at the requesting node using a global timer. Considering, the timing constraints are less strict, it is allowed to divide the time into small and not overlapping units. An operation has to be contained completely in a time unit and serializing these units creates a global sequence. But, it is still possible, that two operations happen in a single unit, making the global ordering hard, due to the unpredictable delays induced by the communication means in WSN and packet collisions. These conditions make it infeasible, to hold the strict consistency requirements. Thus, a usable implementation of this memory consistency model is not feasible in the WSN environment.

5.2.2 Linearizability

Linearizability requires all the operations to be timestamped and uses these timestamps to create a global sequence, all the nodes agree on. It assumes the nodes in the network to have loosely synchronized clocks and the timestamps create a unique and unambiguous sequence of operations. However, if the differences between the local clocks on different nodes become too big, the management of the operation sequence may become unfair, e.g., the requests from nodes with faster running clocks are favored and those from nodes with slower clocks are never executed.

Like the atomic model, the linearizability also requires, that the operation start is defined as the moment of its initialization by the requester node, but linearizability relaxes the time synchronization requirements of the atomic consistency. Time synchronization, even if feasible, because some inaccuracy is allowed, may induce a global operation that reduces the scalability. But, the relaxed temporal requirements makes this consistency model more feasible, compared to the atomic consistency.

The model can be realized in a distributed way, using replicas or in a centralized way, without replicas. These possible solutions can also be differentiated based on the operation that is invalidated in case of conflicts, i.e., either the write or read operation.

In a distributed implementation of the linearizability consistency model, every node manages its own replica and accesses to it. All the replicas are writable and each write request is timestamped and broadcast to all other replica holders. In Figure 5.10, node B issues two write requests and nodes A and C read the shared data item. And since the delivery of the update requests, that follow the write access, is delayed due to transmission, it is necessary to provide a mechanism for conflict solving. Invalidating a write request, once it is sent, would be an expensive task, regarding communication costs. Thus, it sounds more feasible to invalidate the read requests, since these are issued and performed locally, i.e., only the local replicas are read. But, in order to enable the invalidation mechanism, it is necessary to provide a transaction-like mechanism that allows roll-back of a read request. This is a complex task and requires at least for all the nodes to store a history of own read requests for each shared data item. And each time a write request is received, its timestamp is compared with those of the read requests, stored in the history for the particular data item. All the read requests that are newer than the incoming write, are invalidated.

The distributed implementation requires storage for the read requests and the support for invalidation of these requests. In a resource constrained system like a wireless sensor network, both these requirements can introduce memory consistency, as well as scalability problems. If the number of read requests is high and the node runs out of memory, then no new requests can be stored in the read request history. A possible solution for the problem would be to reject the new read requests immediately, in such a case. On the other hand, the invalidation of a read request can become an overkill for the application complexity, since it has to provide the possibility for request invalidation.

The invalidation of read accesses is a complex task, but, in many cases, it can be substituted by an easier solution, i.e., by the delaying of the delivery of the read request processing results. However, the latter assumes, that the application can work with the additional delay. Figure 5.10 shows four possible combinations of timing relations between a read and a write accesses with the application of delayed read. Both, $read_1$ and $read_2$ were issued after $write_1$, but in case of $read_1$, the delay was not sufficient and the invalid response was propagated to the application, before the update for $write_1$ arrived. Similar, both $read_3$ and $read_4$ were issued before $write_2$. In this case it is not necessary to change the result of the read operation, even if an update request for the read data item arrives during the delay period, as it is the case for $read_3$.

If the application accepts delayed responses for read requests, then it is possible to postpone the delivery of the read value until it is clear, that the read request will not be invalidated anymore. This can be realized by introducing an invalidation timeout for the read request history, i.e., once the read request is issued, it is timestamped and stored in the history together with the current response, but this response can still be updated and is delivered after the validation timeout elapses (see Figure 5.10). This solution opens possibilities for memory consistency violation. After the read request is validated and the response is delivered to the application, there is no way to accept a write request older than this already handled read request. This would cause the operation sequence visible on the local node, to be different from the global one and thus, to be invalid. An example of such situation a is depicted by $read_1$ in Figure 5.10. The optimum value for the validation timeout is strongly dependent on the accuracy

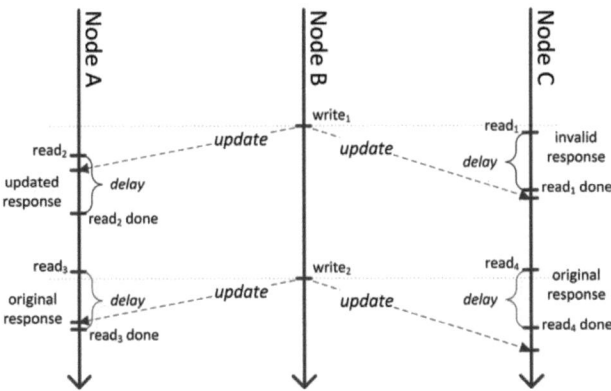

Figure 5.10: An example flow for the linearizability model with replicas (distributed)

of the time synchronization mechanism, but even more on the size of the network and the possible transmission delay.

The implementation of the above mentioned distributed version of the linearizability model with replicas, would require major changes in the tinyDSM middleware. The concept of data item manager had to be redesigned, so that all the nodes posses a writable copy. This settings could be enabled by a new policy parameter–**writable_replicas** (see Table F.1). In such a setting, there is no single manager of a shared data item and the identity of the node included in the update request is used only to distinguish the requests and order them according to the identity, if they were issued at the same moment and thus, have the same timestamp (or version). The write requests are handled immediately, the local copy is changed and the update request is broadcast to the other nodes.

Additionally, the read mechanism had to be adapted as well, i.e., all the local read requests are stored in a read request buffer and are handled after the validation period expires. The later change could be parameterized by an additional policy parameter–**read_delay** (see Table F.3) and could be realized by introducing a delay in the notification on the positively handled read request in the **NOT3** state (see Figure 4.18).

The middleware has to be also modified, so that all the requests are timestamped in the issuing moment with the local time of the requesting node. This could be, for instance, realized by introducing a new policy parameter–**timestamp_issuing**. Enabling this switch parameter for a given variable, turns on the timestamping of requests at the issuing time (see Table F.4).

The definition of variables supporting the linearizability model in the distributed way with replication, is given in Listing 5.1.

```
#define linearizability  fifo_processing \\
                         replication_range:0 \\
                         replication_density:100 \\
                         timestamp_issuing \\
                         writable_replicas \\

distributed global linearizability uint32_t A;
distributed global linearizability uint32_t B;
distributed global linearizability uint32_t C;
```

Listing 5.1: The definition of variables supporting the linearizability model with replication

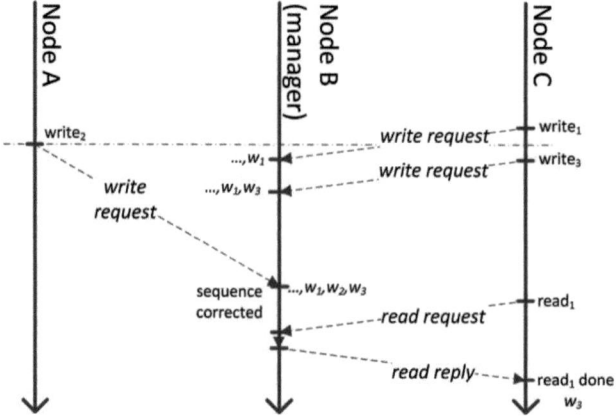

Figure 5.11: An example flow for the linearizability model without replicas (centralized)

In a centralized implementation that tries to assure the linearizability consistency requirements, a single node has to store and manage the shared data item and the data cannot be replicated (defined using the **noreplication** policy parameter). Each access request is transmitted to this manager node and thus, operates on the most recent version of the data item (see Figure 5.11). This solution limits the parallelism of the system, but it also simplifies solving the write-write and write-read conflicts as described in Section 3.9. Two distant nodes (A and C in Figure 5.11) may issue write requests in about the same moment and the messages containing these requests may arrive at the manager node B in incorrect order, regarding their timestamps. In this situation, the write-write conflict can be solved, i.e., the sequence and the value stored in the data item can be corrected, if necessary.

But, if a read operation would be performed between two write operations that require correction, then the value returned by this operation may be invalid, due to the write-read conflict and violates the linearizability model (see Figure 5.12). Thus,

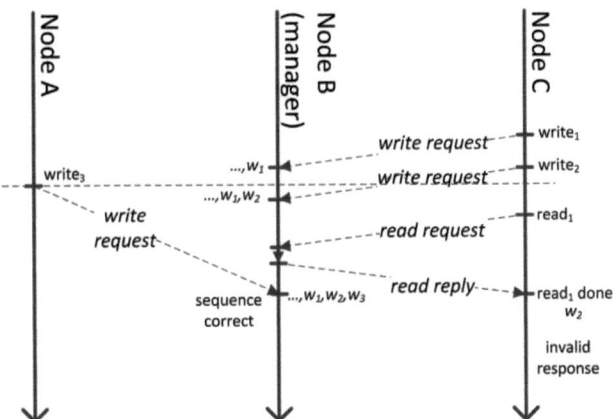

Figure 5.12: A violation of the linearizability model (centralized)

in order to ensure the rules of the model it is either necessary to invalidate all the read requests that happened on the 'dirty' data, or to refuse accepting a write request that is older than the most recently performed read operation. As already mentioned, invalidating read requests is either not practical in wireless sensor networks or substituted by a delayed read (see Figure 5.13). Refusing the write requests is much less complex and resource consuming (see Figure 5.14). Additionally, a realization of the linearizability model that allows large delivery delays and provides small response times at the same time, can combine both, delayed read and rejection of write requests. This can be even realized in an adaptive way, e.g., by adjusting the delay for the read requests according to the delivery delay of the incoming write requests.

Except of the need to have a time synchronization mechanism, only minor changes to the tinyDSM middleware are required, in order to implement the centralized version of the linearizability model. The requests have to be timestamped at the moment of issuing and the timestamps are transmitted to the owner node to order the requests (enabled by the new **timestamp_issuing** policy parameter). Additionally, for each shared data item, it is required to store the timestamp of the most recent read operation. This timestamp is compared with the timestamps of the incoming write requests and requests older than this stored timestamp are rejected. In the tinyDSM middleware, the write operations are by default acknowledged by the manager of the data item, so that the node that issues the write request knows the result of the operation. If the request was issued from within the replication range and the independent forwarding is used, then the corresponding update request is regarded as a positive acknowledgment. Thus, if the requests for the given variable have a defined timeout period, then in case of a refused write operation the owner can skip the sending of

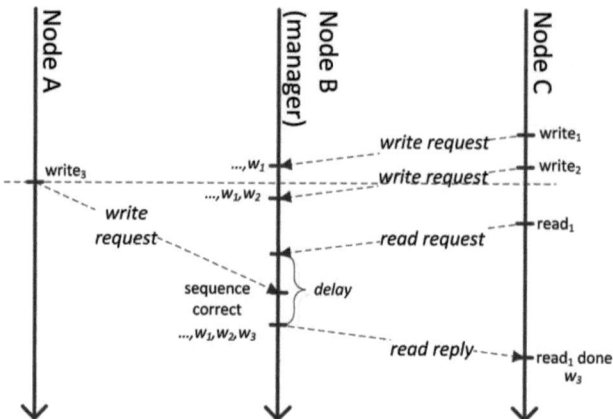

Figure 5.13: An example flow for the delayed read in the linearizability model without replicas (centralized)

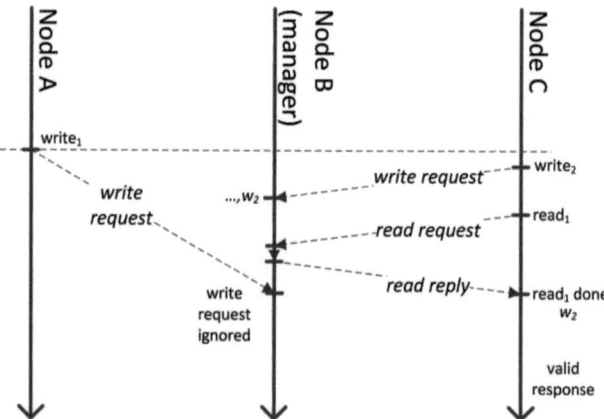

Figure 5.14: An example of refused write request in the linearizability model without replicas (centralized)

the negative acknowledgment message. The unanswered request will timeout on the node that issued the request and the application logic will be notified, that the request failed, so it can be retried.

It is also necessary, that all the correlated variables are owned by a single node, in order to assure the consistency model requirements. This could be realized by introducing another policy parameter–**group_number**, which defines groups of shared variables (see Table F.2). For such a group, the ownership related operations are performed, as if the variables in the group were a single variable, i.e., the owner is set for all of them and the ownership of the whole group is transferred, in case of ownership migration. Actually, it is possible to store a single owner address for all the variables in a single group, if the individual representation of the *local variables and metadata* storage is used.

For multiple variables it becomes even more visible, that the single owner of the all correlated variables becomes a bottleneck in the system. In order to increase the robustness, the shared variables can be replicated, but they can be read only in special cases, e.g., only by the owner, but the ownership can migrate. Such update-only replicas can be also used in case of system recovery, e.g., if the current owner node disappeared.

The definition of variables supporting the linearizability model in the centralized way without replication, is given in Listing 5.2.

```
#define  linearizability  fifo_processing  \\
                          noreplication  \\
                          timestamp_issuing  \\
                          group_number:1  \\

distributed global linearizability uint32_t A;
distributed global linearizability uint32_t B;
distributed global linearizability uint32_t C;
```

Listing 5.2: The definition of variables supporting the linearizability model without replication

The linearizability consistency model was not evaluated practically, due to its strong dependence on the available time synchronization mechanisms, which is out of scope of the presented work. In general, the feasibility of accurate time synchronization mechanisms in WSN is questionable, mainly due to the scalability issues. The linearizability is the memory consistency model that is the closest one to the atomic consistency, from those models discussed in this work. And, if such a strong consistency model is required by the application and an energy efficient, scalable and accurate time synchronization mechanism is available, the linearizability is the best choice. The strong dependence on time synchronization, as well as the definition of the operation start as the request

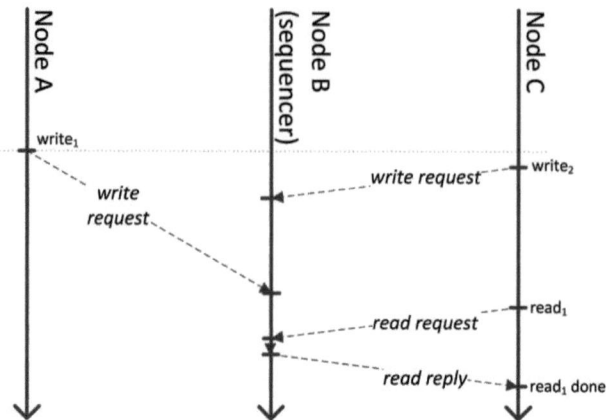

Figure 5.15: An example flow for sequential consistency model without replication

issuing time, can be avoided by using the sequential memory model, described in the following section.

5.2.3 Sequential Consistency

In the sequential consistency model, the order of the operations issued by a single node is fixed and determined by its program, but any sequence of the possible interleaving of operations issued by different nodes is valid, as long as all the nodes agree on this order and it is visible to all of the nodes.

This agreement can be realized either in a distributed or in a centralized way, i.e., it can be implemented as a voting based scheme or the sequence can be managed and determined by a single node. The distributed solution either requires the nodes to communicate extensively, in order to find the consensus, or needs a means that allows for unambiguous ordering of messages in the temporal domain, such as the timestamping in the linearizability model. The single manager solution is shown in Figure 5.15. It is less communication intensive and thus, more attractive, even if it introduces the single point of failure problem. Additionally, to assure that all accesses to all shared data items are sequentially correlated, the single manager node has to manage all the correlated shared data items, defined using the **group_number** policy parameter introduced in Section 5.2.2.

Thus, the implementation of the sequential consistency model is similar to the centralized linearizability. The difference is, that the manager node, also referred to as the sequencer, handles the requests in the sequence as they arrive. Thus, the operation start is not determined by the moment of request issuing, anymore. Additionally,

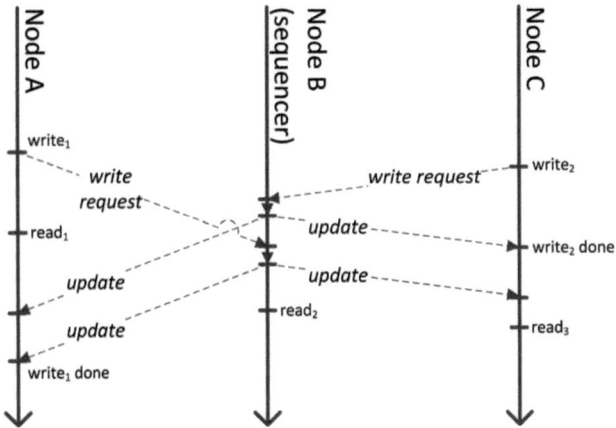

Figure 5.16: An example flow for sequential consistency model with replication

there is no need for a global time synchronization, what improves the scalability of the system.

Similar to the linearizability model, in the sequential model, the sequencer also determines the sequence of the write operations. But defining the start of the operation as the moment, when the request message arrives at the sequencer node, has the advantage, that it removes the delay between the operation start and its inserting into the sequence. Even if a distant node issues a write request and this request is delivered to the sequencer after a relatively long time, it is simply inserted into the sequence. There is no need to reject any write operations and the sequence remains valid.

Additionally, it is possible to enable readable replicas of the shared data items, because the delay between operation start and updating of the replicas, is more predictable (see Figure 5.16). And, if it is necessary to read the most recent value written to the shared data item, it is possible to delay the notification of the result of a read operation, if the read request is handled using a replica (defined using the **read_delay** policy parameter). The value for this policy parameter has to be specified according to the foreseen one-hop delay for update request forwarding and the actual delay depends on the distance to the sequencer (see Table F.3).

The delayed read operation helps to protect from the write-to-read delay in the period, where the operation is regarded as started, but the replicas are not yet updated (see Figure 3.13). The result of the delayed read operation is updated, if a replica update request for the data item in question, is received during the delay period. The disadvantage of the delayed read is, that the read operation takes always at least the amount of time specified by the delay, even if the read operation is performed on the local replica.

Thus, the implementation of the sequential consistency model in the tinyDSM middleware requires either to switch the data replication off, enabling the **noreplication** policy parameter or to enable replication with optional delay for the read operation on local replica, using the **read_delay** policy parameter. The definition of variables supporting the sequential consistency model without and with replication, is given in Listing 5.3 and in Listing 5.4, respectively.

```
#define  sequential  fifo_processing \\
                     noreplication \\
                     group_number:1 \\

distributed  global  sequential  uint32_t  A;
distributed  global  sequential  uint32_t  B;
distributed  global  sequential  uint32_t  C;
```

Listing 5.3: The definition of variables supporting the sequential model without replication

```
#define  sequential  fifo_processing \\
                     replication_range:0 \\
                     replication_density:100 \\
                     replication_copies:16 \\
                     group_number:1 \\

distributed  global  sequential  uint32_t  A;
distributed  global  sequential  uint32_t  B;
distributed  global  sequential  uint32_t  C;
```

Listing 5.4: The definition of variables supporting the sequential model with replication

Both options for the sequential consistency model were implemented and evaluated using the tinyDSM middleware. The implementation without replication contradicts with the basic concept of tinyDSM, because neither the availability of data or the robustness of the storage are increased. But this implementation satisfies the requirements of the sequential model in any case. An example chart presenting the states for the processing of a write request for the implementation of the sequential consistency model without replication, is shown in Figure 5.9 in Section 5.1. In this example, *node16* issues a write request, which uses the request forwarding mechanism to locate the sequencer (*node1*). The sequencer performs the write operation and acknowledges its result back to issuer. The write acknowledgment is forwarded back to *node16* using the path the original request was delivered. Similar procedure applies for read requests. Thus, this realization of the model, has to use the master copy discovery mechanism, introduced in Section 3.4, per default.

Table 5.6: The costs of the sequential model implementation without replication

Operation	Forwarding Costs	Delay
read	1x flood 1x path	2x message forwarding
write	1x flood 1x path	2x message forwarding

Table 5.7: The costs of the sequential model implementation with replication

Operation	Forwarding Costs	Delay
read	0	≈ 0
write without acknowledgments	2x flood	1x message forwarding 1x update convergecast
write with acknowledgments	3x flood 1x path	3x message forwarding 1x update convergecast

In case of read request, the meaning and importance of the acknowledgment (or reply) message is evident, i.e., it contains the read value of the shared data item. But for the realization of sequential consistency model without replicas, it is also absolutely necessary to acknowledge the write requests. This is due to the fact, that at the initialization of the distributed application, the sequencer is not specified and the first node that writes any of the correlated data items, becomes the sequencer. Thus, in order to avoid the situation, where multiple nodes assign themselves as sequencers, it is necessary that the sequencer announces its presence, by issuing acknowledgment messages for all performed requests. Of course, this solution has the drawback, that lost messages can make a writing node think, that it can assign itself as the sequencer. It is necessary to specify the number of failed approaches, before announcing itself as sequencer.

The implementation of the sequential model with replication is not affected by the issue, since all nodes posses a replica of the data item and know, which node is currently the sequencer. But in the tinyDSM implementation without external protocol stack, each write operation is delivered to the sequencer using the request forwarding mechanism, thus a kind of owner discovery is realized in any case.

Table 5.6 and Table 5.7 provide the basic cost figures for the both implementations of sequential consistency. These costs are provided in abstract units, whose exact values dependent on the system settings, like those given in Table 5.4. The costs for the request forwarding depend on the combination of the applied mechanisms. The forwarding can be either a single *path* response propagation or a propagation based on *flooding*, like request forwarding, discovery request or convergecast. The numbers of sent and received messages for each kind of propagation are given in Table 5.5. The costs given in Table 5.6 and in Table 5.7 are the minimum, assuming that the operation was successful without the need of retries. For both realizations, with and without replication, a write request is assumed as failed, if no corresponding message with a positive acknowledgment is received. For the realization without replication, the same applies for the read request.

The values for the write request without acknowledgments are given only for comparison. Such request are not allowed, considering the memory consistency model requirements, because they represent a best effort approach without any feedback.

A lack of reply from the sequencer, or a negative reply, can be caused by a failure at the sequencer. In the realization with replication, the operation is also regarded as failed, if the number of positive acknowledgments collected after the update propagation, did not reach the one defined by the **replication_copies** policy parameter. The application logic on top of the tinyDSM middleware is notified about the result of the operation and the application can decide to retry the failed operation. Thus, the extent of the consistency enforcement arrangements is left to the application engineer and the application logic. Issuing the request repeatedly, causes the basic costs again for each repetition. And since the failures depend mostly on the communication issues, the actual costs of an operation or request processing, depend on the environmental conditions and the ability of the protocol stack to overcome the communication issues. Knowing the abilities of the applied protocol stack, the application engineer can implement the tailor-made consistency enforcement mechanisms in the application logic. If it is absolutely necessary to indicate that the repeated write request is not an individual operation that simply follows the one that failed, it would be necessary to extend the tinyDSM middleware to provide a possibility to re-trigger a request at the moment the result of the processing of this particular request is delivered to the replication logic. This could be realized by introducing an additional policy parameter **repeatable** (see Table F.8). Enabling this switch parameter would allow the application to repeat issuing the request in the moment the notification on this request processing result is provided by the middleware, using the respective callback function (see Section 4.5.1). If the callback function, implemented in the application logic, would return a specified error code, then the request would be automatically reinitialized with the same request number. This feature would be especially interesting for write requests.

In case of the realization with replication, a failed and potentially only partially executed write operation is not canceled. Thus, the replicas can contain inconsistent data. In order to enable partially executed write requests (or actually their update parts), without sacrificing the consistency of the storage, it is necessary to sacrifice the zero costs of the read operation. In such case a read request has to be realized by a mechanism that can be called a *survey convergecast*. This mechanism was already

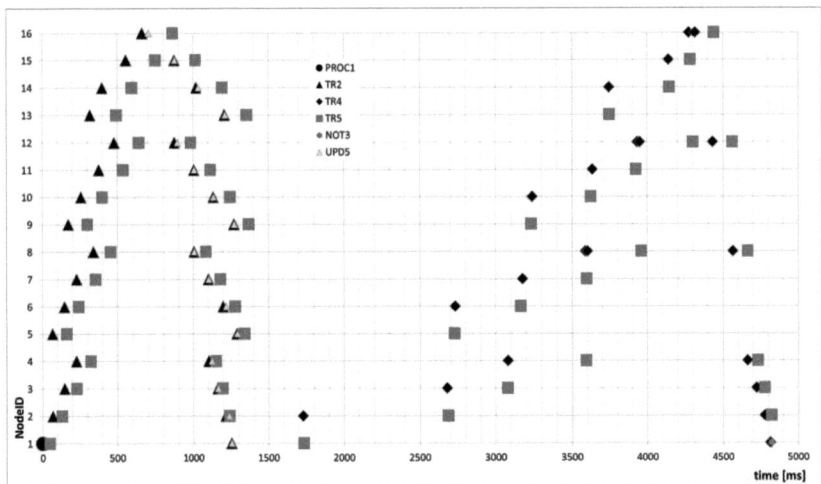

Figure 5.17: The processing of a write request in the realization of sequential consistency model with replication

mentioned in Section 3.1. It is a variation of the convergecast for update acknowledgments, but it differs in the applied aggregation function, i.e., each parent in the forwarding tree, chooses the most recent replica from those received from its children and forwards this replica as an reply to its parent. The convergecast read operation could be enabled by a new policy parameter–**convergecast_read** (see Table F.5 and Table F.6).

Figure 5.8 shows the state chart for a special and optimistic case for the realization with replication. In this special case, the write request is issued by the sequencer itself. In such case, the initial forwarding of the request towards the sequencer, as well as the final forwarding of the result of the operation to the issuing node, are not necessary. Thus, the transmission costs and delay is reduced by 50 per cent, compared to the values for the general case, given in Table 5.7.

The general case of the processing of a write request, is shown in Figure 5.17. In this example, *node1* issues a write request and *node16* is the sequencer. As already mentioned, the progress can be split into four phases. First, the request is forwarded to the sequencer. For the settings given in Table 5.4, this phase takes approximately 700 ms. Then, the update propagation starts. It requires slightly less than the request forwarding and finishes in about 650 ms. The update propagation is followed by the update acknowledgment convergecast, which starts approximately 1350 ms after the request initialization, identified by the **PROC1** state. This is the most time consuming part, due to the relatively large value chosen for the request timeout period. The hop

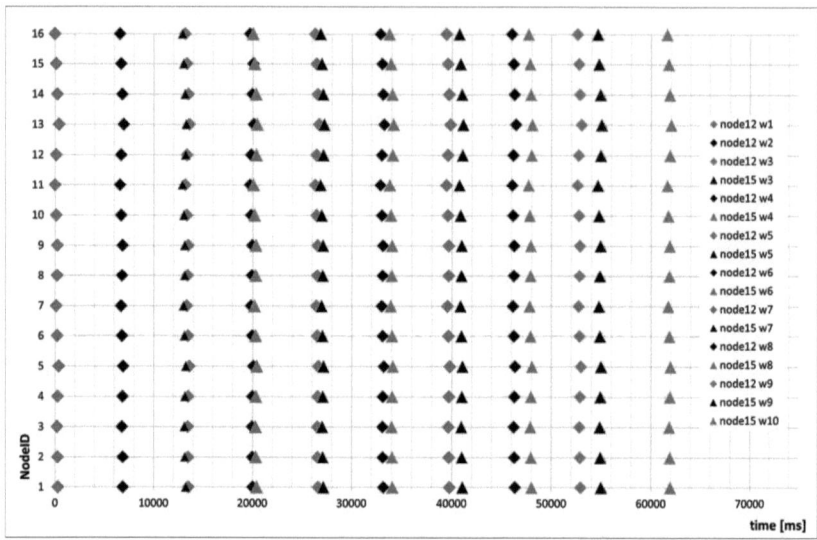

Figure 5.18: The sequence of replication updates for consecutive write request issued by *node12* and *node15* using the implementation of the sequential consistency model with replication

distance between *node1* and *node16* is six hops. Thus, since the request timeout period is equal to 500 ms (see Table 5.4), the time required by the update convergecast shall be approximately 3000 ms. The chart confirms the estimation and about 4300 ms after the request initialization the result of the write operation is available at the sequencer node. At this point, the sequencer (*node16*) forwards the write acknowledgment to the request issuer (*node1*), using the path the request was originally delivered, that again requires about 650 ms.

It can be seen, that the implementation of the sequential consistency with replication requires the nodes to exchange enormous amount of messages. A single write operation requires sending of 51 messages, which are actually received 154 times, according to the forwarding costs in Table 5.5. In order to evaluate how this data traffic influences the consistency of the data storage 10 test runs, 5 minutes each, were performed for the test network and the sequences of replica updates on each nodes were observed. Since the update requests are propagated by a single node, the update forwarding performs well. For the test setup and settings it happened that about 5 percent of the update requests were not delivered to individual nodes. But, it could be observed that the update acknowledgment messages collided with each other causing the returned numbers of updated replicas to be wrong and indicating that an actually successful update was regarded as failed. It was also noticeable, that the delivery of some of the write requests failed on the way to the sequencer. Figure 5.18 present an extract of a test run with *node11* as sequencer and two nodes, *node12* and *node15*, are performing a sequence of 10 write operations, each. Both, *node12* and *node15* write the same shared variable, approximately once every 7 seconds. This period was chosen due to the measured duration of the complete write operation, which requires approximately 5 seconds. In this chosen extract all the update operations were performed successfully, but it is noticeable, that some of the write requests issued by the nodes were not delivered to the sequencer. The *w10* operation by *node12* and the *w1* and *w2* operations by *node15* are missing.

For higher write frequencies, in order to protect the update requests from different write operations from colliding, it is possible to force the requester to process one write operation at a time, disabling the parallel request processing. This could be realized by a new policy parameter–**serialized_processing** (see Table F.7). Enabling this policy parameter would create a queue of requests in the request buffer. The requests from this queue are processed one after another, but the processing of the next one starts after the processing of the current request is completed. This setting would require setting large values for the **external_request_timeout** policy parameter, otherwise the timeout period for the requests stored in the queue elapses and they are regarded as failed, before they can be handled.

5.2.4 Causal Consistency

The causal consistency model assumes the existence of causally dependent operations and reduces the ordering requirement only to these, i.e., the causally related operations have to appear in the global sequence in the defined order, but all other operations are concurrent and thus, can appear in arbitrary order on different nodes. The causal consistency is hard to specify in a general case and its implementations are very application dependent. Thus, this consistency model is not investigated further in the WSN and tinyDSM context.

5.2.5 PRAM or FIFO Consistency

The PRAM and FIFO consistency models are equivalent. The global ordering of operations is reduced only to those issued by a single node, i.e., these operations have to be observed by all other nodes in the sequence as they were issued, but operations issued by different nodes are regarded as concurrent and thus, may be seen in different order by different nodes.

The implementation of this consistency model is similar to the distributed linearizability implementation, but there is no correlation between the write operations issued by different nodes, i.e., each replica is writable and if a node issues a write request,

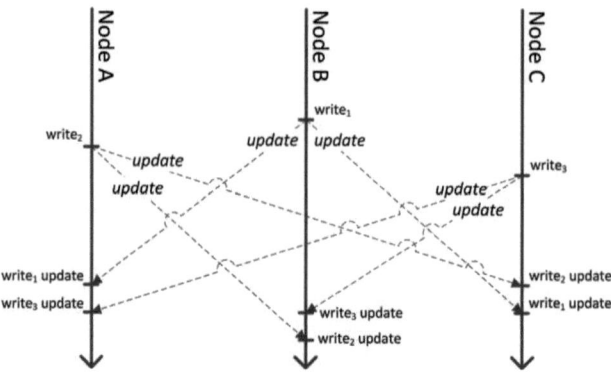

Figure 5.19: An example flow for PRAM/FIFO consistency model

its replica is updated and the update request is broadcast to the other nodes, which update their replicas. Additionally, local writes are immediately visible by the local node. As shown in Figure 5.19, in this implementation, each node is a sequencer of its own write requests, but the global view does not have to be consistent in a strict or sequential sense. After the execution of these example operations in Figure 5.19, the replica of the shared data item on each node has a different value.

The definition of variables supporting the PRAM consistency model is given in Listing 5.5. The implementation based on this definition was evaluated further in this section.

```
#define pram fifo_processing \\
            replication_range:0 \\
            replication_density:100 \\
            replication_copies:16 \\
            writable_replicas \\

distributed global pram uint32_t A;
distributed global pram uint32_t B;
distributed global pram uint32_t C;
```

Listing 5.5: The definition of variables supporting the PRAM consistency model

Table 5.8 gives the cost and delay figures for the tinyDSM PRAM consistency implementation. Again, the values for the write request without acknowledgments are given only for comparison. The PRAM consistency model requires that all the replicas are updated, so all the nodes observe the same order of write operations issued by a single node. If a replica is not updated, then the model is violated. Since the concept of the PRAM model was to speed up the read operation, by reading always from the local replica, it is not advised to provide a cooperative read operation in an

Table 5.8: pram

Operation	Forwarding Costs	Delay
read	0	≈ 0
write without acknowledgments	1x flood	1x request forwarding
write with acknowledgments	2x flood	1x request forwarding 1x update convergecast

implementation of this model. And in the presented tinyDSM implementation, it is actually not possible, because there are no owner informations stored on the nodes to allow restoring the sequence of write requests issued by a given node.

The write operations are simply standard write requests issued by the local nodes and followed by the update request propagation, as already depicted in Figure 5.8. However, what is interesting is the presence of multiple sources of the update requests. Figure 5.20 presents an example sequence of updates performed on the nodes in the test network as a result of a sequence of write requests issued from both *node1* and *node16*. Again, these two nodes perform a write operation approximately every 5 and 7 seconds, respectively. As can be read from the chart in Figure 5.20, the amount of collisions is quite large. This is caused by the fact, that the propagation of update requests and their corresponding acknowledgments generates quite large and, what is maybe more important, non systematic and not coordinated traffic. It also happens that complete update propagations fail, i.e., the write request is issued, the local replica is updated, but the message starting the update propagation collides with another one and none of the other replicas is updated. In the test run presented in Figure 5.20 it can be noticed that the *node9* is not providing any state data.

Similar as it was for the implementation of sequential consistency, the feedback received from the nodes regarding the number of performed updates for a given write request, can be used by the application logic to trigger repetition of the write operation. It was also observed that the number of positively performed write requests was quite low (below 30 per cent). Thus, even if the replicas are updated, the application logic can regard the request as failed and issue the write request again. Similar as it was the case for the implementation of the sequential consistency model, the use of the **repeatable** policy parameter can allow reissuing a failed request, so that it is observed by other nodes as a repetition of the previous request.

In order to investigate, if the avoiding of acknowledgment sending increases the quality of the storage a series of 15 experiment runs, 5 minutes each, with write requests without acknowledgments were performed. These tests have shown that the update rate increased (to about 85 per cent), but as already mentioned such a setting is not

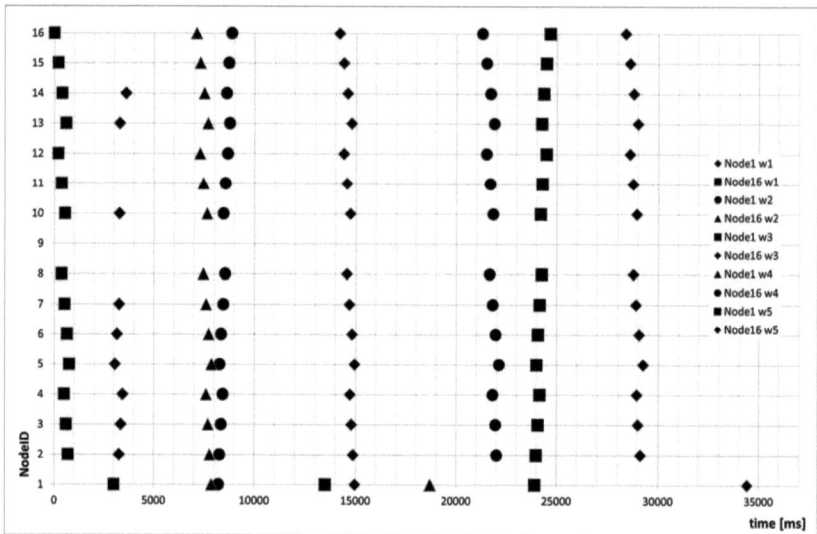

Figure 5.20: The sequence of replication updates for consecutive write request issued by *node1* and *node16* for the implementation of the PRAM consistency model

allowed by the requirements of the consistency model. Figure 5.21 shows an example extract of the sequence of replica updates. It can be noticed, that the number of collisions dropped. This extract also shows, that the CC2520 radio on some of the nodes may stuck, making the node unable to receive the incoming requests. This test exposed the immaturity of the software driver for this radio transceiver.

In case of systems with large number of update issuers it might be necessary to involve more sophisticated coordination mechanisms on the protocol layer, to reduce the collision rate.

5.2.6 Cache Consistency

The cache consistency model is a data related weakening of the sequential consistency. It requires that all nodes observe write operations on a single data item in the same sequence.

This model is the basic model for the tinyDSM and it is supported for the entities of both, global and array variables. The owner of the data item is a sequencer for the write requests on this item and it broadcasts the update requests. The example definitions for variables supporting the cache consistency model are given in Listing 5.6. Variable A is defined as an array, i.e., an entity of this variable is owned by each node in the network. Variables B and C are defined as global and thus, a single entity

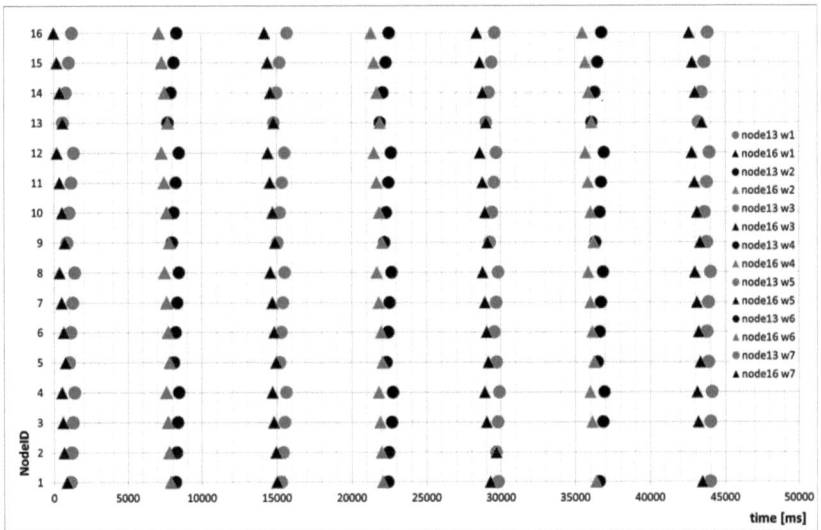

Figure 5.21: The sequence of replication updates for consecutive write request issued by *node13* and *node16* for the implementation of the PRAM consistency model, without write acknowledgments

of these exist in the network. The cache consistency model can be also realized without replication, but, similar as it was already mentioned by the discussion on the sequential consistency model, this realization contradicts to the tinyDSM idea.

```
#define pram fifo_processing \\
               replication_range:0 \\
               replication_density:100 \\
               replication_copies:16 \\

distributed       pram  uint32_t A;
distributed global pram uint32_t B;
distributed global pram uint32_t C;
```

Listing 5.6: The definition of global and array variables supporting the cache consistency model

The operation cost figures for the cache consistency are the same as for the sequential consistency implementation and thus, can be found in Table 5.7, for the realization with replication, or in Table 5.6, for one without replication. The only difference between these implementations is, that for the cache consistency model, the different variables may be owned by different nodes. This distribution of the ownership allows for more scalability, and avoids the single point of failure problem.

5.2.7 Processor Consistency

The processor consistency model combines the requirements of the PRAM and the cache consistency models. It requires, that all the write operations issued by a single node are visible by all other nodes in the same sequence. Additionally, all write operations on a single shared data item are also visible by all the nodes in the same sequence. Thus, it is stronger than each of these models individually, but weaker than the sequential consistency.

These two weaker consistency models (PRAM and cache) can be implemented in a distributed way, as mentioned in previous sections. But, due to the combination of their requirements, the processor consistency model requires a more centralized solution, similar to the one for the sequential model. But, compared to the sequential consistency model, the processor consistency model allows using multiple sequencer nodes, if the accesses from different nodes to different data items create disjoint groups of variables and nodes writing these. However, this implementation does not provide the immediate visibility of locally issued write requests, as they have to be accepted by the sequencer first. The groups of variables can be defined using the new policy parameter **group_number**.

An example definition of variables supporting the processor consistency is provided in Listing 5.7. Variables A and B are defined in the same context, thus, the accesses to these variables will be managed by a single sequencer.

```
#define  processor  fifo_processing \\
                   replication_range:0 \\
                   replication_density:100 \\
                   replication_copies:16 \\

distributed  global  processor  group_number:1  uint32_t A;
distributed  global  processor  group_number:1  uint32_t B;
distributed  global  processor  group_number:2  uint32_t C;
```

Listing 5.7: The definition of variables supporting the processor model with replication

Similar to the cache consistency model, the cost figures for the processing consistency model are the same as those for sequential consistency.

5.2.8 Slow Memory

The slow memory consistency model, like the processor consistency, also involves ordering of the write requests issued from individual nodes on individual shared data items. But, in contrast, the slow memory model, it requires only, that the write operations issued by a single node on a single data item are visible by all the nodes in the same sequence.

Like the PRAM model, slow memory requires, that the local writes are immediately visible locally. Thus, the slow memory model provides weaker consistency than the PRAM model, because it splits the sequencing of all the write requests issued by a single node into multiple independent sequences, one for each data item, the implementation of the slow memory model corresponds to the one of the PRAM model.

Chapter 6
Conclusions

This thesis investigated the feasibility of the provision of the distributed shared memory abstraction in the wireless sensor networks domain. The practical result of this research is the realization of a flexible framework for implementing data consistency for wireless sensor networks, called tinyDSM. This framework consists of two parts, an application specific instantiation of the middleware that provides the shared memory abstraction and a compiler tool, which automates the process of generating the tailor-made middleware and thus, supports the application engineers.

The generation of the application specific middleware instance is controlled by a set of policy parameters specified for the defined shared data. These policy parameters allow defining consistency models or mixing the features of the existing ones. These parameters enable and adjust their corresponding mechanisms and features which are then injected into the specific implementation of the middleware by the already mentioned tool.

tinyDSM allows simplifying the application development, since the data exchanging part is generated automatically according to the chosen policy parameters. Thus, in the application logic the application engineer can focus on the actual data processing. The tinyDSM middleware provides a defined interface, which is independent from its instantiation, what allows evaluating a single application logic using multiple data quality settings without implementing the complete application from scratch. Additionally, the application logic can be involved in the consistency enforcement measures, what gives the application more control over executed mechanisms. This allows more resource aware handling of the data.

In order to prove the results of the theoretical investigation, the chosen consistency models defined for the large scale distributed systems were implemented within the tinyDSM framework and their costs were evaluated for a real network consisting of 16 nodes.

First, the implementation of the sequential consistency model was investigated. In both cases, with and without replication this implementation requires assigning the role of being the sequencer to one of the nodes in the network. The sequencer determines the sequence of the accesses to all the shared data. The other nodes wanting to write the data have to issue a write request to the sequencer. Assuming that the operation was performed successfully for the first time and no retransmission was necessary, both the read and write operations for the sequential model without replication require sending 21 messages, that are actually received 62 times. For write operation for the sequential model with replication the number of send messages grows to 61 and they are received 154 times. This additional cost for writing is compensated by the read operation that is performed without exchanging any message. Already if the ratio of number of read operations to number of the write operations done by the application is larger than two, then it is less expensive to use the sequential model with replication. The delays for the test setup are approximately 5000 ms for the write operations in a system with replicas and approximately 1350 ms for both, read and write operations without replicas. These delays are subject of optimization, but for most of the wireless sensor node applications such operation duration is acceptable.

The second evaluated implementation of a memory consistency model was the PRAM model. In the PRAM model every node possesses a writable replica of the data and thus, every node is able to write its replica and issue update requests. The read operations are performed on the local replica as well and thus, do not require exchanging any messages. The transmission costs for the write operations are 30 sent messages and 92 received.

The implementations of these two models were chosen for the evaluation, because they expose different communication patterns. The sequential consistency with sequencer involves many nodes that issue the requests towards the sequencer, but the sequencer is the only node that issues the update requests. In case of the PRAM model every node may issue the update requests.

It can be noticed, that in the implementation of the PRAM model more messages are corrupted due to collisions. Thus, it is absolutely necessary to involve a more efficient MAC protocol, for both, increasing the throughput and reducing the delay.

These two evaluated models are quite strong consistency models and can experience scalability issues if applied in a network larger than the one used by the tests. This is due to the fact that these models assume that every node has to have a replica and every replica has to be consistent. In a wireless sensor network with an arbitrary size, these two requirements cannot be satisfied. Thus, to enable the application of distributed shared memory in such networks, the memory model requirements have to be weakened.

The two main problems in the wireless sensor networks are the limited resources and the unreliable communication links. Thus, the wireless sensor networks differ dramatically from the large scale distributed systems, on which the distributed shared memory implementations were used to be executed. In order to cope with the specifics of WSNs the initial DSM concepts had to be reconsidered. The main concern is given to reducing the number of transmitted messages, since communication induces the most energy consumption. As already mentioned, the second important factor is the scalability. To cope with these constraints new mechanisms were proposed for the application in DSM implementations. These mechanisms allow weakening the quality of the data storage while reducing the required costs.

Request forwarding A request message represent the wish of one node to perform an operation on another node, what can be reading or writing a data or updating a replica, thus they have to be propagated from node to node. The proposed mechanism combines the best effort broadcast in a specified region with message serialization features. It allows defining the forwarding distance as a number of hops each request will be forwarded in the network. Thus, it helps reducing the global range of the operations increasing the scalability of the system.

The mechanism has very low memory requirements. It requires each forwarding node to store only the forwarded request together with the address of the immediate message source, independent from the size of the network and the forwarding distance. This data is stored only during the forwarding process to avoid loops in the forwarding tree.

During the forwarding of a request a controlled flooding of the chosen part of the network is realized, i.e., a directed tree rooted at the source node is created. The height of the tree is equal to the desired forwarding distance. The advantage of the mechanism is that it can be used to forward a request to a distant node without knowing the route to it, thus independent from the underlying protocol layer. Additionally, if the original request requires a reply message to be forwarded back to the original requester, then the reply message is forwarded back using the path the request was delivered. Additionally, if there are multiple replies forwarded back to the requester, then they are aggregated to reduce the number of sent messages.

Replication strategy If a node that broadcast an update request to its neighbors wants to be sure that the request was really performed, then this node requires an acknowledgment from the nodes that received the request. However, the acknowledgment messages cause additional cost, thus it is possible to disable the sending of these messages. But, completely without a feedback the node has no clue about the actual number of replicas of its data. Thus, in order to reduce the number of transmitted messages, the replication strategy allows defining the ratio between update requests that require acknowledgements and those that do not. Additionally, the procedure is reactive and adapts this ratio to the current situation.

The replication strategy is controlled by the replication goal defined using policy parameters. These parameters define the desired number of the replicas and the replication range that specifies the number of hops the update request is forwarded in the network. What again increases the scalability, by reducing the global character of the replication.

Instance filtering Since in the wireless sensor network a write operation to a shared data can occur very frequently, it is reasonable to limit the number of update requests, in order to save energy. The instance filtering mechanisms is applied on the node that performs the write operation to virtually reduce the amount of write accesses and, as a result, to reduce the costs of updating the replicas of the data, by filtering out data that is redundant or of lower relevance. Thus, this mechanism helps to extract the information out of the written data, decreasing the resource consumption by reducing the processing to the most relevant data only.

6.1 Future work

There are parameters and mechanisms that were not considered during the design phase of the tinyDSM framework. But, during the evaluation of the consistency model within the framework, it was realized that it is reasonable to extend the initial set of policy parameters supported by the tinyDSM. These parameters are provided in Section F. Some of them were already implemented during the evaluation, like the **writable_copies**.

Additional mechanism that could be added to the pool of mechanisms supported by the tinyDSM could be extension to the request forwarding to support hop-by-hop delivery failure detection and recovery. This reliability increasing policy parameter could reduce the number of requests that failed due to lost messages. Such detection reduces the retransmission costs, compared to end-to-end detection.

Another research area that could be investigated is the application of security means in the tinyDSM middleware and in the memory consistency research. The initial step in this direction has already been done and a publication on a lightweight cryptosystem to work together with tinyDSM has been accepted for publication.

In order to allow the tinyDSM compiler to be extensible it would be interesting to provide a possibility to add new mechanisms and policy parameters to the supported pool in a simplified, module like way.

Bibliography

[1] Eistec AB. *Eistec AB - Homepage*, 2011. http://www.eistec.se. [cited at p. 22]

[2] T. Abdelzaher, B. Blum, Q. Cao, Y. Chen, D. Evans, J. George, S. George, L. Gu, T. He, S. Krishnamurthy, et al. Envirotrack: Towards an environmental computing paradigm for distributed sensor networks. In *Distributed Computing Systems, 2004. Proceedings. 24th International Conference on*, pages 582–589. IEEE, 2004. [cited at p. 116]

[3] N. Abramson. THE ALOHA SYSTEM: another alternative for computer communications. In *Proceedings of the November 17-19, 1970, fall joint computer conference*, pages 281–285. ACM, 1970. [cited at p. 30]

[4] G. Acs, L. Buttyán, and I. Vajda. Modelling adversaries and security objectives for routing protocols in wireless sensor networks. In *Proceedings of the fourth ACM workshop on Security of ad hoc and sensor networks*, pages 49–58. ACM, 2006. [cited at p. 31]

[5] S.V. Adve and K. Gharachorloo. Shared memory consistency models: A tutorial. *computer*, 29(12):66–76, 1996. [cited at p. 51]

[6] N. Aes. Advanced encryption standard. *Federal Information Processing Standard, FIPS-197*, 2001. [cited at p. 20]

[7] M. Ahamad, G. Neiger, P. Kohli, J. Burns, P. Hutto, and TE Anderson. Causal Memory: Definitions, Implementation and Programming. *IEEE Transactions on Parallel and Distributed Systems*, 1:6–16, 1990. [cited at p. 53]

[8] S. Ahuja, N. Carriero, and D. Gelernter. Linda and friends. *Computer*, 19(8):26–34, 1986. [cited at p. 11, 41, 63]

[9] K. Akkaya and M. Younis. A survey on routing protocols for wireless sensor networks. *Ad hoc networks*, 3(3):325–349, 2005. [cited at p. 31]

[10] J.N. Al-Karaki and A.E. Kamal. Routing techniques in wireless sensor networks: a survey. *Wireless Communications, IEEE*, 11(6):6–28, 2004. [cited at p. 31]

[11] ZigBee Alliance. *ZigBee Specification*, 2011. http://www.zigbee.org/Specifications.aspx. [cited at p. 19]

[12] T. Arampatzis, J. Lygeros, and S. Manesis. A survey of applications of wireless sensors and wireless sensor networks. In *Intelligent Control, 2005. Proceedings of the 2005 IEEE International Symposium on, Mediterrean Conference on Control and Automation*, pages 719–724. Ieee, 2005. [cited at p. 31]

[13] A. Arora, P. Dutta, S. Bapat, V. Kulathumani, H. Zhang, V. Naik, V. Mittal, H. Cao, M. Demirbas, and M. Gouda. A line in the sand: A wireless sensor network for target detection, classification, and tracking. *Computer Networks*, 46(5):605–634, 2004. [cited at p. 32]

[14] H.E. Bal and A.S. Tanenbaum. Distributed programming with shared data. In *Computer Languages, 1988. Proceedings., International Conference on*, pages 82–91. IEEE, 1988. [cited at p. 41]

[15] P. Bauer, M. Sichitiu, R. Istepanian, and K. Premaratne. The mobile patient: wireless distributed sensor networks for patient monitoring and care. In *Information Technology Applications in Biomedicine, 2000. Proceedings. 2000 IEEE EMBS International Conference on*, pages 17–21. IEEE, 2000. [cited at p. 33]

[16] J.K. Bennett, J.B. Carter, and W. Zwaenepoel. Munin: Distributed shared memory based on type-specific memory coherence. In *Proceedings of the second ACM SIGPLAN symposium on Principles & practice of parallel programming*, pages 168–176. ACM, 1990. [cited at p. 41]

[17] L. Bergamini, C. Crociani, A. Vitaletti, and M. Nati. Validation of WSN simulators through a comparison with a real testbed. In *Proceedings of the 7th ACM workshop on Performance evaluation of wireless ad hoc, sensor, and ubiquitous networks*, pages 103–104. ACM, 2010. [cited at p. 34]

[18] Freie Universitaet Berlin and FeuerWhere project partners. *FeuerWhere Project, Homepage*, 2008. http://www.feuerwhere.de/. [cited at p. 10, 33]

[19] P.A. Bernstein and N. Goodman. Concurrency control in distributed database systems. *ACM Computing Surveys (CSUR)*, 13(2):185–221, 1981. [cited at p. 59]

[20] P.A. Bernstein, V. Hadzilacos, and N. Goodman. *Concurrency control and recovery in database systems*, volume 5. Addison-wesley New York, 1987. [cited at p. 53]

[21] B.N. Bershad and M.J. Zekauskas. Midway: Shared memory parallel programming with entry consistency for distributed memory multiprocessors. Technical Report CMU Report CMU-CS-91-170, 1991. [cited at p. 41, 56]

[22] B.N. Bershad, M.J. Zekauskas, and W.A. Sawdon. *The Midway distributed shared memory system*. IEEE, 1993. [cited at p. 41]

[23] P. A. Bigot. *GCC 4.x toolchain for Texas Instruments MSP430 MCUs*, 2011. http://mspgcc4.sourceforge.net/. [cited at p. 28]

[24] K. Birman and T. Joseph. Exploiting virtual synchrony in distributed systems. *ACM SIGOPS Operating Systems Review*, 21(5):123–138, 1987. [cited at p. 61]

[25] K.P. Birman and T.A. Joseph. Reliable communication in the presence of failures. *ACM Transactions on Computer Systems (TOCS)*, 5(1):47–76, 1987. [cited at p. 61]

[26] R. Bisiani and A. Forin. Multilanguage parallel programming of heterogeneous machines. *Computers, IEEE Transactions on*, 37(8):930–945, 1988. [cited at p. 41]

[27] R. Bisiani and M. Ravishankar. PLUS: A distributed shared-memory system. *ACM SIGARCH Computer Architecture News*, 18(3a):115–124, 1990. [cited at p. 41]

[28] F. Borran and J.P. Hubaux. Data Consistency in Sensor Networks: Secure Agreement. In *Proceedings of The First International Workshop on Wireless Networking for Intelligent Transportation Systems*, 2007. [cited at p. 85]

[29] A. Boulis. Castalia: revealing pitfalls in designing distributed algorithms in WSN. In *Proceedings of the 5th international conference on Embedded networked sensor systems*, pages 407–408. ACM, 2007. [cited at p. 34]

[30] M. Brzozowski, H. Salomon, and P. Langendoerfer. Limiting end-to-end delays in long-lasting sensor networks. In *Proceedings of the 8th ACM international workshop on Mobility management and wireless access*, pages 11–20. ACM, 2010. [cited at p. 31]

[31] M. Brzozowski, H. Salomon, and P. Langendoerfer. On Efficient Clock Drift Prediction Means and their Applicability to IEEE 802.15. 4. In *2010 IEEE/IFIP International Conference on Embedded and Ubiquitous Computing*, pages 216–223. IEEE, 2010. [cited at p. 31]

[32] M. Brzozowski, H. Salomon, K. Piotrowski, and P. Langendoerfer. Cross-platform protocol development for sensor networks: lessons learned. In *Proceeding of the 2nd workshop on Software engineering for sensor network applications*, SESENA '11, pages 7–12, New York, NY, USA, 2011. ACM. [cited at p. 108]

[33] P. Butcher, A. Wood, and M. Atkins. Global synchronisation in Linda. *Concurrency: Practice and Experience*, 6(6):505–516, 1994. [cited at p. 64]

[34] J.B. Carter, J.K. Bennett, and W. Zwaenepoel. Techniques for reducing consistency-related communication in distributed shared-memory systems. *ACM Trans. Comput. Syst.*, 13:205–243, August 1995. [cited at p. 51]

[35] J.B. Carter et al. Design of the Munin distributed shared memory system. *Journal of Parallel and Distributed Computing*, 29(2):219–227, 1995. [cited at p. 41]

[36] L. Casado and P. Tsigas. Contikisec: A secure network layer for wireless sensor networks under the contiki operating system. *Identity and Privacy in the Internet Age*, pages 133–147, 2009. [cited at p. 31]

[37] M. Ceriotti, L. Mottola, G.P. Picco, A.L. Murphy, S. Guna, M. Corra, M. Pozzi, D. Zonta, and P. Zanon. Monitoring heritage buildings with wireless sensor networks: The Torre Aquila deployment. In *Proceedings of the 2009 International Conference on Information Processing in Sensor Networks*, pages 277–288. IEEE Computer Society, 2009. [cited at p. 74]

[38] D. Chaiken and A. Agarwal. *Software-extended coherent shared memory: Performance and cost*, volume 22. IEEE Computer Society Press, 1994. [cited at p. 41, 51]

[39] J.M. Chang and N.F. Maxemchuk. Reliable broadcast protocols. *ACM Transactions on Computer Systems (TOCS)*, 2(3):251–273, 1984. [cited at p. 61]

[40] J. Chase, F. Amador, E. Lazowska, H. Levy, and R. Littlefield. The Amber system: Parallel programming on a network of multiprocessors. *ACM SIGOPS Operating Systems Review*, 23(5):147–158, 1989. [cited at p. 41]

[41] E. Cheong, E.A. Lee, and Y. Zhao. Viptos: a graphical development and simulation environment for tinyos-based wireless sensor networks. In *Proceedings of the 3rd international conference on Embedded networked sensor systems*, pages 302–302. ACM, 2005. [cited at p. 34]

[42] R. Chow and Y.C. Chow. *Distributed operating systems and algorithms*. Addison-Wesley Longman Publishing Co., Inc. Boston, MA, USA, 1997. [cited at p. 34, 51, 59, 60]

[43] Atmel Corp. *Atmel AVR 8- and 32-bit*, 2011. http://www.atmel.com/products/avr/. [cited at p. 14]

[44] Atmel Corp. *Atmel Corp. - Homepage*, 2011. http://www.atmel.com/. [cited at p. 14]

[45] Intel Corp. *Intel Corp., Homepage*, 2011. http://www.intel.com. [cited at p. 17]

[46] MEMSIC Corp. *MEMSIC Corp. - Homepage*, 2011. http://www.memsic.com. [cited at p. 13]

[47] Oracle Corp. *Oracle Corp. - Homepage*, 2011. http://www.oracle.com/us/sun/index.html. [cited at p. 13]

[48] Sentilla Corp. *Sentilla Corp. - Homepage*, 2011. http://www.sentilla.com/. [cited at p. 13]

[49] ATMEL Corporation. *AT86RF231*, 2009. http://www.atmel.com/dyn/resources/prod_documents/doc8111.pdf. [cited at p. 21]

[50] ATMEL Corporation. *AT86RF212*, 2010. http://www.atmel.com/dyn/resources/prod_documents/doc8168.pdf. [cited at p. 21]

[51] ATMEL Corporation. *AT91SAM9G20 Preliminary*, 2010. http://www.atmel.com/dyn/resources/prod_documents/doc6384.pdf. [cited at p. 14, 18]

[52] ATMEL Corporation. *ATmega640/1280/1281/2560/2561 Preliminary*, 2010. http://www.atmel.com/dyn/resources/prod_documents/doc2549.pdf. [cited at p. 14]

[53] ATMEL Corporation. *ATxmega16A4/32A4/64A4/128A4*, 2010. http://www.atmel.com/dyn/resources/prod_documents/doc8069.pdf. [cited at p. 16]

[54] ATMEL Corporation. *ATmega128(L)*, 2011. http://www.atmel.com/dyn/resources/prod_documents/doc2467.pdf. [cited at p. 14]

[55] P. Costa, L. Mottola, A.L. Murphy, and G.P. Picco. Developing sensor network applications using the teenylime middleware. Technical report, 2006. [cited at p. 71, 73]

[56] P. Costa, L. Mottola, A.L. Murphy, and G.P. Picco. TeenyLIME: transiently shared tuple space middleware for wireless sensor networks. In *Proceedings of the international workshop on Middleware for sensor networks*, pages 43–48. ACM, 2006. [cited at p. 11, 71, 116]

[57] P. Costa, L. Mottola, A.L. Murphy, and G.P. Picco. Programming Wireless Sensor Networks with the Teeny Lime Middleware. *Middleware 2007*, pages 429–449, 2007. [cited at p. 71, 74]

[58] AL Cox, S. Dwarkadas, P. Keleher, and W. Zwaenepoel. TreadMarks: Distributed Shared Memory on Standard Workstations and Operating Systems. In *Proceedings of the Winter 94 Usenix Conference*, pages 115–131, 1994. [cited at p. 41]

[59] D. Culler. *Berkeley NEST (Network Embedded Systems Technology)*, 2011. http://nest.cs.berkeley.edu/. [cited at p. 13]

[60] D. Culler. *Berkeley WEBS (Wireless Embedded Systems)*, 2011. http://webs.cs.berkeley.edu/. [cited at p. 13]

[61] C. Curino, M. Giani, M. Giorgetta, A. Giusti, A.L. Murphy, and G.P. Picco. Mobile data collection in sensor networks: The TinyLime middleware. *Pervasive and Mobile Computing*, 1(4):446–469, 2005. [cited at p. 70]

[62] C. Curino, M. Giani, M. Giorgetta, A. Giusti, A.L. Murphy, and G.P. Picco. Tinylime: Bridging mobile and sensor networks through middleware. 2005. [cited at p. 69]

[63] R. de Paz Alberola and D. Pesch. AvroraZ: extending Avrora with an IEEE 802.15.4 compliant radio chip model. In *Proceedings of the 3nd ACM workshop on Performance monitoring and measurement of heterogeneous wireless and wired networks*, pages 43–50. ACM, 2008. [cited at p. 33]

[64] G.S. Delp, D.J. Farber, R.G. Minnich, J.M. Smith, and M.C. Tam. Memory as a network abstraction. *Network, IEEE*, 5(4):34–41, 1991. [cited at p. 41]

[65] A. Demers, D. Greene, C. Hauser, W. Irish, J. Larson, S. Shenker, H. Sturgis, D. Swinehart, and D. Terry. Epidemic algorithms for replicated database maintenance. In *Proceedings of the sixth annual ACM Symposium on Principles of distributed computing*, pages 1–12. ACM, 1987. [cited at p. 57]

[66] A. Demers, K. Petersen, M. Spreitzer, D. Terry, M. Theimer, and B. Welch. The bayou architecture: Support for data sharing among mobile users. *Mobile Computing Systems and Applications, IEEE Workshop on*, 0:2–7, 1994. [cited at p. 57]

[67] J. Deng, R. Han, and S. Mishra. Secure code distribution in dynamically programmable wireless sensor networks. In *Proceedings of the 5th international conference on Information processing in sensor networks*, pages 292–300. ACM, 2006. [cited at p. 31]

[68] R. Di Pietro, C. Soriente, A. Spognardi, and G. Tsudik. Collaborative authentication in unattended WSNs. In *Proceedings of the second ACM conference on Wireless network security*, pages 237–244. ACM, 2009. [cited at p. 31]

[69] D. Diky and Ch. Liechti. *The GCC toolchain for the Texas Instruments MSP430 MCUs*, 2011. http://mspgcc.sourceforge.net/. [cited at p. 28]

[70] G. Dilin. Survey on Routing Protocols in Wireless Sensor Networks. *World Sci-tech R & D*, 4, 2005. [cited at p. 31]

[71] N. Dimokas, D. Katsaros, and Y. Manolopoulos. Cache consistency in wireless multimedia sensor networks. *Ad Hoc Networks*, 8(2):214–240, 2010. [cited at p. 84]

[72] A. Douglas, A. Wood, and A. Rowstron. Linda implementation revisited. In *Transputer and occam developments: WoTUG-18: proceedings of the 187th world occam and Transputer User Group Technical Meeting, 9th-13th April 1995, Manchester, UK*, page 125. Ios Pr Inc, 1995. [cited at p. 64]

[73] M. Dubois, C. Scheurich, and F. Briggs. Memory access buffering in multiprocessors. In *Proceedings of the 13th annual international symposium on Computer architecture*, pages 434–442. IEEE Computer Society Press, 1986. [cited at p. 54]

[74] A. Dunkels, B. Grönvall, and T. Voigt. Contiki - a lightweight and flexible operating system for tiny networked sensors. In *Proceedings of the First IEEE Workshop on Embedded Networked Sensors (Emnets-I)*, Tampa, Florida, USA, November 2004. [cited at p. 26, 117]

[75] P. Dutta. *Epic: An Open Mote Platform for Application-Driven Design*, 2011. http://www.cs.berkeley.edu/ prabal/projects/epic/. [cited at p. 16, 23]

[76] E. Egea-Lopez, J. Vales-Alonso, AS Martinez-Sala, P. Pavon-Marino, and J. García-Haro. Simulation tools for wireless sensor networks. In *Proceedings of the International Symposium on Performance Evaluation of Computer and Telecommunication Systems (SPECTS05)*, 2005. [cited at p. 34]

[77] A. El-Hoiyi, J.D. Decotignie, and J. Hernandez. Low power MAC protocols for infrastructure wireless sensor networks. In *Proceedings of the Fifth European Wireless Conference*, pages 563–569. Citeseer, 2004. [cited at p. 30]

[78] D. Estrin. *Center for Embedded Networked Sensing (CENS)*, 2011. http://www.cens.ucla.edu/. [cited at p. 13]

[79] G. Fang and E. Dutkiewicz. BodyMAC: energy efficient TDMA-based MAC protocol for wireless body area networks. In *Communications and Information Technology, 2009. ISCIT 2009. 9th International Symposium on*, pages 1455–1459. IEEE, 2009. [cited at p. 31]

[80] B. Fleisch and G. Popek. Mirage: A coherent distributed shared memory design. In *Proceedings of the twelfth ACM symposium on Operating systems principles*, pages 211–223. ACM, 1989. [cited at p. 41]

[81] S. Floyd, V. Jacobson, C.G. Liu, S. McCanne, and L. Zhang. A reliable multicast framework for light-weight sessions and application level framing. *IEEE/ACM Transactions on Networking (TON)*, 5(6):784–803, 1997. [cited at p. 61]

[82] C.L. Fok, G.C. Roman, and G. Hackmann. A lightweight coordination middleware for mobile computing. In *Coordination Models and Languages*, pages 135–151. Springer, 2004. [cited at p. 67]

[83] R. Fonseca, P. Dutta, P. Levis, and I. Stoica. Quanto: Tracking energy in networked embedded systems. In *Proceedings of the 8th USENIX conference on Operating systems design and implementation*, pages 323–338. USENIX Association, 2008. [cited at p. 34]

[84] IHP-Innovations for High Performance Microelectronics. *IHP–Innovations for High Performance Microelectronics - Homepage*, 2011. http://www.ihp-microelectronics.com/. [cited at p. 13, 19]

[85] K. Gharachorloo, A. Gupta, and J. Hennessy. Performance evaluation of memory consistency models for shared-memory multiprocessors. *ACM SIGARCH Computer Architecture News*, 19(2):245–257, 1991. [cited at p. 51]

[86] K. Gharachorloo, A. Gupta, and J. Hennessy. *Two techniques to enhance the performance of memory consistency models.* 1991. [cited at p. 51]

[87] K. Gharachorloo, D. Lenoski, J. Laudon, P. Gibbons, A. Gupta, and J. Hennessy. Memory consistency and event ordering in scalable shared-memory multiprocessors. *ACM SIGARCH Computer Architecture News*, 18(3a):15–26, 1990. [cited at p. 54, 55]

[88] J. Girao, D. Westhoff, E. Mykletun, and T. Araki. Tinypeds: Tiny persistent encrypted data storage in asynchronous wireless sensor networks. *Ad Hoc Networks Journal (Elsevier).*, to appear. [cited at p. 116]

[89] J.R. Goodman. CACHE CONSISTENCY AND SEQUENTIAL CONSISTENCY. Technical report, SCI Committee, 1989. [cited at p. 54]

[90] A. Grilo, K. Piotrowski, P. Langendoerfer, and A. Casaca. A Wireless Sensor Network Architecture for Homeland Security Application. *Ad-Hoc, Mobile and Wireless Networks*, pages 397–402, 2009. [cited at p. 32]

[91] R. Gummadi, O. Gnawali, and R. Govindan. Macro-programming wireless sensor networks using kairos. *Distributed Computing in Sensor Systems*, pages 126–140, 2005. [cited at p. 116]

[92] W.B. Heinzelman, A.P. Chandrakasan, and H. Balakrishnan. An application-specific protocol architecture for wireless microsensor networks. *Wireless Communications, IEEE Transactions on*, 1(4):660–670, 2002. [cited at p. 31]

[93] M.P. Herlihy and J.M. Wing. Linearizability: A correctness condition for concurrent objects. *ACM Transactions on Programming Languages and Systems (TOPLAS)*, 12(3):463–492, 1990. [cited at p. 52]

[94] T.W. Hnat, T.I. Sookoor, P. Hooimeijer, W. Weimer, and K. Whitehouse. Macrolab: a vector-based macroprogramming framework for cyber-physical systems. In *Proceedings of the 6th ACM conference on Embedded network sensor systems*, pages 225–238. ACM, 2008. [cited at p. 79, 121]

[95] P. Hurni and T. Braun. Calibrating Wireless Sensor Network Simulation Models with Real-World Experiments. *NETWORKING 2009*, pages 1–13, 2009. [cited at p. 34]

[96] P.W. Hutto and M. Ahamad. Slow memory: Weakening consistency to enhance concurrency in distributed shared memories. In *Distributed Computing Systems, 1990. Proceedings., 10th International Conference on*, pages 302–309. IEEE, 1989. [cited at p. 54]

[97] L. Iftode, J.P. Singh, and K. Li. Scope consistency: A bridge between release consistency and entry consistency. *Theory of Computing Systems*, 31(4):451–473, 1998. [cited at p. 41]

[98] M. Imran, A.M. Said, and H. Hasbullah. A survey of simulators, emulators and testbeds for wireless sensor networks. In *Information Technology (ITSim), 2010 International Symposium in*, volume 2, pages 897–902. IEEE, 2010. [cited at p. 34]

[99] Marvell Technology Group Inc. *Marvell Technology Group Inc., Homepage*, 2011. http://www.marvell.com. [cited at p. 17]

[100] MEMSIC Inc. *Imote2 High-Performance Wireless Sensor Network Node*, 2011. http://www.memsic.com/support/documentation/wireless-sensor-networks/category/7-datasheets.html?download=134:imote2. [cited at p. 13]

[101] MEMSIC Inc. *IRIS Wireless Measurement System*, 2011. http://www.memsic.com/support/documentation/wireless-sensor-networks/category/7-datasheets.html?download=135:iris. [cited at p. 13]

[102] MEMSIC Inc. *MICA2 Wireless Measurement System*, 2011. http://www.memsic.com/support/documentation/wireless-sensor-networks/category/7-datasheets.html?download=147:mica2. [cited at p. 13]

[103] MEMSIC Inc. *MICAz Wireless Measurement System*, 2011. http://www.memsic.com/support/documentation/wireless-sensor-networks/category/7-datasheets.html?download=148:micaz. [cited at p. 13]

[104] MEMSIC Inc. *TELOSB Mote Platform*, 2011. [cited at p. 13]

[105] Oracle America Inc. *SunSPOT Main Board Technical Datasheet*, 2010. http://www.sunspotworld.com/docs/Yellow/eSPOT8ds.pdf. [cited at p. 13, 117]

[106] Oracle America Inc. *Oracle Technology Network for Java Developers*, 2011. http://www.oracle.com/technetwork/java/index.html. [cited at p. 18]

[107] Texas Instruments Inc. *MSP430x1xx Family User's Guide*, 2006. http://www.ti.com/litv/pdf/slau049f. [cited at p. 14]

[108] Texas Instruments Inc. *2.4 GHz IEEE 802.15.4 / ZigBee-Ready RF Transceiver*, 2007. http://www.ti.com/lit/gpn/cc2420. [cited at p. 14]

[109] Texas Instruments Inc. *2.4 GHz IEEE 802.15.4/ZIGBEE RF TRANSCEIVER*, 2007. http://www.ti.com/lit/gpn/cc2520. [cited at p. 14]

[110] Texas Instruments Inc. *Single-Chip Very Low Power RF Transceiver*, 2007. http://www.ti.com/lit/gpn/cc1000. [cited at p. 14, 18]

[111] Texas Instruments Inc. *Low-Cost Low-Power 2.4 GHz RF Transceiver*, 2009. http://www.ti.com/lit/gpn/cc2500. [cited at p. 14, 19]

[112] Texas Instruments Inc. *CC1101 Low-Power Sub-1 GHz RF Transceiver*, 2010. http://www.ti.com/lit/gpn/cc1101. [cited at p. 14, 19]

[113] Texas Instruments Inc. *CC430 Family User's Guide*, 2010. http://www.ti.com/litv/pdf/slau259b. [cited at p. 14]

[114] Texas Instruments Inc. *CC430F613x, CC430F612x, CC430F513x MSP430 SoC With RF Core*, 2010. http://www.ti.com/lit/gpn/cc430f6137. [cited at p. 14]

[115] Texas Instruments Inc. *eZ430-Chronos Development Tool User's Guide*, 2010. http://www.ti.com/lit/pdf/slau292. [cited at p. 13]

[116] Texas Instruments Inc. *MSP430F543xA, MSP430F541xA Mixed Signal Microcontroller*, 2010. http://www.ti.com/lit/gpn/msp430f5438a. [cited at p. 14, 17]

[117] Texas Instruments Inc. *MSP430x5xx/MSP430x6xx Family User's Guide*, 2010. http://www.ti.com/litv/pdf/slau208h. [cited at p. 14]

[118] Texas Instruments Inc. *Code Composer Studio (CCStudio) Integrated Development Environment (IDE)*, 2011. http://focus.ti.com/docs/toolsw/folders/print/ccstudio.html. [cited at p. 28, 149, 158]

[119] Texas Instruments Inc. *MSP430F15x, MSP430F16x, MSP430F161x Mixed Signal Microcontroller*, 2011. http://www.ti.com/lit/gpn/msp430f1611. [cited at p. 14, 16]

[120] Texas Instruments Inc. *Texas Instruments Inc. - Homepage*, 2011. http://www.ti.com/. [cited at p. 13]

[121] D.V. James. The scalable coherent interface: scaling to high-performance systems. In *Compcon Spring'94, Digest of Papers.*, pages 64–71. IEEE, 1994. [cited at p. 41]

[122] C. Jardak, K. Rerkrai, A. Kovacevic, J. Riihijarvi, and P. Mahonen. Email from the vineyard. In *Testbeds and Research Infrastructures for the Development of Networks & Communities and Workshops, 2009. TridentCom 2009. 5th International Conference on*, pages 1–6. IEEE, 2009. [cited at p. 32]

[123] M. Johnson, M. Healy, P. van de Ven, M.J. Hayes, J. Nelson, T. Newe, and E. Lewis. A comparative review of wireless sensor network mote technologies. In *Sensors, 2009 IEEE*, pages 1439–1442. IEEE. [cited at p. 13]

[124] P. Juang, H. Oki, Y. Wang, M. Martonosi, L.S. Peh, and D. Rubenstein. Energy-efficient computing for wildlife tracking: Design tradeoffs and early experiences with zebranet. In *Proceedings of the 10th international conference on Architectural support for programming languages and operating systems*, pages 96–107. ACM, 2002. [cited at p. 33]

[125] A. Judge, P.A. Nixon, V.J. Cahill, B. Tangney, and S. Weber. Overview of distributed shared memory. Technical report, Trinity College Dublin, 1998. [cited at p. 34, 51]

[126] M.F. Kaashoek, A.S. Tanenbaum, and S.F. Hummel. An efficient reliable broadcast protocol. *ACM SIGOPS Operating Systems Review*, 23(4):5–19, 1989. [cited at p. 60]

[127] C. Karlof, N. Sastry, and D. Wagner. TinySec: a link layer security architecture for wireless sensor networks. In *Proceedings of the 2nd international conference on Embedded networked sensor systems*, pages 162–175. ACM, 2004. [cited at p. 31]

[128] C. Karlof and D. Wagner. Secure routing in wireless sensor networks: Attacks and countermeasures. *Ad hoc networks*, 1(2-3):293–315, 2003. [cited at p. 31]

[129] P. Keleher, A.L. Cox, and W. Zwaenepoel. Lazy release consistency for software distributed shared memory. In *Proceedings of the 19th annual international symposium on Computer architecture*, pages 13–21. ACM, 1992. [cited at p. 56]

[130] J. Kuskin, D. Ofelt, M. Heinrich, J. Heinlein, R. Simoni, K. Gharachorloo, J. Chapin, D. Nakahira, J. Baxter, M. Horowitz, et al. The stanford flash multiprocessor. In *Proceedings of the 21ST annual international symposium on Computer architecture*, pages 302–313. IEEE Computer Society Press, 1994. [cited at p. 41]

[131] L. Lamport. How to make a multiprocessor computer that correctly executes multiprocess programm. *IEEE transactions on computers*, pages 690–691, 1979. [cited at p. 52]

[132] P. Langendoerfer, S. Peter, K. Piotrowski, R. Nunes, and A. Casaca. A Middleware Approach to Configure Security in WSN. 2007. [cited at p. 31]

[133] D Lenoski, J. Laudon, K. Gharachorloo, W.D. Weber, A. Gupta, J. Hennessy, M. Horowitz, and M.S. Lam. The stanford dash multiprocessor. *COMPUTER,*, pages 63–79, 1992. [cited at p. 41]

[134] B.N. Levine and J.J. Garcia-Luna-Aceves. A comparison of reliable multicast protocols. *Multimedia Systems*, 6(5):334–348, 1998. [cited at p. 61]

[135] P. Levis and N. Lee. Tossim: A simulator for tinyos networks. *UC Berkeley, September*, 2003. [cited at p. 33]

[136] P. Levis, N. Lee, M. Welsh, and D. Culler. TOSSIM: Accurate and scalable simulation of entire TinyOS applications. In *Proceedings of the 1st international conference on Embedded networked sensor systems*, pages 126–137. ACM, 2003. [cited at p. 33]

[137] P. Levis, S. Madden, J. Polastre, R. Szewczyk, K. Whitehouse, A. Woo, D. Gay, J. Hill, M. Welsh, E. Brewer, et al. Tinyos: An operating system for sensor networks. *Ambient Intelligence*, pages 115–148, 2005. [cited at p. 25, 117]

[138] P. Levis, N. Patel, D. Culler, and S. Shenker. Trickle: A self-regulating algorithm for code propagation and maintenance in wireless sensor networks. In *Proceedings of the 1st conference on Symposium on Networked Systems Design and Implementation-Volume 1*, pages 2–2. USENIX Association, 2004. [cited at p. 62]

[139] D. Li, K. Wong, Y.H. Hu, and A. Sayeed. Detection, classification and tracking of targets in distributed sensor networks. *IEEE signal processing magazine*, 19(2):17–29, 2002. [cited at p. 32]

[140] K. Li. Shared virtual memory on loosely coupled multiprocessors. 1986. [cited at p. 34]

[141] K. Li. Ivy: A shared virtual memory system for parallel computing. In *Proceedings of the 1988 International Conference on Parallel Processing*, volume 2, pages 94–101, 1988. [cited at p. 41]

[142] K. Li and P. Hudak. Memory coherence in shared virtual memory systems. *ACM Transactions on Computer Systems (TOCS)*, 7(4):321–359, 1989. [cited at p. 44]

[143] R.J. Lipton and J.S. Sandberg. *PRAM: A scalable shared memory*. Princeton University, Dept. of Computer Science, 1988. [cited at p. 53]

[144] T. Liu, C.M. Sadler, P. Zhang, and M. Martonosi. Implementing software on resource-constrained mobile sensors: experiences with impala and zebranet. In *Proceedings of the 2nd international conference on Mobile systems, applications, and services*, pages 256–269. ACM, 2004. [cited at p. 33]

[145] ARM Ltd. *ARM Ltd. - Homepage*, 2011. http://www.arm.com/. [cited at p. 14]

[146] L. Luo, T.F. Abdelzaher, T. He, and J.A. Stankovic. Envirosuite: An environmentally immersive programming framework for sensor networks. *ACM Transactions on Embedded Computing Systems (TECS)*, 5(3):543–576, 2006. [cited at p. 116]

[147] S.R. Madden, M.J. Franklin, J. Hellerstein, and W. Hong. TinyDB: an acquisitional query processing system for sensor networks. *ACM Transactions on Database Systems*, 30(1):122–173, 2005. [cited at p. 116]

[148] C. Maples and L. Wittie. MERLIN. A superglue for multicomputer systems. In *Compcon Spring'90. Intellectual Leverage. Digest of Papers. Thirty-Fifth IEEE Computer Society International Conference.*, pages 73–81. IEEE. [cited at p. 41]

[149] K. Martinez, R. Ong, and J. Hart. Glacsweb: a sensor network for hostile environments. In *Sensor and Ad Hoc Communications and Networks, 2004. IEEE SECON 2004. 2004 First Annual IEEE Communications Society Conference on*, pages 81–87. IEEE, 2004. [cited at p. 32]

[150] Marvel. *PXA27x Specification Update*, 2010. http://www.marvell.com/products/processors/applications/pxa_family/pxa_27x_emts.pdf. [cited at p. 14, 17]

[151] M. Mogensen. Epidemic protocols for pervasive computing systems: moving focus from architecture to protocol. In *Proceedings of the International Workshop on Middleware for Pervasive Mobile and Embedded Computing*, pages 1–4. ACM, 2009. [cited at p. 57]

[152] C. Morin and I. Puaut. A survey of recoverable distributed shared virtual memory systems. *Parallel and Distributed Systems, IEEE Transactions on*, 8(9):959–969, 1997. [cited at p. 59]

[153] D. Mosberger. Memory consistency models. *ACM SIGOPS Operating Systems Review*, 27(1):18–26, 1993. [cited at p. 51]

[154] L. Mottola, A.L. Murphy, and G.P. Picco. Pervasive games in a mote-enabled virtual world using tuple space middleware. In *Proceedings of 5th ACM SIGCOMM workshop on Network and system support for games*, pages 29–es. ACM, 2006. [cited at p. 71]

[155] L. Mottola and G.P. Picco. Programming wireless sensor networks: Fundamental concepts and state of the art. *ACM Computing Surveys*, 2010. [cited at p. 31]

[156] A.L. Murphy, G.P. Picco, and G-C. Roman. Lime: A middleware for physical and logical mobility. *Distributed Computing Systems, International Conference on*, 0:0524, 2001. [cited at p. 64, 66]

[157] A.L. Murphy, G.P. Picco, and G.C. Roman. LIME: A coordination model and middleware supporting mobility of hosts and agents. *ACM Transactions on Software Engineering and Methodology (TOSEM)*, 15(3):279–328, 2006. [cited at p. 64, 66]

[158] B. Nitzberg and V. Lo. Distributed shared memory: A survey of issues and algorithms. *Computer*, 24(8):52–60, 1991. [cited at p. 34, 40, 51]

[159] The Institute of Electrical and Inc. Electronics Engineers. *IEEE 802.15.4*, 2011. http://www.ieee802.org/15/pub/TG4.html. [cited at p. 19]

[160] C. Otto, A. Milenkovic, C. Sanders, and E. Jovanov. System architecture of a wireless body area sensor network for ubiquitous health monitoring. *Journal of Mobile Multimedia*, 1(4):307–326, 2006. [cited at p. 33]

[161] E. Pagani and G.P. Rossi. Reliable broadcast in mobile multihop packet networks. In *Proceedings of the 3rd annual ACM/IEEE international conference on Mobile computing and networking*, pages 34–42. ACM, 1997. [cited at p. 60]

[162] G. Pei and C. Chien. Low power TDMA in large wireless sensor networks. In *Military Communications Conference, 2001. MILCOM 2001. Communications for Network-Centric Operations: Creating the Information Force. IEEE*, volume 1, pages 347–351. IEEE, 2001. [cited at p. 31]

[163] St. Peter, P. Langendoerfer, and K. Piotrowski. Public key cryptography empowered smart dust is affordable. *International Journal of Sensor Networks*, 4(1/2), 2008. [cited at p. 16]

[164] St. Peter, K. Piotrowski, and P. Langendoerfer. In-network-aggregation as case study for a support tool reducing the complexity of designing secure wireless sensor networks. In *Proc. of the Third IEEE International Workshop on Practical Issues in Building Sensor Network Applications (SenseApp)*, 2008. [cited at p. 31]

[165] H.N. Pham, D. Pediaditakis, and A. Boulis. From simulation to real deployments in WSN and back. 2007. [cited at p. 34]

[166] G.P. Picco, A.L. Murphy, and G.C. Roman. LIME: Linda meets mobility. In *Proceedings of the 21st international conference on Software engineering*, pages 368–377. ACM, 1999. [cited at p. 64, 66]

[167] G.P. Picco, A.L. Murphy, and G.C. Roman. Developing mobile computing applications with LIME. In *Software Engineering, 2000. Proceedings of the 2000 International Conference on*, pages 766–769. IEEE, 2000. [cited at p. 66]

[168] S. Pingali, D. Towsley, and J.F. Kurose. A comparison of sender-initiated and receiver-initiated reliable multicast protocols. In *ACM SIGMETRICS Performance Evaluation Review*, volume 22, pages 221–230. ACM, 1994. [cited at p. 61]

[169] K. Piotrowski, P. Langendoerfer, and St. Peter. How public key cryptography influences wireless sensor node lifetime. In *SASN '06: Proceedings of the fourth ACM workshop on Security of ad hoc and sensor networks*, pages 169–176, New York, NY, USA, 2006. ACM Press. [cited at p. 16, 24]

[170] K. Piotrowski, P. Langendoerfer, and St. Peter. tinyDSM: A highly reliable cooperative data storage for Wireless Sensor Networks. In *Collaborative Technologies and Systems, 2009. CTS'09. International Symposium on*, pages 225–232. IEEE, 2009. [cited at p. 115]

[171] K. Piotrowski, A. Sojka, and P. Langendoerfer. Body area network for first responders-a case study. In *Proceedings of the Fifth International Conference on Body Area Networks*, BodyNets '10. ICST (Institute for Computer Sciences, Social-Informatics and Telecommunications Engineering), 2010. [cited at p. 13, 28, 33]

[172] K. Piotrowski, A. Sojka, and P. Langendoerfer. Wireless Sensor Networks Can Save Lives-Benefits and Open Issues. *Sensoren und Messsysteme 2010*, 2010. [cited at p. 33]

[173] K. Pister. *SMART DUST*, 2011. http://robotics.eecs.berkeley.edu/p̃ister/SmartDust/. [cited at p. 13]

[174] J. Polastre, J. Hill, and D. Culler. Versatile low power media access for wireless sensor networks. In *Proceedings of the 2nd international conference on Embedded networked sensor systems, November*, pages 03–05. Citeseer, 2004. [cited at p. 30]

[175] J. Polley, D. Blazakis, J. McGee, D. Rusk, and J.S. Baras. Atemu: A fine-grained sensor network simulator. In *Sensor and Ad Hoc Communications and Networks, 2004. IEEE SECON 2004. 2004 First Annual IEEE Communications Society Conference on*, pages 145–152. IEEE, 2004. [cited at p. 34]

[176] J. Portilla, A. De Castro, E. De La Torre, and T. Riesgo. A modular architecture for nodes in wireless sensor networks. *Journal of Universal Computer Science*, 12(3):328–339, 2006. [cited at p. 23]

[177] UBISEC&SENS project partners. *UBISEC&SENS Project, Homepage*, 2006. http://www.ist-ubisecsens.org/. [cited at p. 32]

[178] WSAN4CIP project partners. *WSAN4CIP Project, Homepage*, 2009. http://www.wsan4cip.eu/. [cited at p. 32]

[179] J. Protic, M. Tomasevic, and V. Milutinovic. A survey of distributed shared memory systems. In *hicss*, page 74. Published by the IEEE Computer Society, 1995. [cited at p. 34, 41, 42, 43, 51, 273]

[180] J. Protić, M. Tomašević, M. Tomasevic, and V. Milutinović. *Distributed Shared Memory: concepts and systems*. Wiley-IEEE Computer Society Pr, 1998. [cited at p. 34, 44, 51]

[181] V. Rajendran, JJ Garcia-Luna-Aveces, and K. Obraczka. Energy-efficient, application-aware medium access for sensor networks. In *IEEE International Conference on Mobile Adhoc and Sensor Systems Conference, 2005.*, page 630. IEEE, 2005. [cited at p. 31]

[182] U. Ramachandran and M.Y.A. Khalidi. An implementation of distributed shared memory. *Software: Practice and Experience*, 21(5):443–464, 1991. [cited at p. 41]

[183] A.M.V. Reddy, A.V.U.P. Kumar, D. Janakiram, and G.A. Kumar. Wireless sensor network operating systems: a survey. *International Journal of Sensor Networks*, 5(4):236–255, 2009. [cited at p. 25]

[184] Q. Ren and Q. Liang. Secure media access control (MAC) in wireless sensor networks: Intrusion detections and countermeasures. In *Personal, Indoor and Mobile Radio Communications, 2004. PIMRC 2004. 15th IEEE International Symposium on*, volume 4, pages 3025–3029. IEEE, 2004. [cited at p. 31]

[185] Shimmer Research. *Shimmer Research - Homepage*, 2011. http://www.shimmer-research.com/. [cited at p. 13]

[186] A.M. Ricciardi and K.P. Birman. Using process groups to implement failure detection in asynchronous environments. In *Proceedings of the tenth annual ACM symposium on Principles of distributed computing*, pages 341–353. ACM, 1991. [cited at p. 61]

[187] I. Schoinas, B. Falsafi, A.R. Lebeck, S.K. Reinhardt, J.R. Larus, and D.A. Wood. Fine-grain access control for distributed shared memory. In *Proceedings of the sixth international conference on Architectural support for programming languages and operating systems*, pages 297–306. ACM, 1994. [cited at p. 41]

[188] K. Sha and W. Shi. Modeling Data Consistency in Wireless Sensor Networks. In *Distributed Computing Systems Workshops, 2007. ICDCSW'07. 27th International Conference on*. IEEE. [cited at p. 82]

[189] A. Sheth, C.A. Thekkath, P. Mehta, K. Tejaswi, C. Parekh, T.N. Singh, and U.B. Desai. Senslide: a distributed landslide prediction system. *ACM SIGOPS Operating Systems Review*, 41(2):75–87, 2007. [cited at p. 32]

[190] V. Shnayder, M. Hempstead, B. Chen, G.W. Allen, and M. Welsh. Simulating the power consumption of large-scale sensor network applications. In *Proceedings of the*

2nd international conference on Embedded networked sensor systems, pages 188–200. ACM, 2004. [cited at p. 34]

[191] J. Silcock, Deakin University. School of Computing, and Mathematics. *Distributed Shared Memory: A Survey*. Citeseer, 1995. [cited at p. 34, 51]

[192] E. Speight and J.K. Bennett. Brazos: A third generation DSM system. In *Proceedings of the USENIX Windows NT Workshop on The USENIX Windows NT Workshop 1997*, pages 13–13. USENIX Association, 1997. [cited at p. 41]

[193] E. Stavrou and A. Pitsillides. A survey on secure multipath routing protocols in WSNs. *Computer Networks*, 54(13):2215–2238, 2010. [cited at p. 31]

[194] D. Sundarraj, P.B. Gibbons, and P.S. Pillai. Ensuring spatio-temporal consistency in distributed networks of smart cameras. In *Proceedings of the First Workshop on Distributed Smart Cameras*. Citeseer, 2006. [cited at p. 83]

[195] S. Sundresh, W. Kim, and G. Agha. SENS: A sensor, environment and network simulator. In *Proceedings of the 37th annual symposium on Simulation*, page 221. IEEE Computer Society, 2004. [cited at p. 34]

[196] A.S. Tanenbaum. *Distributed operating systems*. Prentice Hall, 1995. [cited at p. 52]

[197] A.S. Tanenbaum and M. Van Steen. *Distributed systems: principles and paradigms*, volume 130888931. Prentice Hall Upper Saddle River, NJ:, 2002. [cited at p. 34, 51, 52, 58, 61]

[198] A.S. Tanenbaum and A.S. Woodhull. Operating systems: design and implementation. 1987. [cited at p. 34]

[199] K. Tang and M. Gerla. MAC reliable broadcast in ad hoc networks. In *Military Communications Conference, 2001. MILCOM 2001. Communications for Network-Centric Operations: Creating the Information Force. IEEE*, volume 2, pages 1008–1013. IEEE, 2001. [cited at p. 60]

[200] J. Tateson, C. Roadknight, A. Gonzalez, T. Khan, S. Fitz, I. Henning, N. Boyd, C. Vincent, and IW Marshall. Real World Issues in Deploying a Wireless Sensor Network. *Refereed REALWSN 2005 proceedings*, 2005. [cited at p. 32]

[201] D.B. Terry, A.J. Demers, K. Petersen, M.J. Spreitzer, M.M. Theimer, and B.B. Welch. Session guarantees for weakly consistent replicated data. In *Parallel and Distributed Information Systems, 1994., Proceedings of the Third International Conference on*, pages 140–149. IEEE, 1994. [cited at p. 57]

[202] D.B. Terry, K. Petersen, M. Spreitzer, and M. Theimer. The case for non-transparent replication: Examples from Bayou. *Data Engineering Bulletin*, 21(4):12–20, 1998. [cited at p. 57]

[203] B.L. Titzer, D.K. Lee, and J. Palsberg. Avrora: scalable sensor network simulation with precise timing. In *Proceedings of the 4th international symposium on Information processing in sensor networks*, pages 67–es, 2005. [cited at p. 33]

[204] T. Van Dam and K. Langendoen. An adaptive energy-efficient MAC protocol for wireless sensor networks. In *Proceedings of the 1st international conference on Embedded networked sensor systems*, pages 171–180. ACM, 2003. [cited at p. 30]

[205] M. Varshney, D. Xu, M. Srivastava, and R. Bagrodia. sQualNet: A scalable simulation and emulation environment for sensor networks. In *Proceedings of the International Conference on Information Processing in Sensor Networks, New York, NY, USA*. Citeseer, 2007. [cited at p. 34]

[206] K. Walther and J. Nolte. A flexible scheduling framework for deeply embedded systems. In *Proceedings of the 21st International Conference on Advanced Information Networking and Applications Workshops - Volume 01*, AINAW '07, pages 784–791, Washington, DC, USA, 2007. IEEE Computer Society. [cited at p. 27, 117]

[207] M. Welsh and G. Mainland. Programming sensor networks using abstract regions. In *Proceedings of the 1st conference on Symposium on Networked Systems Design and Implementation-Volume 1*, pages 3–3. USENIX Association, 2004. [cited at p. 77, 123]

[208] G. Werner-Allen, J. Johnson, M. Ruiz, J. Lees, and M. Welsh. Monitoring volcanic eruptions with a wireless sensor network. In *Wireless Sensor Networks, 2005. Proceeedings of the Second European Workshop on*, pages 108–120. IEEE, 2005. [cited at p. 32]

[209] G. Werner-Allen, K. Lorincz, J. Johnson, J. Lees, and M. Welsh. Fidelity and yield in a volcano monitoring sensor network. In *Proceedings of the 7th symposium on Operating systems design and implementation*, pages 381–396. USENIX Association, 2006. [cited at p. 32]

[210] K. Whitehouse, C. Sharp, E. Brewer, and D. Culler. Hood: a neighborhood abstraction for sensor networks. In *MobiSys '04: Proceedings of the 2nd international conference on Mobile systems, applications, and services*, pages 99–110, New York, NY, USA, 2004. ACM Press. [cited at p. 75, 123]

[211] A.S. Xu and Massachusetts Institute of Technology. Laboratory for Computer Science. *A fault-tolerant network kernel for Linda*. 1988. [cited at p. 64]

[212] Y. Yao and J. Gehrke. The cougar approach to in-network query processing in sensor networks. *SIGMOD record*, 31(3):9–18, 2002. [cited at p. 116]

[213] W. Ye, J. Heidemann, and D. Estrin. An energy-efficient MAC protocol for wireless sensor networks. In *INFOCOM 2002. Twenty-First Annual Joint Conference of the IEEE Computer and Communications Societies. Proceedings. IEEE*, volume 3, pages 1567–1576. IEEE, 2002. [cited at p. 30]

[214] W. Ye, F. Silva, and J. Heidemann. Ultra-low duty cycle MAC with scheduled channel polling. In *Proceedings of the 4th international conference on Embedded networked sensor systems*, pages 321–334. ACM, 2006. [cited at p. 31]

[215] YU Yong-chang and WEI Gang. Survey on routing protocols for wireless sensor networks. *Application Research of Computers*, 6:1616–1621, 2008. [cited at p. 31]

[216] O. Younis and S. Fahmy. HEED: a hybrid, energy-efficient, distributed clustering approach for ad hoc sensor networks. *IEEE Transactions on Mobile Computing*, pages 366–379, 2004. [cited at p. 31]

[217] P. Zhang, C.M. Sadler, S.A. Lyon, and M. Martonosi. Hardware design experiences in ZebraNet. In *Proceedings of the 2nd international conference on Embedded networked sensor systems*, pages 227–238. ACM, 2004. [cited at p. 33]

[218] S. Zhou, M. Stumm, and T. McInerney. Extending distributed shared memory to heterogeneous environments. In *Distributed Computing Systems, 1990. Proceedings., 10th International Conference on*, pages 30–37. IEEE, 1990. [cited at p. 41]

Appendix A

Policy Parameters–Identification

Table A.1: The policy parameter–global

Parameter name	**global**
Description	This parameter indicates that the variable is a global one.
Parameter class	Identification
Usage	global
Default setting	off–an array variable
Dependencies	—
Influenced functions	$var\_isGlobal()$

Table A.2: The policy parameter–migration

Parameter name	**migration**
Description	Specifies the number of consecutive write operations from an external node that result in a transfer of the ownership. Applies for global variables only.
Parameter class	Identification
Usage	migration : integer
Default setting	0
Dependencies	Requires **global**.
Influenced functions	$repLogic\_shallBeSent()$

Table A.3: The policy parameter–timestamp

Parameter name	**timestamp**
Description	This switch parameter specifies the identification of the instances of the variable. If it is enabled the time-stamping is used, otherwise, the instances are identified by a version number. The version numbers of individual entities of the variable are independent.
Parameter class	Identification
Usage	timestamp
Default setting	off–version number identifies the instances
Dependencies	—
Influenced functions	*repLogic_setTimestamp()*

Table A.4: The policy parameter–timestamp_size

Parameter name	**timestamp_size**
Description	Specifies the size of the version number or timestamp in bytes.
Parameter class	Identification
Usage	timestamp_size : integer
Default setting	2
Dependencies	—
Influenced functions	—

Table A.5: The policy parameter–timestamp_tolerance

Parameter name	**timestamp_tolerance**
Description	Defines the allowed timestamp difference for a read request.
Parameter class	Identification
Usage	timestamp_tolerance : integer
Default setting	0
Dependencies	—
Influenced functions	*repLogic_isTsInRange()*

Table A.6: The policy parameter–request_number_size

Parameter name	**request_number_size**
Description	Defines the required size of the request sequence number in bytes.
Parameter class	Identification
Usage	request_number_size : integer
Default setting	2
Dependencies	—
Influenced functions	—

Appendix B

Policy Parameters–Replication

Table B.1: The policy parameter–replication_range

Parameter name	**replication_range**
Description	Defines the replication range for the variable. The range is defined in hops.
Parameter class	Replication
Usage	replication_range : integer
Default setting	Undefined–the replication is switched off
Dependencies	—
Influenced functions	*repLogic_shallForward()* *repLogic_shallBeSent()*

Table B.2: The policy parameter–replication_density

Parameter name	**replication_density**
Description	Specifies the desired density of replicas depending on the distance from the owner of the master copy. Is used as the probability of replication depending on the distance from the owner node.
Parameter class	Replication
Usage	replication_density : {integer, ..., integer}
Default setting	50
Dependencies	Requires **replication_range**.
Influenced functions	*repLogic_shallBeStored()* *repLogic_shallBeAcked()*

Table B.3: The policy parameter–replication_copies

Parameter name	**replication_copies**
Description	Defines the desired number of replicas.
Parameter class	Replication
Usage	replication_copies : integer
Default setting	0
Dependencies	Requires **replication_range**.
Influenced functions	*repLogic_requestedUpdateCount()* *repLogic_shallBeAcked()*

Table B.4: The policy parameter–update_pattern

Parameter name	**update_pattern**
Description	Defines the sequence of data advertisement update requests, plain update requests and verified update requests.
Parameter class	Replication
Usage	update_pattern : {integer, integer, integer}
Default setting	0, 1, 0 (*ADVERTISE, UPDATE, VERIFY*)
Dependencies	—
Influenced functions	*repLogic_shallBeSent()*

Table B.5: The policy parameter–replication_history

Parameter name	**replication_history**
Description	Defines the number of historical instances of the entities of the variable to be stored in the historical storage depending on the distance to the owner node.
Parameter class	Replication
Usage	replication_history : {integer, ..., integer}
Default setting	1
Dependencies	Requires **replication_range**. May be modified by **replication_density**.
Influenced functions	*repLogic_historySize()*

Table B.6: The policy parameter–independent_update_forward

Parameter name	**independent_update_forward**
Description	Enables the forwarding of update requests independent from the replication.
Parameter class	Replication
Usage	independent_update_forward
Default setting	Off–dependent forwarding is used
Dependencies	May be enabled by the **replication_density**. May be disabled by the **replication_range**.
Influenced functions	*repLogic_shallForward()*

Appendix C

Policy Parameters–Reliability

Table C.1: The policy parameter–permanent

Parameter name	**permanent**
Description	Specifies that the most recent instance of the variable shall be stored in a non-volatile memory.
Parameter class	Reliability
Usage	permanent
Default setting	Off–data stored in RAM
Dependencies	—
Influenced functions	*var_setValueTsOwner()* *var_getValueTS()*

Table C.2: The policy parameter–variable_timeout

Parameter name	**variable_timeout**
Description	Defines the timeout period for the instances of the variable in milliseconds. If the value is equal to zero, there is no timeout period for the variable.
Parameter class	Reliability
Usage	variable_timeout : integer
Default setting	0
Dependencies	—
Influenced functions	*var_setValueTsOwner()*

Table C.3: The policy parameter–answer_not_local_gets

Parameter name	**answer_not_local_gets**
Description	Allows a node to answer a remote read request about foreign entity.
Parameter class	Reliability
Usage	answer_not_local_gets
Default setting	Off–only queries on own data are answered
Dependencies	—
Influenced functions	*repLogic_answerNotLocalGets()*

Appendix D

Policy Parameters–Optimization

Table D.1: The policy parameter–local_request_timeout

Parameter name	**local_request_timeout**
Description	Defines the timeout for locally sourced requests in milliseconds. Reduces the possibility of request buffer overflow.
Parameter class	Optimization
Usage	local_request_timeout : integer
Default setting	500
Dependencies	—
Influenced functions	*repLogic_setBufferTimeout()*

Table D.2: The policy parameter–external_request_timeout

Parameter name	**external_request_timeout**
Description	Defines the timeout for external requests in milliseconds. Reduces the possibility of request buffer overflow.
Parameter class	Optimization
Usage	external_request_timeout : integer
Default setting	500
Dependencies	—
Influenced functions	*repLogic_setBufferTimeout()*

Table D.3: The policy parameter–local_request_retries

Parameter name	**local_request_retries**
Description	Defines the number of delivery retries for local requests. Reduces the possibility of request buffer overflow.
Parameter class	Optimization
Usage	local_request_retries : integer
Default setting	5
Dependencies	—
Influenced functions	*repLogic_setRetriesCount()*

Table D.4: The policy parameter–external_request_retries

Parameter name	**external_request_retries**
Description	Defines the number of delivery retries for external requests. Reduces the possibility of request buffer overflow.
Parameter class	Optimization
Usage	external_request_retries : integer
Default setting	5
Dependencies	—
Influenced functions	*repLogic_setRetriesCount()*

Table D.5: The policy parameter–fifo_processing

Parameter name	**fifo_processing**
Description	Indicates that the variable requires sequential processing of requests.
Parameter class	Optimization
Usage	fifo_processing
Default setting	Off
Dependencies	—
Influenced functions	—

Table D.6: The policy parameter–discovery_hops

Parameter name	**discovery_hops**
Description	Specifies the forwarding distance for the master copy owner discovery requests.
Parameter class	Optimization
Usage	discovery_hops : integer
Default setting	0
Dependencies	—
Influenced functions	*repLogic_shallBeSent()*

Table D.7: The policy parameter–min_store_delta_time

Parameter name	**min_store_delta_time**
Description	Defines the minimum time difference between two consecutive writes in the history storage. Setting to zero disables the filter.
Parameter class	Optimization
Usage	min_store_delta_time : integer
Default setting	0
Dependencies	Requires **timestamp**.
Influenced functions	*repLogic_shallBeStored()*

Table D.8: The policy parameter–min_store_delta_value

Parameter name	**min_store_delta_value**
Description	Defines the minimum allowed difference between the values of two consecutive instances to store in the history storage. Setting to zero disables the filter.
Parameter class	Optimization
Usage	min_store_delta_value : integer
Default setting	0
Dependencies	—
Influenced functions	*repLogic_shallBeStored()*

Table D.9: The policy parameter–per mille_store_delta_value

Parameter name	**permille_store_delta_value**
Description	These parameters specify the way the value delta filter is realized.
Parameter class	Optimization
Usage	permille_store_delta_value
Default setting	Off–the delta is defined as an absolute value
Dependencies	Requires **min_store_delta_value**.
Influenced functions	*repLogic_shallBeStored()*

Table D.10: The policy parameter–min_update_delta_time

Parameter name	**min_update_delta_time**
Description	Defines the minimum time difference between two consecutive update requests. Setting to zero disables the filter.
Parameter class	Optimization
Usage	min_update_delta_time : integer
Default setting	0
Dependencies	Requires **timestamp**. May be influenced by **min_store_delta_time**.
Influenced functions	*repLogic_shallBeSent()*

Table D.11: The policy parameter–min_update_delta_value

Parameter name	**min_update_delta_value**
Description	Defines the minimum allowed difference between the values of the instances of two consecutive update requests. Setting to zero disables the filter.
Parameter class	Optimization
Usage	min_update_delta_value : float
Default setting	0
Dependencies	May be influenced by **min_store_delta_value**.
Influenced functions	*repLogic_shallBeSent()*

Table D.12: The policy parameter–per mille_update_delta_value

Parameter name	**permille_update_delta_value**
Description	This parameter specifies the way the value delta filter is realized.
Parameter class	Optimization
Usage	permille_update_delta_value
Default setting	Off–the delta is defined as an absolute value
Dependencies	Requires **min_update_delta_value**.
Influenced functions	*repLogic_shallBeSent()*

Appendix E

Policy Parameters–Access rights

Table E.1: The policy parameters–local_access_readonly and local_access_writeonly

Parameter name	local_access_readonly
	local_access_writeonly
Description	Specifies the allowed operations to be performed on local entity of the variable.
Parameter class	Access rights
Usage	local_access_readonly or local_access_writeonly
Default setting	None–read and write access is allowed
Dependencies	—
Influenced functions	*repLogic_isAllowedToWrite()*
	repLogic_isAllowedToRead()

Table E.2: The policy parameters–external_access_readonly and external_access_writeonly

Parameter name	external_access_readonly
	external_access_writeonly
Description	Specifies the allowed operations to be performed on external entity of the variable.
Parameter class	Access rights
Usage	external_access_readonly or external_access_writeonly
Default setting	None–read and write access is allowed
Dependencies	—
Influenced functions	*repLogic_isAllowedToWrite()*
	repLogic_isAllowedToRead()

Appendix F

Policy Parameters–Future improvements

Table F.1: The policy parameter–writable_replicas

Parameter name	**writable_replicas**
Description	Disables the ownership for a global variable, i.e., every replica is writable, and every node may issue the write request directly to its copy and broadcasts the update requests. The timestamps, if present and the source node identities, included in the write requests, may be used for the ordering of the requests.
Parameter class	Reliability
Usage	writable_replicas
Default setting	undefined–only one copy of each entity is writable.
Dependencies	requires **global** requires **replication_range** disables **migration**
Influenced functions	TBD

Table F.2: The policy parameter–group_number

Parameter name	**group_number**
Description	Assigns the variable to the group identified by the input integer. All variables in a group are owned by a single node. All ownership related operations are done for all the variables in the group.
Parameter class	Identification
Usage	group_number : integer
Default setting	undefined–the variable does not belong to any group.
Dependencies	requires **global**
Influenced functions	TBD

Table F.3: The policy parameter–read_delay

Parameter name	**read_delay**
Description	Defines the delay for the application notification for locally handled read requests. If ownership is enabled, then the value specified for this parameter is multiplied by the hop distance to the owner of the data. The result of the read operation is updated, if for the data item in question a replica update request is received during the delay period.
Parameter class	Reliability
Usage	read_delay : integer
Default setting	undefined–the application is notified immediately as the result is available.
Dependencies	requires **global**
Influenced functions	TBD

Table F.4: The policy parameter–timestamp_issuing

Parameter name	**timestamp_issuing**
Description	Enables the timestamping of read and write requests at the issuing time. If enabled, the timestamp is transmitted with every read and write request toward the data owner. In case of read requests about historical data, the timestamp that represents the desired data, not the issue time is transmitted. This parameter is independent from the **timestamp** policy parameter.
Parameter class	Identification
Usage	timestamp_issuing
Default setting	Off–standard operation span is used, i.e., the request start is identified by the moment the request arrives at the data owner node.
Dependencies	—
Influenced functions	TBD

Table F.5: The policy parameter–convergecast_read

Parameter name	**convergecast_read**
Description	Enables the aggregation of responses from multiple replicas for the read request.
Parameter class	Reliability
Usage	convergecast_read
Default setting	Off–standard read operation from a single source is used.
Dependencies	requires **replication_range**
Influenced functions	TBD

Table F.6: The policy parameter–convergecast_quorum

Parameter name	**convergecast_quorum**
Description	Enables the quorum-like aggregation of responses from multiple replicas for the read request, i.e., a parent in the forwarding tree chooses the most frequent answer, it receives from it children and forwards this answer together with the number of repetitions (stored in *noACKS* field of the *radiodata_t*).
Parameter class	Reliability
Usage	convergecast_quorum
Default setting	Off–each parent in the forwarding tree forwards the most recent value from those, it received from its children nodes.
Dependencies	requires **convergecast_read**
Influenced functions	TBD

Table F.7: The policy parameter–serialized_processing

Parameter name	**serialized_processing**
Description	Enables the serialization of the request processing, so that the processing of one request is not interrupted by processing of another one. The second request is handled as soon as the processing of the first one is completed.
Parameter class	Reliability
Usage	serialized_processing
Default setting	Off–the requests are processed in parallel, if possible.
Dependencies	requires **fifo_processing**
Influenced functions	TBD

Table F.8: The policy parameter–repeatable

Parameter name	**repeatable**
Description	Enables the reinitialization of a request at the moment of the delivery of the processing result. The reinitialized request is then identified by the same request sequence number.
Parameter class	Reliability
Usage	repeatable
Default setting	Off–the requests cannot be reinitialized.
Dependencies	–
Influenced functions	TBD

Used Abbreviations

ACK	Positive Acknowledgment
API	Application Programming Interface
ASIC	Application Specific Integrated Circuit
BAN	Body Area Network
MBAN	Medical Body Area Network
WBAN	Wireless Body Area Network
CCA	Clear Channel Assessment
CPS	Cyber-Physical System
CTU	Common Timeout Unit
DSM	Distributed Shared Memory
DSSS	Direct Symbol Spread Spectrum
DUI	Data Update Interval
FIFO	First In First Out
FPGA	Field Programmable Gate Array
IC	Integrated Circuit
IDE	Integrated Development Environment
ITS	Interface Tuple Space
JNI	Java Native Interface
LIME	Linda In Mobile Environment

LPM	Low Power Mode
MAC	Medium Access Control
MCM	Memory Coherency Manager
MDT	Minimum Delta Time
MDV	Minimum Delta Value
MMU	Memory Management Unit
MRMW	Multiple Reader / Multiple Writer
MRSW	Multiple Reader / Single Writer
MSDT	Minimum Store Delta Time
MSDV	Minimum Store Delta Value
MUDT	Minimum Update Delta Time
MUDV	Minimum Update Delta Value
NACK	Negative Acknowledgment
PC	Program Counter
PDA	Personal Digital Assistant
PER	Packet Error Rate
PHY	Physical Layer
PRAM	Pipelined Random Access Memory
RAM	Random Access Memory
RC	Replication Copies
RD	Replication Density
RR	Replication Range
RSSI	Received Signal Strength Indication
RTC	Real Time Clock
RTS	Run Time System
RX	Receive Mode

SACK	Set Acknowledgment
SRSW	Single Reader / Single Writer
TS	Tuple Space
TTL	Time To Live
TX	Transmit Mode
UACK	Update Acknowledgment
ULP	Ultra Low Power
UP	Update Pattern
WSAN	Wireless Sensor and Actor Network
WSN	Wireless Sensor Network

List of Figures

2.1	High level idea of a WSN application	12
2.2	A simplified architecture of a wireless sensor node	13
2.3	An extended architecture of a wireless sensor node	13
2.4	The IHPNode hardware platform	14
2.5	The Tandem Stack hardware platform	23
2.6	The simplified WSN protocol stack	29
2.7	A shared memory system	34
2.8	A loosely coupled multiprocessor system	35
2.9	A distributed shared memory system	35
2.10	The flow of a *central server* algorithm	37
2.11	The flow of a *single copy migration* algorithm	38
2.12	The flow of a *read replication* algorithm	39
2.13	The flow of a *full replication* algorithm	40
2.14	An example of a system with replicated data	48
3.1	An example of a request forward tree	89
3.2	The state diagram of the proposed replication strategy	93
3.3	Update request forwarding tree–independent forwarding	95
3.4	Update request forwarding tree–dependent forwarding	96
3.5	The ownership discovery mechanism	98
3.6	Master copy migration–updating the replicas	99
3.7	Master copy migration–the new replication area	100
3.8	The algorithm of filtering the instances to reduce the frequency of storing and update requests	102
3.9	An idealized flow of a distributed operation	104
3.10	The blocking flow of a distributed operation	105
3.11	The split-phase flow of a distributed operation	105
3.12	An architecture including the operating system independent DSM system	108
3.13	The flow of a write operation in a system with replicas	109

3.14	Write-write access conflict example flow	110
3.15	A time flow of master-read and any-read operations	112
3.16	A time flow of a quorum-read operation	113
4.1	The architecture of a system based on the tinyDSM middleware	118
4.2	The internal architecture of the tinyDSM Core	119
4.3	The logical division of the tinyDSM Core	119
4.4	The tinyDSM interfaces	120
4.5	The two-step compilation approach	121
4.6	The structure of an instance of a variable	122
4.7	Addressing of the data in the tinyDSM middleware	123
4.8	Replication of data in the tinyDSM middleware	124
4.9	The structure of the source folders of the tinyDSM middleware	132
4.10	The Operating System adaptation layer–its location and interfaces in a tinyDSM based system	137
4.11	Data structures and processes in tinyDSM	138
4.12	The request buffer	139
4.13	The 3D visualization of the external variables and history storage	166
4.14	Serialization of the three dimensional matrix–a sketch	167
4.15	State diagram for the request buffer–local request	177
4.16	State diagram for the request buffer–external request	177
4.17	The *external variables and history* storage access state diagrams	178
4.18	The notification state diagram	179
4.19	The transmission state diagram	179
4.20	The state diagram for the initial processing of a GET request	181
4.21	The state diagram for the initial processing of a SET request	182
4.22	The state diagram for the initial processing of an UPDATE request	183
4.23	The request processing state diagram	185
5.1	The topology of the network used for the evaluation on IHPNode nodes	188
5.2	The states during the processing of a read request	191
5.3	The states during the processing of a write request without update acknowledgments	193
5.4	The states during the processing of a write request with update acknowledgments	194
5.5	The monitored states of a write request without update acknowledgments	195
5.6	The monitored states of a write request with update acknowledgments	196
5.7	The update forwarding tree used for accumulative convergecast of acknowledgments	197

5.8 The monitored states of a write request with update acknowledgments for the optimized settings 198

5.9 An example of a propagated write request followed by a forwarded write acknowledgment 199

5.10 An example flow for the linearizability model with replicas (distributed) . . 203

5.11 An example flow for the linearizability model without replicas (centralized) 204

5.12 A violation of the linearizability model (centralized) 205

5.13 An example flow for the delayed read in the linearizability model without replicas (centralized) 206

5.14 An example of refused write request in the linearizability model without replicas (centralized) 206

5.15 An example flow for sequential consistency model without replication . . . 208

5.16 An example flow for sequential consistency model with replication 209

5.17 The processing of a write request in the realization of sequential consistency model with replication 213

5.18 The sequence of replication updates for consecutive write request issued by *node12* and *node15* using the implementation of the sequential consistency model with replication 214

5.19 An example flow for PRAM/FIFO consistency model 216

5.20 The sequence of replication updates for consecutive write request issued by *node1* and *node16* for the implementation of the PRAM consistency model 218

5.21 The sequence of replication updates for consecutive write request issued by *node13* and *node16* for the implementation of the PRAM consistency model, without write acknowledgments 219

List of Tables

2.1	Sensor node hardware platforms build from off-the-shelf components	14
2.2	The energy consumption profile of the Atmel AT128L microcontroller	15
2.3	The energy consumption profile of the Atmel AT1281 microcontroller	15
2.4	The energy consumption profile of the Atmel ATx128A4 microcontroller	15
2.5	The energy consumption profile of the Texas Instruments MSP430F1611 microcontroller	16
2.6	The energy consumption profile of the Texas Instruments MSP430F5438A microcontroller	16
2.7	The energy consumption profile of the Marvell PXA271 microprocessor	17
2.8	The energy consumption profile of the Atmel AT915SAM9G20 microprocessor	17
2.9	Energy consumption profiles of the processing units used in WSN hardware platforms	18
2.10	The energy consumption profile of the Texas Instruments CC1000 transceiver	19
2.11	The energy consumption profile of the Texas Instruments CC1101 transceiver	20
2.12	The energy consumption profile of the Texas Instruments CC2500 transceiver	20
2.13	The energy consumption profile of the Texas Instruments CC2420 transceiver	21
2.14	The energy consumption profile of the Texas Instruments CC2520 transceiver	21
2.15	The energy consumption profile of the Atmel AT86RF212 transceiver	22
2.16	The energy consumption profile of the Atmel AT86RF231 transceiver	22
2.17	Energy consumption profiles of the radio transceivers used in WSN hardware platforms	23
2.18	Hardware DSM implementations [179]	41
2.19	Software DSM implementations [179]	42
2.20	Hybrid DSM implementations [179]	43
4.1	Complexity of the request buffer access functions	150
4.2	Clock cycles required by the access operations of the *local variables and metadata* storage	159

4.3	Code size and initialization data size requirements of the *local variables and metadata* storage representations	161
4.4	The complexity of the validation check for the *local variables and metadata* storage	162
4.5	Message fields required by the tinyDSM requests	171
4.6	Measured size of request messages and the complexity of request encoding and decoding	172
5.1	The content of the state notification data	189
5.2	The initial settings chosen for the evaluation and the resulting parameters	190
5.3	The state marks chosen to be monitored in the test network	192
5.4	The optimized settings chosen for the evaluation and the resulting parameters	197
5.5	The number of messages sent and received during the request forwarding .	200
5.6	The costs of the sequential model implementation without replication . . .	211
5.7	The costs of the sequential model implementation with replication	211
5.8	pram	217
A.1	The policy parameter–global	245
A.2	The policy parameter–migration	245
A.3	The policy parameter–timestamp	246
A.4	The policy parameter–timestamp_size	246
A.5	The policy parameter–timestamp_tolerance	246
A.6	The policy parameter–request_number_size	247
B.1	The policy parameter–replication_range	249
B.2	The policy parameter–replication_density	249
B.3	The policy parameter–replication_copies	250
B.4	The policy parameter–update_pattern	250
B.5	The policy parameter–replication_history	250
B.6	The policy parameter–independent_update_forward	251
C.1	The policy parameter–permanent	253
C.2	The policy parameter–variable_timeout	253
C.3	The policy parameter–answer_not_local_gets	254
D.1	The policy parameter–local_request_timeout	255
D.2	The policy parameter–external_request_timeout	255
D.3	The policy parameter–local_request_retries	256
D.4	The policy parameter–external_request_retries	256
D.5	The policy parameter–fifo_processing	256
D.6	The policy parameter–discovery_hops	257

D.7   The policy parameter–min_store_delta_time 257
D.8   The policy parameter–min_store_delta_value 257
D.9   The policy parameter–per mille_store_delta_value 258
D.10 The policy parameter–min_update_delta_time 258
D.11 The policy parameter–min_update_delta_value 258
D.12 The policy parameter–per mille_update_delta_value 259

E.1   The policy parameters–local_access_readonly and local_access_writeonly . . 261
E.2   The policy parameters–external_access_readonly and external_access_writeonly 261

F.1   The policy parameter–writable_replicas 263
F.2   The policy parameter–group_number 264
F.3   The policy parameter–read_delay 264
F.4   The policy parameter–timestamp_issuing 265
F.5   The policy parameter–convergecast_read 265
F.6   The policy parameter–convergecast_quorum 266
F.7   The policy parameter–serialized_processing 266
F.8   The policy parameter–repeatable 266

List of Listings

4.1	The constants defined for the trigger parameter	126
4.2	The tinyDSMAppInterface.h header file	133
4.3	The tinyDSMOSInterface.h header file	136
4.4	The definition of the request buffer	139
4.5	The functional interface to the request buffer	140
4.6	A SQL like description of the request buffer	141
4.7	The definition of the *request_t* structure	142
4.8	The tinyDSM operation constants	142
4.9	The example constants for the operation flags	143
4.10	The example constants for internal request flags	143
4.11	The definitions of the buffer element state flags	146
4.12	The definitions of request state flags	146
4.13	Definitions of the result constants	148
4.14	A SQL like description of the local variables and metadata structure . .	151
4.15	The functional interface to the local variables and metadata storage module	151
4.16	The *variable_t* structure and definition of the *local variables and metadata* storage in the array representation	153
4.17	Example constants for the configuration of a variable - ignoring the sign	155
4.18	Example constants for the configuration of a variable - respecting the sign	155
4.19	Example constants for the state of a local instance	155
4.20	The individual representation of an example shared variable	156
4.21	The definition of the *varinfo_t* structure type	156
4.22	Definition of the *local variables and metadata* storage in the individual-array representation	157
4.23	A SQL like description of the external variables and history structure .	164
4.24	The functional interface of the external variables and history storage . .	164
4.25	Definition of the *flashdata_t* structure type	168
4.26	Constants used for the *flags* field in the *flashdata_t* structure type . . .	168

4.27 Definition of the *radiodata_t* structure type 169
4.28 Example definition of an alternative *radiodata_t* structure type 170
4.29 Example type definitions for the message size related measurements . . 172
4.30 The definition of the *serialdata_t* structure type 173
4.31 The functions of the Replication Logic module 174
4.32 The functional interface of the Event Logic module 175
4.33 Functions used for constructing the evaluated equations in the Event Logic 175
4.34 The definition of the *eval_t* structure type 175
4.35 The *event()* function 176
5.1 The definition of variables supporting the linearizability model with replication 204
5.2 The definition of variables supporting the linearizability model without replication 207
5.3 The definition of variables supporting the sequential model without replication 210
5.4 The definition of variables supporting the sequential model with replication 210
5.5 The definition of variables supporting the PRAM consistency model . . 216
5.6 The definition of global and array variables supporting the cache consistency model 219
5.7 The definition of variables supporting the processor model with replication 220

i want morebooks!

Buy your books fast and straightforward online - at one of world's fastest growing online book stores! Environmentally sound due to Print-on-Demand technologies.

Buy your books online at
www.get-morebooks.com

Kaufen Sie Ihre Bücher schnell und unkompliziert online – auf einer der am schnellsten wachsenden Buchhandelsplattformen weltweit! Dank Print-On-Demand umwelt- und ressourcenschonend produziert.

Bücher schneller online kaufen
www.morebooks.de

VDM Verlagsservicegesellschaft mbH
Heinrich-Böcking-Str. 6-8   Telefon: +49 681 3720 174   info@vdm-vsg.de
D - 66121 Saarbrücken   Telefax: +49 681 3720 1749   www.vdm-vsg.de

Printed by Books on Demand GmbH, Norderstedt / Germany